The **WHEN**

Case

for **WELFARE**

Economic

Human **DISAPPEARS**

Rights

KENNETH J. NEUBECK

Routledge
Taylor & Francis Group
New York   London

Routledge is an imprint of the
Taylor & Francis Group, an informa business

Published in 2006 by
Routledge
Taylor & Francis Group
270 Madison Avenue
New York, NY 10016

Published in Great Britain by
Routledge
Taylor & Francis Group
2 Park Square
Milton Park, Abingdon
Oxon OX14 4RN

Printed in the United States of America on acid-free paper
10 9 8 7 6 5 4 3 2 1

International Standard Book Number-10: 0-415-94779-0 (Hardcover) 0-415-94780-4 (Softcover)
International Standard Book Number-13: 978-0-415-94779-4 (Hardcover) 978-0-415-94780-0 (Softcover)
Library of Congress Card Number 2005031275

Library of Congress Cataloging-in-Publication Data

Neubeck, Kenneth J.
    When welfare disappears : the case for economic human rights / by Kenneth J. Neubeck.
        p. cm.
    Includes bibliographical references and index.
    ISBN-13: 978-0-415-94779-4 (hardback)
    ISBN-13: 978-0-415-94780-0 (pbk.)
    1. Public welfare--Economic aspects--United States. 2. Welfare recipients--United
States--Economic conditions. 3. Poverty--Government policy--United States. I. Title.

HV91.N443 2006
330--dc22   2005031275

Taylor & Francis Group
is the Academic Division of Informa plc.

Visit the Taylor & Francis Web site at
http://www.taylorandfrancis.com

and the Routledge Web site at
http://www.routledge-ny.com

WHEN

WELFARE

DISAPPEARS

To my grandchildren Dylan Christopher Neubeck, Harper Clancy Neubeck, and Lucy Sinclair Neubeck, and to the memory of my granddaughter Yssis Amina Neubeck. Loving thoughts from Grampa.

Contents

Preface

After Hurricane Katrina hit the Gulf Coast region of the United States in late August 2005, it quickly became clear that its enormous impact was disproportionately being felt by people living in poverty. Katrina did terrible damage to large areas of Louisiana, Mississippi, and Alabama—areas in which many poverty-stricken families lived. Most mass media attention focused on residents of the city of New Orleans, which had a high poverty rate in comparison to most other U.S. cities its size. While much of the city was flooded and wind damaged, the hurricane almost totally destroyed those sections of New Orleans where impoverished families were concentrated. Many of these families were not only displaced but were rendered homeless.

People throughout the United States were shocked to learn that numerous families in New Orleans had no means of escaping the approaching hurricane and no way to sustain themselves outside the city. Many did not own cars and lacked money for bus or train transportation. Few had money to pay for housing in a distant motel or hotel, or could afford to buy meals while living away from home. Some were so impoverished and socially isolated that they had never been out of New Orleans and had no idea where they could even go. While these families were in deep economic trouble even before the hurricane hit, their poverty circumstances made them particularly vulnerable to further harm. Many people in New Orleans and elsewhere in the Gulf Coast region died in Hurricane Katrina because they were so poor that they lacked the resources and means to evacuate and stay out of harm's way.

Lone mothers and their children were disproportionately present among the large numbers of poverty-stricken families who were traumatized and harmed by Hurricane Katrina. In the Gulf Coast region of the United States, as is true elsewhere across the nation, lone-mother-headed families are far more likely than those headed by dual partners to be living in poverty, especially extreme poverty. The high poverty rate for lone-mother-headed families is a major contributor to the fact that nearly one in five U.S. children lives in a household with an annual income below the federal poverty line. The United States lacks policies designed to effectively reduce such poverty. In this regard, it is an outlier in comparison with virtually every other affluent nation.

Mass media coverage of Hurricane Katrina drew public attention to the poverty circumstances of many of those that the hurricane displaced, injured, and even killed. Many members of the public were shocked and disturbed. For a brief moment it appeared that public reaction to the deep impoverishment that the coverage of the hurricane brought to light might move U.S. political elites to take poverty up as a national issue. But in the months immediately following Hurricane Katrina, the U.S. Congress adopted a budget agreement aimed at reducing federal expenditures for several key programs serving low-income families. While Congress ultimately rejected reducing food stamp benefits, it cut the budgets for Medicaid and child support enforcement—programs of particular importance to impoverished lone mothers. Congress also reauthorized Temporary Assistance for Needy Families (TANF), the major welfare program on which many lone mothers must rely. It required the individual states to sharply increase work participation rates for adult TANF recipients but did not provide funding to assist states with the implementation of this expensive federal mandate. Nor did Congress provide states with funds to accommodate an increase in working parents needing help with child care expenses. Some states are likely to reduce the numbers of low-income families they assist, or the benefits they provide to such families, as a way of meeting the costs of these changes in federal policy.[1]

At the national level, the U.S. government's failure to ensure that the basic subsistence needs of families are met has left tens of millions of people struggling to sustain themselves. Victimization by natural (or humanly induced) disasters only exacerbates the sense of oppression and deprivation that those living in poverty experience daily. I believe that the principal problem that must be addressed is the refusal of U.S. political elites (powerful, influential elected and non-elected government officials) to recognize that everyone within the United States has fundamental human rights that deserve respect, protection, and fulfillment. Political elites are especially resistant to the notion that people have economic human rights—rights to work, food, housing, health care, social security, and an adequate standard of living.

When disasters such as Hurricane Katrina occur, emergency government assistance is temporarily provided to the victims. However, attention to their subsistence needs is typically fleeting. There is no permanent and long-term government commitment to programs that would end the economic deprivation to which the victims, who had been living in poverty, usually return. In my view, and that of increasing numbers of others in the United States, the U.S. government's refusal to take steps toward ending poverty is a human rights violation for which political elites must be held accountable.

Recent U.S. welfare reform goes in the reverse policy direction from that required of a nation that respects economic human rights. Under welfare reform, impoverished lone-mother-headed families are denied entitlement to even the most minimal income assistance, no less that which would provide for an adequate standard of living. Lone mothers are told that it is their own personal responsibility to achieve self-sufficiency. For many this is impossible to do, given that they must simultaneously meet responsibilities associated with parenting and overcome formidable barriers to above-poverty-wage employment. The high percentage of this nation's lone mothers and their children who live in poverty is a national scandal and should be cause for international embarrassment.

The Internet has helped to rapidly globalize the distribution of knowledge, including knowledge of international human rights and human rights violations. A movement has now arisen in the United States that seeks to create a human rights culture, pressure the U.S. government to sign and abide by international human rights treaties, and address human rights violations that are occurring at home. Ending domestic poverty is one of the human rights goals to which this movement is committed. I hope that the readers of this book come to see the crucial importance of framing poverty and its elimination in human rights terms, and see themselves as part of the U.S. human rights movement.

Acknowledgments

In 2001, Routledge published *Welfare Racism: Playing the Race Card Against America's Poor*, which I co-authored with University of Connecticut colleague Noel A. Cazenave. The book examined the impact of racism on the conception, formulation, and implementation of U.S. welfare policy and received an extremely positive response, including five book awards. Ilene Kalish, my Routledge editor at the time, urged me to write another book, one that analyzed the outcomes of present-day U.S. welfare reform. I am grateful to Ilene for that invitation and for the encouragement that she immediately gave me when I proposed to frame a critique of U.S. welfare reform in a human rights context. Thanks also to Sanford F. Schram of Bryn Mawr College for his careful review and strong endorsement of my book proposal.

At the time that I committed to writing this book, I was directing the University of Connecticut's newly established undergraduate Human Rights minor and participating in a faculty human rights reading group. Many of the arguments that I make in the book were influenced by the wide-ranging discussions that took place within the reading group on the topic of economic human rights. I wish to extend my appreciation to the group's members, especially Davita Silfen Glasberg, Veronica Makowsky, Lanse Minkler, Bandana Purkayastha, Susan Randolph, Eleni Coundouriotis, and Richard Wilson.

During the course of writing this book, I was invited to contribute to an edited volume of articles on economic human rights and to attend a conference at which the volume's contributors would discuss drafts of their articles. Involvement in this interdisciplinary project gave me a much greater understanding of the stubborn gap between economic human rights ideals and current social policies in the United States. I wish to express my gratitude to the volume editors and conference organizers, international human rights scholars Rhoda E. Howard-Hassmann of Wilfrid Laurier University and Claude Welch of State University of New York at Buffalo.

Other colleagues and friends have been consistently interested in my work and deserve mention. They include Marcia Bok, Bob Fisher, Nancy Naples, Louise Simmons, Marita McComiskey, Helen Raisz, and Keith Kilty. I was pleased to present some of my ideas on the contradiction between welfare reform and economic human rights at the University of Oregon's Center for the Study of Women in Society, and wish to thank Sandra Morgen, Joan Acker, and Ellen Scott for inviting me to join the Center's Welfare, Work, and Economic Restructuring Research Interest Group.

Writers always benefit from talented research assistance. My thanks in this regard go to University of Connecticut graduate student Sicelo Makapela, who helped me to identify and locate key documents bearing on the conceptualization of economic human rights in the international arena. I owe a particularly special thank-you to Katherine A. Kandetzki, who worked with me just after her graduation from the university. Katherine sifted through, selected from, and organized a large body of reports and articles on the outcomes of U.S. welfare reform. Her research skills and informed judgment in the selection of materials covering diverse topics proved invaluable to my writing. My research for this book was also greatly facilitated by helpful staff at the University of Connecticut's Homer Babbidge Library and at the University of Oregon's Knight Library.

I want to thank the acquisitions editors at Routledge, both Ilene Kalish and Michael Bickerstaff, for their enthusiastic support of this book and their faith in me as an author. Thanks also to project editor Richard Tressider for the efficient way in which he guided the final manuscript through the production process.

My spouse, Mary Alice Neubeck, displayed great understanding and patience as I completed this most recent book. She has always appreciated the importance that I place upon my writing and I count upon her to lend me a sympathetic ear when my progress seems fitful or too slow. Mary Alice never lets me down.

Finally, I want to thank those who are engaged daily in the struggle to build respect for economic human rights and to end poverty in the United States. In this regard, I continue to be deeply inspired by the commitment and leadership shown by Cheri Honkala, Willie Baptist, Mary Bricker-Jenkins, and other members of the Kensington Welfare Rights Union. Thank you for all your good work on behalf of economic human rights, and remember, "What goes around, comes around."

1
Introduction: Combating Poverty, Respecting Economic Human Rights

> Nora reached her 60-month lifetime limit [of eligibility for welfare benefits] and had her $499 monthly cash assistance discontinued. She is a single mother with three children, ages 6, 3, and 2 months. Nora faces the following barriers to becoming self-supporting: She does not have a high school diploma. She works as a school crossing guard—a job that pays only $460 monthly. She receives only $200 per month in child-care assistance, while the cheapest child care she can find for her two youngest costs $774 per month. Nora will not be able to look for a better-paying job until she can find affordable child care.[1]

Nora is but one of millions of "lone mothers" in the United States, mothers who "are potentially the sole [caregivers] and sole supporters of their children."[2] While being in a family headed by two adult partners is clearly no guarantee that a family will avoid poverty, families headed by lone mothers in the United States are far more likely than two-parent families to experience economic deprivation. The Urban Institute compared the economic hardships experienced by U.S. families with children headed by noncohabiting single parents (the vast majority of whom are women) to the hardships experienced by families headed by married couples. It found that 57.3 percent of single-parent families were "low income" in 2002, having incomes below 200 percent of the federal poverty line, compared with

1

22.8 percent of married-couple families. Almost 30 percent of U.S. families headed by noncohabiting single parents were living in poverty in 2002, compared with only 6.6 percent of families headed by married couples.[3]

To obtain cash assistance to help meet her family's basic subsistence needs, Nora was forced to seek admission to the welfare rolls. Welfare's existence derives from federal legislation authorizing "Temporary Assistance for Needy Families" (TANF). Applicants for TANF must meet strict means tests in order to receive cash benefits. Some two million families were receiving such benefits in 2002.[4] While TANF is jointly funded by the federal government and the fifty states, each individual state has created and administers its own TANF program. Although states must abide by general federal guidelines, programs vary in terms of eligibility requirements and benefit levels; however, all TANF programs are similar in that their cash assistance does little to lift lone-mother-headed families, such as Nora's, out of poverty.

Connecticut, where Nora resides, is an extremely affluent state, and its TANF program is generous compared to other such programs. Nora and her three children received almost $6,000 per year in income assistance from the state of Connecticut before their benefits were discontinued. Still, her yearly welfare payments were less than a third of the federally-set poverty line. In 2002 a family consisting of an adult and three children under 18 was considered poor by the federal government if its annual income was under $18,307.[5] Nora's yearly welfare payments, when supplemented by her earnings from employment as a crossing guard during the school year, barely brought her family above 50 percent of the federal poverty line.

Under individual state TANF programs, cash assistance to poverty-stricken mothers and children is only minimal. Regardless of the seriousness of a family's economic needs, such aid also is provided only for a temporary period of time. Federal legislation sets a lifetime limit of sixty months for cash TANF benefits. Individual states are, however, free to be more restrictive, and many are. Connecticut, for example, has a twenty-one-month time limit for cash assistance. In 2002 it ended a policy of granting six-month extensions—not to exceed the five-year federal time limit—to those TANF families found to be in especially chronic need, replacing it with a policy that allows families only three such six-month extensions. Nora and her family are among many thousands of impoverished lone mothers and children across the United States who have hit their state's maximum time limits and been cut off from further cash welfare benefits.

It is important to stress that TANF legislation allows welfare to be extended only to those impoverished families who can meet eligibility requirements, one of which involves work outside the home. Regardless of whether mothers want or need to be with their children, or have other family members in their household needing care (e.g., elders who are ill or disabled), in order to receive TANF cash benefits mothers must engage in work activity. They must put the responsibilities of being a worker before those of mother and caregiver. If mothers cannot or refuse to do so, they risk loss of their family's cash benefits, either wholly or in part. At the time of this writing, federal legislation required that most TANF recipients work a minimum of thirty hours per week—a minimum many members of Congress have sought to increase.[6]

Most TANF recipients, whose physical and mental health permit, show willingness to accept employment outside the home, even without the threatened loss of TANF benefits. Indeed, many lone mothers receiving TANF have a history of work experience. But large numbers of those on the welfare rolls are like Nora; they do not have much formal education or they lack the kinds of skills or job experience in demand by employers. Moreover, they frequently cannot find affordable (as well as accessible and dependable) child care that would facilitate their working outside the home. Those mothers on the TANF rolls, who place their children with caregivers and hold down jobs, typically earn poverty-level wages. Low earnings likewise plague mothers who leave the rolls because their TANF eligibility has ended. For lone mothers, moving from welfare to work more often than not means being trapped in the economically precarious and vulnerable ranks of the nation's working poor, a sector of the U.S. labor force that has grown markedly in recent years.

Over a quarter of families headed by noncohabiting single parents live below the poverty line. The economic deprivation experienced by lone mothers is one reason that almost one in five children under 18 lives in poverty in the United States, a rate higher than that of any other affluent nation. Moreover, in recent years the numbers of children living in "severe poverty" (children living in families who have incomes below 50 percent of the federal poverty line) have been on the increase.

Yet, despite this chronic and severe impoverishment, the number of mothers and children on the TANF rolls has dropped by more than half over the last decade or so. While some families have used up their eligibility for TANF under state time limits, many lone-mother families eligible for TANF are simply not receiving assistance. Moreover, the number of families, who are eligible but who are not on the TANF rolls, has been on the rise. In short, while millions of poverty-stricken lone mothers and their children struggle to meet basic subsistence needs, the safety net that should be providing cash assistance toward meeting these needs delivers little or even no help at all.

Like many other impoverished lone mothers, Nora clearly is going to need a lot of aid and support if she is to overcome the serious barriers that stand in the way of her ability to provide adequately for herself and her children. In light of the barriers Nora faces, should the meager cash benefits that she and her children were receiving have been summarily discontinued? In principle, shouldn't a lone mother who finds herself unable to adequately provide for herself and her children receive some type of income assistance? And why should cash assistance be both inflexibly time limited and so small as to do little more than maintain lone mothers and their children below the federal poverty line? Doesn't living in severe and chronic poverty circumstances harm both mothers and their children? What happens to impoverished families when welfare disappears? Shouldn't access to an adequate standard of living be a fundamental human right?

International Acknowledgment of Economic Human Rights

Some sixty years ago, nations around the world collectively agreed that every person on earth possesses certain fundamental rights simply on the basis of being a member of the human species.[7] Without respect for their rights as human beings, these nations held, individuals cannot live in freedom or with dignity. The establishment of a broad consensus as to the existence and importance of universal human rights stands as perhaps the most significant international development following World War II. Indeed, the horrors of and destruction stemming from that war, including the genocidal Holocaust, played a major role in galvanizing international sentiment as to the desirability of codifying fundamental human rights and of establishing ways to respect, protect, and fulfill them.

A broad multinational consensus on the existence of human rights was formalized in 1948 when the General Assembly of the newly established United Nations (UN) adopted and proclaimed a Universal Declaration of Human Rights. The opening words of this historic document call for "recognition of the inherent dignity and of the equal and inalienable rights of all members of the human family."[8] The Universal Declaration was unanimously approved by forty-eight members of the UN General Assembly. Eight other member nations abstained from voting, but there were no negative votes. The United States was a leader in the drafting of the Universal Declaration's provisions and voted for its adoption.

Provisions of the Universal Declaration of Human Rights address a wide range of fundamental human rights, such as the right to be free from torture, slavery, or arbitrary arrest and detention and the right to freedom of expression and to participation in elections. Beyond such civil and political rights, provisions of the Universal Declaration also address economic rights—human rights that involve people's basic subsistence needs. These are presented as no less deserving of respect by nation–states than civil and political rights.

Article 25 of the Universal Declaration is of particular importance to the plight of impoverished lone mothers and their children. It states, "Everyone has the right to a standard of living adequate for the health and well-being of himself and of his family, including food, clothing, housing, and medical care, and necessary social services, and the right to security in the event of unemployment, sickness, disability, widowhood, old age or other lack of livelihood in circumstances beyond his control."[9] This article goes on to say that "motherhood and childhood are entitled to special care and assistance. All children, whether born in or out of wedlock, shall enjoy the same social protection."[10]

In the United States, support for the concept of economic human rights had been voiced by President Franklin D. Roosevelt as early as 1941.[11] In that year's State of the Union Address to the U.S. Congress, he reflected on the goals of the United States and its World War II allies in terms of the need to collectively pursue the universal establishment of "four freedoms." President Roosevelt considered freedom of speech and freedom of religion to be essential, along with freedom from fear. But economic security was identified as equally important, as evidenced in his fourth freedom, "the freedom from want, which, translated into world terms, means economic understandings, which will secure to every nation a healthy peacetime life for its inhabitants everywhere in the world."[12]

Later, in a 1944 State of the Union Address, President Roosevelt advocated the adoption of an Economic Bill of Rights; in effect, a second bill of rights to supplement that protecting civil and political rights under the U.S. Constitution.[13] Voicing the need to plan for both peace and the establishment of a high domestic standard of living in a post-World War II United States, President Roosevelt stated, "We cannot be content, no matter how high that general standard of living may be, if some fraction of our people—whether it be one-third or one-fifth or one-tenth—is ill-fed, ill-clothed, ill-housed, and insecure." While noting the crucial importance of protecting people's political and civil rights, he held that these rights had "proved inadequate to assure us equality in the pursuit of happiness."

In his 1944 address, President Roosevelt stressed that "true individual freedom cannot exist without economic security and independence." He went on to declare that "necessitous men are not free men" and called for "a new basis of security and prosperity for all—regardless of station, race, or creed."[14] President Roosevelt's Economic Bill of Rights included the right to employment and to wages high enough to provide adequate food, clothing, and recreation; the right to a decent home, education, and health care; and protection from economic fears due to problems over which people had no control. President Roosevelt died in 1945, but his economic human rights concerns, shared by others worldwide, were directly reflected in the drafting of the Universal Declaration of Human Rights adopted by the UN General Assembly in 1948.

The creation of the Universal Declaration benefited greatly from leadership provided by Mrs. Eleanor Roosevelt, President Roosevelt's widow, who served on the Commission on Human Rights created by the United Nations. The Universal Declaration is a statement of human rights ideals and principles—a declaration of aspirations and goals. It provides common standards for how all people should be treated, regardless of who they are or where they live. However, while the forty-eight nations that officially sanctioned its adoption in 1948 were presumably in favor of its provisions, the Universal Declaration was not actually a treaty to which nations were legally bound under international law. It was instead a step toward treaty creation. Even so, its themes have been incorporated into the constitutions and laws of most of the 191 members of the present-day United Nations, and it is considered to have achieved the status of "customary international law." From its creation, the Universal Declaration has carried great moral force for people worldwide and has frequently been cited by oppressed groups seeking to justify and to legitimate their struggles against governmental policies and actions that violate its provisions.

Once the Universal Declaration was adopted in 1948, the UN Commission on Human Rights moved forward with drafts of treaties that would legally obligate nations to implement the human rights provisions it contained. Accordingly, the commission produced what is known as the International Bill of Human Rights. It includes two major treaties, each addressing a different set of rights. One treaty is known as the International Covenant on Civil and Political Rights. The second, of more immediate importance to this discussion, is called the International Covenant on Economic, Social, and Cultural Rights. These two human rights treaties were adopted by the UN General Assembly in 1966 and, once having received the number of nation–state ratifications required under the United Nations' rules, they entered into force in 1976.

The International Covenant on Economic, Social, and Cultural Rights states that "the widest possible protection and assistance should be accorded to the family," particularly "while it is responsible for the care and education of dependent children."[15] The covenant recognizes freedom from hunger as a "fundamental right of everyone," as is "the enjoyment of the highest attainable standard of physical and mental health." It provides for "the right to work, which includes the right of everyone to gain his living by work which he freely chooses or accepts." The covenant states that work must be carried out "under just and favorable conditions" and must include remuneration that provides workers with "fair wages," wages that allow them and their families a "decent living."

Echoing Article 25 of the Universal Declaration, the Covenant provides for "the right of everyone to an adequate standard of living for himself and his family, including adequate food, clothing, and housing, and to the continuous improvement of living conditions."[16] In ratifying this treaty, nations agree to take immediate and appropriate steps, in keeping with their resources, to progressively ensure the realization of the human rights it addresses.[17]

U.S. Actions Mixed Regarding Respect for Human Rights

By helping to draft and then by voting for the UN General Assembly's adoption of the Universal Declaration of Human Rights in 1948, the United States acceded to that document's human rights ideals, including those pertaining to economic human rights.[18] But in actual practice the United States has not shown a willingness to consistently respect the full range of human rights enumerated in the Universal Declaration.[19] U.S. political elites have been unevenly supportive of the protection of individuals' civil and political rights in other nations. And, with few exceptions, they have not been champions of economic human rights.[20] Moreover, U.S. political elites have resisted allowing the United States to be scrutinized for human rights violations of any type—whether civil, political, or economic, nor do they use human rights language or rhetoric when discussing problematic domestic events or conditions. As a consequence, people in the United States largely assume that human rights violations are carried out only in or by other nations.[21]

It seems fair to say that U.S. political elites have been prone to pay lip service to human rights violations on the part of other nations when they believe it to be politically pragmatic and convenient to do so. Otherwise, they have been apt to frame violations in nonhuman-rights language or to simply remain silent or soft-spoken in the face of such violations.[22] The United States has been slow to define or condemn even some of the most visibly horrific situations of genocide (e.g., Rwanda) as human rights violations. It has restrained its condemnation of human rights violations by powerful former enemies with which it wishes to maintain good relations (e.g., China), while vociferously condemning human rights violations in less powerful nations with which it is at serious odds (e.g., Cuba, North Korea). National self-interest, at least as it is defined by U.S. political elites, plays a role. The United States has routinely allowed human rights violations to go largely unchallenged in nations where important U.S. political, economic, or military interests are at stake (e.g., Saudi Arabia).

Over the past sixty years, the United States has refused to ratify all but a few of over twenty principal international human rights treaties.[23] It has ratified the International Covenant on Civil and Political Rights; the International Convention on the Elimination of All Forms of Racial Discrimination; the Convention on the Prevention and Punishment of the Crime of Genocide; and the Convention against Torture and Other Cruel, Inhuman, or Degrading Treatment or Punishment. These treaties were ratified long after most other nations had already done so. The United States has not, however, joined the overwhelming majority of nations that have ratified other important human rights treaties, including the International Covenant on Economic, Social, and Cultural Rights; the Convention on the Elimination of All Forms of Discrimination against Women; or the Convention on the Rights of the Child.

U.S. Senate ratification, a step required under the U.S. Constitution, generally has occurred only after the insertion of legalistic "reservations" to treaty language. Such reservations have the effect of limiting the vulnerability of the United States to charges of or sanctions for human rights violations under international law. When a nation as powerful and central to global affairs as the United States refuses to ratify treaties or ratifies them with reservations that render it an exception to treaty provisions to which other nations are bound, the credibility and authority of international human rights law is undermined and weakened. Why should other nations ratify treaties or take their treaty obligations seriously when the behavior of the United States challenges the very concept of human rights?

U.S. "exceptionalism" in the human rights arena extends even further, however. While U.S. political elites have frequently portrayed the United States as a leading champion of human rights, they have by and large refused to recognize the possibility of human rights violations by or within the United States. Policies, practices, and incidents that could reasonably be considered violations of international human rights law are typically defined by U.S. political elites in other terms. Policymakers routinely deny or ignore charges of U.S. human rights violations made by critics at home or abroad and generally reject the idea that the United States could ever commit violations for which it deserves to be held accountable to international bodies. At the same time, the United States has not resisted the notion that other nations need to be held to judgment and made accountable for human rights violations.

Broad international consensus exists that every individual on earth has human rights that must be respected, including economic human rights.[24]

The whole notion of human rights rests upon a belief in their universality, a belief U.S. political elites seem to hold only when it suits them. When coupled with U.S. political elites' uneven and selective attention to other nations' human rights violations, the posture adopted by the United States has invited charges of hypocrisy and bad faith from human rights advocates. While the United States has been criticized for its mixed support for civil and political rights in other nations, critics have been even more struck by the fact that it has failed to champion economic human rights at all, either at home or abroad.

U.S. Rejection of Economic Human Rights

U.S. indifference or hostility to economic human rights exists in the face of a general international acceptance of the need to respect such rights equally with civil and political rights.[25] Economic human rights are not inferior to or subsidiary to civil and political rights, nor are they deserving of a lower priority or emphasis. Rather, the two sets of rights are mutually supportive and interdependent. People whose civil and political rights are protected are in a better position to press their governments to address problems such as poverty than those who are politically oppressed. Similarly, people who must struggle endlessly simply to subsist are far less likely than those who are economically secure to have the energy to demand and to exercise civil and political rights. As Nobel Prize-winning economist Amartya Sen put it, "Economic unfreedom, in the form of extreme poverty, can make a person a helpless prey in the violation of other kinds of freedom... Economic unfreedom can breed social unfreedom, just as social or political unfreedom can also foster economic unfreedom."[26]

Since its adoption by the UN General Assembly in 1966, the International Covenant on Economic, Social, and Cultural Rights has been ratified by 151 nations. However, as already mentioned, the United States is not among them. The U.S. government's failure to ratify this covenant illustrates the second-class status the United States has generally accorded economic human rights in comparison to its support (albeit uneven and selective) for civil and political rights. Among the U.S. presidents who have followed Franklin D. Roosevelt (1933–1945), only Jimmy Carter (1977–1981) displayed a credible commitment to economic human rights, if actions are the measure of commitment.

Economic Human Rights and the Carter Administration

President Carter viewed poverty amelioration as a government responsibility. In 1977 he proposed to Congress legislation entitled Program for Better Jobs and Income. It offered all of those living in poverty—including two-parent families and families with heads already working—a guaranteed minimum income. Public service jobs of last resort were to be provided for those adults who could work but who were unable to find employment. Cash benefits were to go to both those who were able to work and those who could not. Although the plan contained a work requirement for those receiving benefits, it would have exempted mothers with preschool children from employment and would have required mothers of school-age children up to age 14 to work only part time. While Congress subsequently failed to support the president's proposals, Carter's belief that poor people in the United States were entitled to a job and income assistance was consistent with his support for an economic human rights approach to poverty at the international level.[27]

In 1977—the same year in which he introduced his domestic antipoverty legislation—President Carter signed the International Covenant on Economic, Social, and Cultural Rights on behalf of the United States. He also signed the International Covenant on Civil and Political Rights and sent both treaties to the U.S. Senate for ratification. The Senate subsequently ratified the International Covenant on Civil and Political Rights—but not until 1992, and only then with reservations. However, the Senate has never ratified the International Covenant on Economic, Social, and Cultural Rights and to this day shows little inclination to do so. The United States thus does not consider itself subject to that covenant's provisions.[28]

President Carter's efforts to have the United States recognize and respect economic human rights at the international level never gained much domestic political traction and had little influence over the actions of subsequent presidential administrations. This has been true for both Republican and Democratic presidencies, conservative and liberal alike. Indeed, a representative of liberal Democrat Bill Clinton's administration (1993–2001) told participants at the 1996 UN World Food Summit that the United States could not endorse the "right to food." The rationale for this not only rejected the notion of such a right but also included the claim that cutbacks in assistance mandated by the welfare reform bill passed by Congress and signed by President Clinton that year would put the United States in violation of international law.[29] The rationale for the lack of U.S. support for economic human rights has been made especially clear by the administration of Clinton's successor as president, conservative Republican George W. Bush (2001–present).

The Bush Administration's Dismissal of Economic Human Rights

David Weissbrodt, a human rights expert and advocate, in analyzing the U.S. stance on economic human rights has depicted the Bush administration as "inclined to support freedoms rather than rights, and opportunities rather than entitlements."[30] As one illustration to support this, Weissbrodt cites a representative of the Bush administration to the UN World Food Summit in 2002, who essentially reiterated a stated objection in connection with the right to food made by a Clinton administration representative in 1996: "[T]he U.S. believes that the attainment of the right to an adequate standard of living is a goal or aspiration to be realized progressively that does not give rise to any international obligation or any domestic legal entitlement... Additionally, the U.S. understands the right of access to food to mean the *opportunity* to secure food and not guaranteed entitlement."[31] Repeating the isolated position it occupied at the earlier World Food Summit, in 2002 the United States stood alone among the 182 nations represented in refusing to sign a declaration referring to food as a human right.

In discussing the reasoning underlying the Bush administration's rejection of economic human rights, Weissbrodt finds evidence of several arguments.[32] First, casting aside the premise that economic human rights are as vital to protect as civil and political rights, the Bush administration has argued that protection of civil and political rights *per se* will allow individuals the freedom to fulfill their economic goals and aspirations. It is true that impoverished people have the same political and civil rights under the law as do the wealthy in the United States, notwithstanding their racially and class-biased treatment within the nation's criminal justice system.[33] However, possession of such rights is not in and of itself a ticket out of poverty for those who lack access to adequate education and training opportunities, quality health care, affordable child care, and jobs that pay a living wage. Moreover, people who must deal daily with the wearing effects of impoverishment are less likely than the affluent to vote, and many who struggle with poverty have little confidence that voting will help them in any event. In turn, the political estrangement of the impoverished allows the major political parties and elected office holders to place a low priority on spending to improve the conditions under which poor people live and has even allowed them to support "welfare reform" policies that shred the safety net on which many of the poor are forced to rely.

Second, the Bush administration has argued that by enhancing the protection of free trade and reducing government interference in the market economy, new jobs and new income will be created that will reduce poverty. In its view, allowing the market to take care of poverty is a far more appropriate way of addressing the problem than direct state intervention. Unfortunately, in recent decades economic growth in the United States has not proven to be an answer to poverty. The growing economy, as in the boom period of the 1990s, has been accompanied by the disappearance of better-paying industrial jobs (many of which have been exported to poor underdeveloped nations) and a concomitant increase in the numbers of low-paying jobs in the expanding service sector. Together, these trends have contributed to an increase in the numbers of working poor. In addition, since the 1980s, there have been a series of federal tax cuts—justified in part as stimulants of economic growth—that have disproportionately benefited the wealthy. Consequently, poverty has not been meaningfully reduced by growth and the income gap between the most affluent and everyone else, the poor included, has progressively widened even in good economic times.

Third, the Bush administration has argued that incurring an obligation to accede to international law regarding economic human rights would conflict with U.S. national sovereignty along with the legal authority individual states and localities have to handle their own affairs. Certainly this argument contains some truth. When a nation ratifies a treaty, it always agrees to abide by international norms. In conforming to international human rights norms, sovereignty is affected in that a nation cannot simply do whatever it wishes, to whomever it wishes, whenever it wishes. In effect, human rights overcome sovereignty. Human rights norms require conformity to a set of commonly agreed-upon behaviors and the willingness to be held accountable for behaviors that deviate from the norms. In some instances conformity may require that a nation cease or refrain from engaging in offensive acts (e.g., religious persecution, torture, denial of suffrage), as is often the case when a treaty calls for the protection of civil and political rights. In other instances, conformity may require that a nation initiate new and more positive policies (e.g., to provide food, health care, housing), as is frequently the case when a treaty addresses economic human rights.

Under the U.S. Constitution, international treaties into which the United States enters are the "law of the land." If the United States were to accede to international law on economic human rights, no unit of government—whether federal, state, or local—would have the legal authority to ignore this law. Respecting the rights enumerated in the International Covenant on Economic, Social, and Cultural Rights would require that the United States change its current approach to poverty. Viewing poverty as a human rights issue would mean rejecting the notion that it is the personal responsibility of the impoverished individual. The very presence of impoverished people in the United States to whom assistance was being denied would be a human rights violation. Governmental units at all levels would have to take responsibility, whenever appropriate, for addressing poverty. Present-day federal-state programs, such as Temporary Assistance for

Needy Families, would have to be replaced with policies that treat poverty as a systemic problem requiring society-wide solutions that reach out to all who were in need.

Finally, the Bush administration has argued that economic human rights, unlike civil and political rights, are not legally *justiciable* (settled by applying the principles of law). Economic human rights are said to be too vague to implement, thus making it impossible to know when they have been realized (e.g., the right to an "adequate standard of living"). In this view, economic human rights are like lofty promises or pipe dreams that realistically cannot be fulfilled, and thus they must remain on the level of aspirations and goals. How, for example, could the United States function if its millions of ill-housed or homeless people could go to court and sue the government for failure to respond to their human right to adequate housing? What if the millions of hungry people in the United States were to sue because government policies were denying them their human right to food? The tens of millions who cannot afford health insurance could likewise sue in the face of their inadequate health care. Who would pay for and who would produce and provide these things? How could such rights ever possibly be respected?

The justiciability argument begs a more serious problem, which is the failure of U.S. courts, including the Supreme Court, to take international human rights law seriously in their decision-making. Unlike what occurs in the courts of many other nations, such as those in the European Union, rarely is this law even cited or alluded to by U.S. judges when rendering legal decisions. This is the case with regard to international human rights law pertaining to civil and political rights, as well as economic human rights. The failure of U.S. courts to acknowledge or draw upon international law is particularly a problem when it comes to economic human rights, since domestic law simply does not address such matters as the right to an adequate income or the right to food. In contrast, protection of individuals' civil and political rights is covered by a strong body of domestic law. This is no doubt why the Senate eventually found it possible to ratify the International Covenant on Civil and Political rights (albeit with reservations).

While varying widely in the effectiveness of their policies and the seriousness with which they respect economic human rights, 151 other nations have not used the alleged lack of justiciability or vagueness of such rights as a reason to reject ratification of the International Covenant on Economic, Social, and Cultural Rights. Were the United States to ratify this treaty, the nation's courts and other units of government would no doubt find ways to abide by the "law of the land." Model indicators and measures of progress toward the fulfillment of economic human rights are being discussed internationally, and indicators and measures specifically tailored to conditions in the United States certainly could be developed and progressively improved upon over time. It is not unreasonable to imagine that a workable definition of "an adequate standard of living" could be created, just as the U.S. government was able to create the long-used (but badly in need of revision) federal poverty line.

The chronically high rates of severe impoverishment among lone-mother-headed families in the United States is a direct reflection of the failure of U.S. political elites to conceive of poverty as a human rights issue. The way in which a problem is conceptualized and defined shapes the solutions that logically follow. If all individuals have a fundamental human right to an adequate standard of living, then governments committed to respecting human rights must address the subsistence needs of those who struggle in poverty. Yet, instead of treating poverty as a human rights issue, U.S. political elites have come to define poverty as a matter of personal responsibility. When poverty is conceptualized and defined in this way, government need not act to end poverty. Poverty-stricken individuals are blamed for their own plight, and they bear their own burden of finding ways out. Thus, in the United States, individuals have the "right" to live in poverty but do not have the right to government assistance that would get them out of it.[34] The failure to frame poverty as a human rights issue perpetuates the suffering made possible by governmental indifference to the plight of impoverished lone mothers and their families.

The Scope and Organization of This Book

This book examines U.S. welfare policy affecting lone mothers and children, with particular emphasis on the impact of recent "welfare reform." The analysis to be undertaken is intended to underscore the vast gap between current U.S. welfare policy and its effects and the very different conditions for lone-mother-headed families that could prevail were the United States to operate under the premise that all people possess fundamental economic human rights deserving of respect.

No nation can be cited as an economic human rights nirvana. The ratification of the International Covenant on Economic, Social, and Cultural Rights by 151 nations has to date led to very uneven results in terms of the initiation of policies that have effectively reduced poverty. Nonetheless, some nations' successful inroads into the amelioration of poverty among lone-mother-headed families sharply contrast with the level of chronic impoverishment that prevails among such families in the United States. While the conditions under which income and other assistance are provided to these families vary, in most instances where success in poverty reduction has occurred, the aid lone mothers and their children receive is provided as a matter of right.

If other nations can achieve success in reducing suffering and struggles for subsistence by lone-mother-headed families through policies informed by respect for economic human rights, there is no reason the United States cannot do so as well. But why should it do so? What possible benefits could be extended to U.S. society? It goes without saying that respecting economic human rights involves acting with moral integrity and fairness in the treatment of people who are impoverished. However, the benefits of doing so are not simply limited to increased freedom and dignity among those who are economically oppressed, which is the intended outcome. Significant benefits in terms of an improved quality of life for all members of society occur when economic human rights are respected.[35]

Chapter 2 provides a brief historical overview of U.S. welfare policy from the early twentieth century to the present. As will be shown, at no point in time has this policy—in any of its various transformations—meaningfully addressed poverty or adequately provided for the subsistence needs of impoverished lone mothers and their children. Indeed, over time the extension of assistance has grown more begrudging, meager, and punitive, as exemplified by the "welfare reform" initiatives that have taken place over the past two decades. This chapter will close with discussion of some of the reasons U.S. welfare policy looks like it does, addressing key factors shaping it that include this nation's systemic racial, gender, and class inequalities.

In chapter 3, a portrait of the overall outcomes of welfare reform in the United States will be presented. It is common for lone mothers and their children who move off the welfare rolls to remain impoverished. This chapter will examine welfare recipients' and welfare leavers' employment and income situations; the problems mothers face in providing their families with food, housing, health care, and child care both while on and off welfare; and ways in which welfare reform has adversely affected child and family well-being. The chapter will close by addressing questions of how and whether welfare reform can be considered a success, and for whom.

No generic welfare recipient exists in the United States. Data on the overall outcomes of welfare reform, including data discussed in chapter 3, tend to ignore or underplay the diversity of the recipient population. Various sectors of this population often face discriminatory treatment or are subject to other disadvantages on the basis of race, ethnicity, gender, sexual orientation, ablebodiedness, citizenship or immigration status, rural versus urban residency, or having been caught up in the criminal justice system, all reflected in the diverse ways in which families have experienced welfare reform. Chapter 4 deconstructs the welfare recipient population to show ways in which its different segments have been adversely affected by present-day U.S. welfare policy.

Affluent nations that have ratified the International Covenant on Economic, Social, and Cultural Rights have developed policies to aid those who are impoverished. Poverty rates in the United States are quite a bit higher than in most other affluent nations, such as those in Western Europe, particularly where lone-mother-headed families are concerned. In chapter 5, the following questions will be addressed: How do these other affluent nations define and address poverty? Why are they apparently more successful than the United States in reducing rates of poverty among lone mothers and children? What can the United States learn from other nations in this regard?

Chapter 6 addresses the question of "What is to be done?" Human rights have rarely simply been handed out by a society's powers-that-be, but are usually the product of conflict and struggle. The chapter points to some avenues through which citizen activism on behalf of economic human rights can be channeled. In the United States there is a growing movement to view poverty and welfare reform in human rights terms. Various groups are pointing to the contradiction between the human rights rhetoric espoused by U.S. political elites and the nation's failure to recognize and to address economic human rights. Readers who believe in respecting economic human rights as a route to the elimination of poverty in the United States will be introduced to groups, resources, and strategies than can help transform this belief into action.

2

U.S. Welfare Policy: From Supporting Motherhood to a War against the Poor

As discussed in chapter 1, the international recognition of economic human rights occurred as part of a post-World War II global movement to define and codify human rights more generally. The United States played a leadership role in the UN General Assembly's 1948 adoption of the Universal Declaration of Human Rights, an historic document addressing fundamental economic as well as civil and political rights. However, in the decades since its adoption, U.S. political elites' record of respect for human rights abroad has been uneven and often self-serving. Moreover, elites have ignored or resisted efforts to frame conditions within the United States in ways that would allow the U.S. government to be held accountable for violation of international human rights standards.

A particularly sharp gap has occurred between the economic human rights ideals enumerated in the Universal Declaration (and implemented through UN treaties, such as the International Covenant on Economic, Social, and Cultural Rights) and the U.S. government's treatment of impoverished people in the United States.[1] The United States's welfare policy for lone-mother-headed families has never been about such economic human rights as the right to food, housing, health care, or an adequate standard of living. Instead, U.S. political elites have typically taken the position that those who are poor—with few exceptions—are largely responsible for their own plight. Consequently, it is argued, they must escape poverty through their own efforts. This dominant ideology of *competitive individualism* has

17

helped to temper and to limit the substance of U.S. welfare policy and has contributed to its restrictive and meager offerings. In rejecting a rights-based approach to addressing the subsistence needs of those who are impoverished, U.S. political elites have accepted chronically high rates of poverty among lone mothers and their children that many other affluent Western nations are unwilling to tolerate.

This chapter will provide an historical overview of U.S. welfare policy, from its beginnings in the mothers' pension movement to the Aid to Families with Dependent Children program and its recent transformation under welfare reform. Contemporary welfare policy can be traced back to the early part of the twentieth century when mothers' pension programs were established in most individual states. Under these state-approved programs, localities were encouraged to provide income assistance to impoverished lone mothers to help them care for their children. However, not all states supported such programs, and in those that did, localities typically reserved mothers' pensions for small numbers of carefully selected families. Assistance was by no means considered a right, and local officials could simply deny aid to needy mothers or take it away from those to whom it was granted.

During the Depression of the 1930s, the federal government began jointly financing welfare programs with the individual states. Federal assistance was extended to states under a New Deal program called Aid to Dependent Children, or ADC. Later renamed Aid to Families with Dependent Children (AFDC), the program effectively replaced mothers' pensions. The availability of federal contributions for states' welfare programs encouraged all states to become participants in ADC and significantly increased the numbers of impoverished lone-mother-headed families being served at the local level.

Under ADC, all families who met means-tested eligibility requirements were theoretically considered to be entitled to income assistance. However, many eligible families were refused aid or were discouraged from applying for it, while others were simply left unaware of their eligibility. Near the end of the twentieth century, even this nominal entitlement to welfare would be abolished by federal welfare reform legislation. Clearly, even during the singular phase of U.S. welfare policy when needy families were supposedly entitled to income assistance, this policy was not informed by a concept of human rights. Welfare reform legislation of the 1990s abolished entitlement. In contrast, by definition human rights cannot be taken away.

One might well ask why income assistance for impoverished U.S. lone-mother-headed families has, throughout U.S. welfare history, been limited, difficult to obtain, meager, and begrudgingly extended. Aside from the dominant ideology of competitive individualism often expressed by U.S. political elites—that poverty and its resolution are primarily the responsibility of those who are poor—what other social factors have helped shape the features of U.S. welfare policy? This policy has undergone alterations in form and content over time, but it has always reflected the presence of class, gender, and racial inequalities. This chapter will close with observations on some ways in which U.S. welfare policy not only reflects, but also reinforces, such systemic inequalities.

When Poor Mothers and Children Mattered: The Movement toward Mothers' Pensions

One might assume that the United States has always had some kind of welfare safety net or system to care for impoverished lone mothers and their children. The key word at issue here should be *system.* Throughout U.S. history there have certainly always been those whose individual or collective moral leanings, religious obligations, sense of enlightened self-interest, or charitable impulses have led them to extend a hand to others in need. At the beginning of the twentieth century, however, no federal- or state-level system of income assistance existed to help poor families. Local private charitable and church-based help existed, and some aid for the most destitute was at times provided by local governments. But it was all very limited, even in the many areas of the United States, both urban and rural, in which poverty was widespread.[2]

Lone mothers, who were far more likely in the early twentieth century to be widowed, divorced, or deserted by their husbands than never married, faced formidable challenges and hardships. They were forced to deal simultaneously with child-care responsibilities and finding a way for their families to survive economically.[3] If mothers lacked extended family ties and assistance, the strain was especially great, and for many women it turned out to be overwhelming. It was not unusual for impoverished lone mothers to turn their children over to orphanages or to offer them up to foster homes or for adoption in the desperate hope that their children would have a better life.[4]

The overall U.S. poverty rate is estimated to have been 40 percent in 1900,[5] over three times the annual rate in recent decades. While most poor families at that time contained two adult parents, certainly plenty of poverty-stricken lone mothers and children existed. Indeed, during the Progressive Era (1890–1920) the extreme poverty conditions under which many mothers and children were living was deemed a national scandal. Prominent Progressive Era social reformers argued that the nation's children should be treated as an asset. Assuring the well-being and adequate mothering of children in poor families was said to be an investment in the nation's future. Many held that the public sector had to play a more concrete role in the protection of children who were living in poverty.[6]

The growing clamor around the issue of child poverty received a response at the highest levels of government, signaled by the convening of a White House Conference on Dependent Children in 1909. This unprecedented conference, which attracted child welfare advocates and charity officials from across the United States, functioned to underscore the extent and seriousness of the issue. While some conference participants held to the position that solutions to child poverty rested with traditional charitable and private philanthropic organizations and their activities, others among the participants felt that this approach was insufficient. The latter were convinced that government had to get involved in addressing the plight of poor children.

Shortly thereafter, reform-minded women's civic organizations took the leadership in propagandizing the issue of child poverty and in lobbying state legislatures to do something about it. Such groups proved relentless in seeking out political allies and pressing legislators to pass bills approving what were broadly referred to as mothers' pensions.[7] In state legislature after state legislature, activists and lobbyists from women's groups were successful in arguing on behalf of mothers' pension laws. Income assistance to impoverished lone mothers with children, they held, would allow mothers to reduce or to eliminate their economic reliance on poorly paid, often debilitating jobs. Mothers' pensions would allow women instead to remain at home to properly nurture their children. Many legislators were sympathetic, but even more were swayed by the argument that financial savings would result from keeping children at home with their mothers, thus avoiding the more costly alternative of maintaining them in orphanages or other institutional settings.[8]

Over the course of the two decades following the 1909 White House conference, just about every state legislature passed some form of mothers' pension law endorsing local community programs of income assistance to impoverished lone mothers and their children. This might seem like it was a tremendous victory for mothers' pension advocates' child-centered and maternalist values. But in most instances the state laws left the decision to set up mothers' pensions to local option, and many communities were uninterested in initiating such programs. Moreover, while endorsing income assistance for poor mothers, few state legislatures actually budgeted any funds to support local mothers' pensions programs. Thus, despite all the legislative activity, relatively few mothers actually ended up receiving any income assistance. Moreover, the assistance mothers did receive was so extremely meager, especially in comparison to the magnitude of their families' subsistence needs, that it usually did not allow them to completely withdraw from low-wage labor in order to engage in full-time, at-home mothering.[9]

In addition, biases on the part of local community officials administering mothers' pensions often led to aid being channeled to a highly select few recipients.[10] To be awarded a pension, mothers had to be considered members of the "deserving" poor. Only those poor mothers whose lifestyles were thought to be in accordance with the highest moral standards were even deemed eligible for consideration. They alone were thought to be capable of maintaining suitable homes for their children—homes worthy of community support. Upstanding white widows were given preference as mothers' pension recipients. The character of white mothers who had been divorced or abandoned by their husbands was usually considered more morally ambiguous and likely to be flawed, while unwed mothers were simply deemed morally bankrupt and unworthy of assistance. Regardless of their marital status, African-American mothers and other mothers of color, and at times immigrant mothers from white ethnic groups popularly held at that time to be racially inferior, were by definition considered to be undeserving and were systematically excluded.[11]

When examined today, mothers' pensions can hardly be interpreted as an approach to poverty that included respect for impoverished families' economic human rights. No mother had a right to a mother's pension, regardless of her level of economic deprivation. The income assistance mothers' pensions provided did little to secure an adequate standard of living for recipient families. And, in practice, mothers' pensions were primarily reserved for "gilt-edge widows,"[12] white widowed mothers singled out as deserving from among the far larger population of allegedly undeserving lone mothers with children. The rights-blind approach to family impoverishment taken by mothers' pension programs in the early twentieth century would set the tone and provide a template for the federal–state program that became popularly known as *welfare*.

From Mothers' Pensions to Aid to Families with Dependent Children

During the Great Depression of the 1930s, the extraordinary economic suffering that accompanied soaring rates of unemployment across the United States threatened widespread social and political unrest. Consequently, many U.S. political elites became reluctant supporters of welfare state activities, including programs of income assistance, that most would have otherwise eschewed.[13] Path-breaking legislation enacted during the early years of President Franklin D. Roosevelt's administration (1933–1945) offered a "New Deal" to many individuals and families who were severely impoverished. Under the Social Security Act of 1935, the federal government would, for the first time, join with states to help them provide an income safety net for children in needy families.[14]

New Deal programs introduced under the Social Security Act included Aid to Dependent Children, a program aimed at helping states provide income assistance to those lone-mother-headed families who could satisfy a means test verifying their economic need. All families who met ADC eligibility requirements were entitled to income assistance under the act so long as they remained in need. While the assistance was to be channeled through mothers, the funds were intended to help meet the subsistence needs of children. The creation of what amounted to a minimum (albeit minimal) guaranteed income for a portion of the nation's poor became possible, however, only after significant political compromises between the Roosevelt administration and powerful southern politicians whose appointed committee positions and seniority gave them control of the U.S. Congress.

Southern members of Congress, as well as many of their Northern colleagues, were concerned with the impact of ADC on local labor markets.[15] Many feared that ADC-eligible mothers would use this income assistance to reduce their participation in the low-wage labor force, particularly in the agricultural and domestic service sectors of the economy. Many members of Congress had concerns and fears that were clearly racially charged, particularly when it came to the possibility of ADC benefits prompting a drop in the supply of African-American women who previously had no choice but to work for the extremely low wages employers wished to pay.[16] If southern white employers were forced to compete with ADC by raising wages for women of color, it was feared that this in turn would create pressures to increase the higher wages they ordinarily paid their white workers. A failure to maintain the existing racial pay gap would threaten white economic dominance and could undermine the existing racial hierarchy as a whole.

The political compromises that shaped ADC reflected a willingness on the part of the Roosevelt administration to allow individual state's rights to trump centralized control over ADC by federal officials. Compromises reached before passage of the Social Security Act of 1935 included:

1. The removal of legislative language that would have directly prohibited racial discrimination in states' administration of ADC.
2. Granting the individual states permission to set benefit levels under ADC at whatever level they wished, rather than requiring that states abide by a nationwide federal standard.
3. Allowing the states to turn day-to-day administration of their ADC programs over to local communities, which effectively meant decisions

regarding eligibility for aid would be informally influenced by locally prevailing norms and prejudices regarding who was to be defined as "deserving." [17]

The states' rights approach to income assistance for poor families almost guaranteed discriminatory treatment, and it took root as states' ADC programs began to sluggishly evolve. For some thirty years, until the mid-1960s, the program that became popularly known as *welfare* provided aid to some eligible families and not others. Early on, white widows and their children received priority over other white lone-mother-headed families. African-American families and other families of color were grossly underrepresented on the ADC rolls over this thirty-year period, despite their overrepresentation in the poverty population.[18] Whereas ADC benefits were low in every state, benefit levels were especially meager in those states where people of color made up a high percentage of the poverty population. In some locales, officials granted higher benefits to white families than to equally needy families of color.[19]

More often than not racial bias in the administration of ADC was quite subtle and thus difficult to detect because the policies through which the bias was expressed did not necessarily appear to be based upon race. For example, in keeping with the precedent established earlier by mothers' pension programs, many states required local welfare officials to restrict ADC to those households in which mothers were providing morally suitable homes for their children. When local employers were in need of seasonal workers, as when crops had to be planted or harvested, families were often cut off from ADC under the rationale that jobs for mothers were available. Families were also cut off from ADC benefits under the so-called "man-in-the-house rule." If local officials had any reason to believe that a mother had entered into a relationship with a man, the presumption was that he was assisting the household financially and that ADC was not needed. While these policies appeared to be blind to race, in actual practice they were primarily directed at African-American mothers.[20]

In short, until the mid-1960s, lone-mother-headed families' entitlement to income assistance under the Social Security Act of 1935 was tempered by discriminatory and exclusionary practices that were often little more than expressions of institutional racism. As sociologist Theda Skocpol put it, "The great leeway left to the states in the legislation of the 1930s ensured that conservative or racist interests would be able to control welfare coverage, benefit levels, and methods of administration in large stretches of the nation, and especially in the South, where the vast majority of blacks lived in poverty and political disenfranchisement."[21] While racial bias may have meant that many eligible white lone-mother-headed families were able to exercise their lawful entitlement to ADC benefits, no family really had a fundamental human right to income assistance. Moreover, the income assistance made available to such families at best did little more than maintain them in the depths of poverty. It did nothing to respect families' economic human right to an adequate standard of living.

Welfare Rights and Backlash Politics

The 1960s proved to be a key turning point for U.S. welfare policy.[22] Amendment of the Social Security Act allowed mothers, in addition to their children, to be included on the AFDC rolls. In recognition of this change, Aid to Dependent Children was renamed Aid to Families with Dependent Children (AFDC) in 1962. More significantly, in the 1960s strides were made toward fulfilling the promise of entitlement to income assistance for lone-mother-headed families regardless of their skin color. Thirty years of racially exclusionary practices began to be abolished and bureaucratic obstacles that hampered families' access to the welfare rolls were eased, resulting in marked changes in both the overall size and racial composition of the nation's welfare recipient population.

The process of change in the welfare rolls began with successful attacks by the 1960s civil rights movement on the U.S. version of racial apartheid.[23] The movement's successes in breaking down legally sanctioned racial segregation helped to energize grassroots antipoverty and welfare rights advocates. These advocates, who drew a great deal of support from within poverty-stricken African-American communities, worked with legal services attorneys supported by the federal War on Poverty (1964–1974). Through their combined efforts, impoverished lone-mother-headed families won class-action suits and U.S. Supreme Court decisions that overturned such well-established exclusionary practices as the man-in-the-house rule. Organized welfare rights protests, coupled with street-level rebelliousness and rioting by African Americans in cities across the nation, also put pressure on political elites to reduce the dense thicket of bureaucratic obstacles that discouraged needy families from applying for and receiving aid.[24]

Consequently, by the end of the 1960s the size of the U.S. welfare recipient population had greatly increased. Even in the face of discriminatory practices, the proportion of the welfare rolls made up of African Americans had been on the increase since the 1930s.[25] When the overall size of the rolls expanded in the 1960s, many more white lone-mother-headed families were added. However, with the breakdown of race-based exclusionary practices and other obstacles to accessing the rolls, the most significant increase in terms of numbers of recipients came from the

African-American community. Finally, more than three decades after the passage of the Social Security Act of 1935, the color composition of the welfare population had begun to more closely resemble the color composition of those lone-mother-headed families whose poverty rendered them eligible for assistance.[26]

Even as legal actions and the threat of greater social unrest progressively put an end to much of the racial exclusion from welfare and made its benefits available to more lone-mother-headed families, a significant backlash against AFDC began to develop. It is no understatement to say that income assistance to lone-mother-headed families had never been a wildly popular cause in the United States. The public had long been keenly concerned that welfare be limited to those who were truly needy, but had the suspicion that this was not necessarily occurring. By the 1960s widespread public sentiment existed that many, if not most, lone mothers who received welfare were at heart malingerers, fraudulently living off the labor of hardworking taxpayers, and enjoying indolent if not immoral lifestyles.[27] With the rapid expansion of the AFDC rolls, by the end of the 1960s what to do about welfare had become a national political issue for the first time. The backlash against AFDC that ensued would be helped along by U.S. political elites who were highly critical of the nation's "welfare mess." Many found AFDC to be a reliable lightening rod for all manner of public dissatisfactions and did not hesitate to denounce welfare and its recipients in their quest for voter support.

U.S. political elites were helped greatly in this regard by the changing characteristics of the growing welfare recipient population. One important change was in the marital status of most of the mothers whose families received income assistance.[28] Over the course of the twentieth century, an ever larger proportion of impoverished families had become headed by women. In the past, lone-mother-headed families living in poverty were most frequently headed by widows. But by the 1960s such families were far more likely to be headed by mothers whose marriages had dissolved or who had never married at all. This shift was reflected in the characteristics of the mothers helped by AFDC, of whom widows constituted only a small percentage. In little more than three decades, the welfare rolls had become dominated by mothers whose life circumstances brought them far less public sympathy.

We have already alluded to the second major change in welfare recipient characteristics, namely the rise in both the proportion and in the numbers of AFDC recipients who were African American. When African Americans migrated out of economically depressed rural areas of the deep South, largely to settle in northern and midwestern states, they often found themselves forced to live in city neighborhoods turned into ghettos. Their choice of household location was dictated by long-entrenched, white-enforced patterns of residential racial segregation.[29] The obvious concentration of large numbers of impoverished African Americans in certain city neighborhoods contributed to whites' awareness of their significant physical presence and whereabouts.

Yet racial segregation also kept whites from gaining a realistic understanding of the everyday struggles and lifestyles of the African-American poor and thus contributed to the resilience of long-standing racist stereotypes.[30] Common stereotypes held by many whites included beliefs that African Americans were lazy, immoral, dishonest, and promiscuous. Many whites also believed that African-American mothers preferred receiving welfare over work, even to the point of conceiving and bearing children in order to obtain or to increase the size of cash welfare benefits. Political elites played on such racist stereotypes by subtly portraying AFDC as a "black problem," conveniently ignoring the fact that large numbers of whites were also on the AFDC rolls.[31]

The connection in whites' eyes between African Americans and AFDC was further strengthened by mass media coverage showing African-American leadership and rank-and-file participation in welfare rights groups. During the 1960s, militant welfare rights protest activities often emerged out of ghetto sections of central cities. Protestors' demands frequently included more adequate and comprehensive benefits, humane treatment by welfare caseworkers, access to meaningful training and education programs, and jobs that would pay a decent living wage. The mass media, however, tended to devote little attention to analyzing the validity of protestors' concerns. Instead, whites were presented with images of (ostensibly undeserving) African-American advocates of welfare rights engaging in disruptive protest tactics, thus meriting the police repression and arrests with which their protests were met. Other negative reporting, including hyped-up stories of welfare fraud in which African Americans were prominently featured, also helped to inflame white antipathy toward welfare recipients.[32]

One effect of widespread antiwelfare attitudes was to restrain the rate of increase in the growth of AFDC rolls. In the ensuing decades many families who were technically entitled to receive AFDC would remain outside the program. Some poverty-stricken lone mothers failed to apply because they were unaware or unsure of their entitlement. Neither the federal government nor the individual states had anything to gain by seeking to expand the rolls and the costs to taxpayers, and welfare officials did not conduct outreach activities, widely disseminate eligibility information, or otherwise encourage AFDC applications. Other lone mothers were unwilling to endure the often humiliating and invasive AFDC application process, during which they were at the mercy of welfare agency workers and their often hostile attitudes. Yet others could not take the loss of personal privacy that often accompanied required supervision of recipients by caseworkers or were unwilling to endure the negatively stigmatized social status associated with being termed a welfare mother.

Still other lone mothers found that, when all was said and done, the cash benefits their families received were so low they were not worth applying for. Most mothers had to find ways to supplement AFDC benefits, legally or illegally, given that they were generally not enough for a family to live on.[33] Indeed, from the 1960s to the 1990s states allowed the purchasing power of the benefit levels attached to AFDC to progressively erode in the face of increases in the costs of living.

Calls for Welfare Reform: From Guaranteed Incomes to Personal Responsibility

By the end of the 1960s, the electoral successes and popularity of conservatives who made condemnation of AFDC recipients a component of their campaign strategies virtually guaranteed that welfare would remain a potent political issue in the United States. Attacks on AFDC by conservative political figures such as Arizona's senator Barry Goldwater, Alabama's governor George Wallace, and West Virginia's senator Robert C. Byrd helped to energize the debate. Prior to the 1960s, providing welfare benefits to lone-mother-headed families had largely been a political issue in individual states. During the 1960s, the view that welfare was a problem gained such national political salience that it could no longer be downplayed or ignored at the highest levels of government. Legislative proposals to alter U.S. welfare policy began to emanate from the White House. Such proposals would continue during both conservative and liberal presidential administrations for the next thirty years.[34]

At least initially, the most significant proposals to overhaul the welfare system called for guaranteed cash benefits for those mothers who could not work, while those who could work would be provided with supplemental cash benefits if they were earning low wages.[35] Work would be expected of those able to do so. Top politicians' increasing willingness to consider linking work requirements to benefits reflected the public's concern with welfare freeloaders. But it also subtly addressed employers' long-standing fears that easily available cash benefits could disrupt labor markets by providing mothers with an alternative to low-wage jobs.[36]

The first presidential proposals for addressing the "welfare mess" were actually somewhat radical when compared to the actual directions in which contemporary U.S. welfare policy would ultimately evolve. In 1969 President Richard M. Nixon's administration (1969–1974) sought to replace AFDC with the Family Assistance Plan, a negative income tax that would have provided a national minimum welfare benefit coupled with a work requirement. It died in Congress. In 1977 President Jimmy Carter's administration (1977–1981) proposed an alternative to AFDC that was similarly unsuccessful. Carter's Program for Better Jobs and Income likewise was a negative income tax, combining cash benefits with a work requirement, but Carter's proposal also would have provided public service jobs for those who could not find work. Objections to the notion of a federally guaranteed minimum income, even one with work requirements and the specter of greatly increased costs to government, played a major role in the lack of support that these proposals received in the U.S. Congress.

President Ronald Reagan's administration (1981–1989) took a different approach to welfare, one that in retrospect proved to be a key precursor to recent welfare reforms. Reagan rejected the idea of a negative income tax or a guaranteed minimum income, along with the notion of government-subsidized public service jobs. Poverty reduction was not the goal of his administration. Instead it placed emphasis on the much more limited but politically popular objective of reducing the AFDC rolls. In 1981 Reagan signed off on Congressional budget legislation that cut real spending on AFDC cash benefits and tightened program eligibility requirements, briefly cutting the growth of the welfare rolls. In 1988 Congress passed the Reagan administration's Family Support Act, which continued the tightening-up process by pushing new work requirements for mothers receiving AFDC.

The provisions of the Family Support Act of 1988 involved shared responsibilities between government and AFDC recipients. Mothers were responsible for abiding by AFDC's work requirements, while states in turn were responsible for providing mothers with supportive services. To help hasten the movement of mothers from welfare to work—thus reducing the size of the AFDC rolls—the act called for states to provide mothers with necessary skills training, education, job placement, transportation, and child care. In the end, however, Congress failed to provide the federal funding states needed to adequately expand and carry out such services; consequently, they ended up being unavailable to many mothers on the AFDC rolls. Since in many instances the states did not fulfill their responsibilities, lone mothers who were unable to access needed supportive services through no fault of their own could not be penalized if they failed to find employment.

With the passage of the Family Support Act of 1988, conservative political elites had won an important victory. Mandatory work requirements for lone mothers who were AFDC recipients were now enshrined into federal law. While liberals in Congress had insisted that government maintain its responsibility to AFDC recipients by providing job-related services for mothers, they did not have the clout to make sure the services were funded. This imbalance between work requirements and the absence of adequate supportive services for working lone mothers would become a hallmark of subsequent policies of welfare reform.

Although President George H. Bush's administration (1989–1993) did not push for major changes in U.S. welfare policy, it did decide to approve waivers to the Social Security Act of 1935 for individual states wishing to experiment with various types of welfare-to-work programs. Approval of such waivers continued into the early years of President Bill Clinton's administration (1993–2001). One experimental approach taken to move AFDC recipients into the work force was called Work First, which took the position that any job is a good job, regardless of the nature of the work involved or the wages the job paid. In Work First programs, lone mothers were required to take any employment offered to them or to suffer penalties, such as reduced AFDC benefits. Work First advocates asserted that going directly into the labor market was a much better route to developing good work habits and job skills, thus permanently escaping the AFDC rolls, than was spending time in training or education activities.

The Work First philosophy appealed to conservative political elites, whose principal concern was reducing the AFDC rolls and who had little interest in what happened to lone mothers once they were in the labor force.[37] The program also avoided the substantial costs involved in providing lone mothers with extensive job-related training and other supportive services. Liberals, on the other hand, while willing to accept mandatory work requirements, were insistent that such services were necessary in order to increase the probability of lone mothers' labor market success. Thus, when President Clinton's administration unveiled his proposed welfare reform legislation in the early 1990s—legislation he stated would "change welfare as we know it"—work requirements were included. But so was substantial federal funding for supportive services, including education and training.[38]

When the Republican Party gained control of Congress in 1994, conservatives lost little time in issuing counterproposals to those of the Democratic Clinton administration. Their policy statement, called the Contract for America, powerfully shaped the debate around welfare reform in ways that ended up fostering unprecedented changes in U.S. welfare policy.

Congressional Republicans were far less concerned with addressing the responsibility of government to help lone mothers toward economic self-sufficiency than they were in making mothers take on this responsibility themselves. Their ideas carried over into the Personal Responsibility and Work Opportunity Reconciliation Act (PRWORA), legislation amending the 1935 Social Security Act in ways that created a sea change in U.S. welfare policy.

The PRWORA, signed by President Clinton in 1996, retained joint federal–state funding of states' welfare programs. However, the act markedly reduced the responsibility of government for ensuring the well-being of impoverished lone-mother-headed families. Welfare, many of the act's advocates argued, was addictive much like a habit-forming drug. AFDC was said to entrap and enslave mothers, its cash benefits undermining their work ethic. Conservative political elites portrayed the PRWORA as a form of tough love necessary to wean mothers away from their welfare dependency, thus ending their enslavement. Securing their families' well-being, henceforth, was going to be the mothers' responsibility, not the government's.

Under the PRWORA:

1. Aid to Families with Dependent Children was abolished and replaced by a new program called Temporary Assistance for Needy Families (TANF). Under AFDC, lone mothers and their children had been legally entitled to cash assistance so long as they met means tests and other eligibility standards. Any such entitlement to assistance was abolished by the PRWORA. In general, the question of who the states would assist, how, and for how long would now be up to them. In minimizing its control over individual states' TANF programs, the federal government made a u-turn toward the states' rights approach that U.S. welfare policy had earlier emphasized.

2. The individual states were given a great deal of latitude in determining how they wished to administer their own TANF programs and were encouraged by provisions of the PRWORA to find ways to divert applicants away from their TANF rolls. States were permitted, for example, to keep impoverished lone-mother-headed families off the rolls until they could provide proof they had exhausted familial as well as private charitable and faith-based resources.

3. Fixed time limits were instituted for TANF assistance, eliminating AFDC's open-ended policy of aiding families as long as they were in need. Families meeting TANF eligibility criteria could receive federally-subsidized cash assistance for a cumulative total of no more than five years. PRWORA allowed individual states to limit families to even fewer years of assistance under TANF, and many took advantage

of this opportunity. Connecticut, for example, instituted a twenty-one-month TANF time limit.

4. Lone mothers receiving TANF benefits had to engage in work activities for thirty hours per week, a level of mandatory participation that had not existed under AFDC. If they failed to meet work requirements, the individual states could impose sanctions on TANF families. Sanctions could include partial or even total loss of TANF benefits. Sanctions could also be levied for such rule violations as a failure by mothers to file TANF paperwork properly or in a timely manner or for missing scheduled appointments with TANF program staff.

5. If a lone mother gave birth to an additional child while she and her children were receiving AFDC, in most instances the family would receive a small cash supplement to its regular benefits. Under the PRWORA, however, the individual states were allowed to adopt family-cap policies that eliminated or reduced this small cash supplement. The existence of a family cap meant that family members would effectively experience a per-capita reduction in benefits in the event of a new birth.

6. Under the PRWORA, the access to cash benefits allowed to legal immigrants was sharply restricted. While aid to legal immigrants who could meet eligibility requirements was not restricted, immigrants arriving after 1996 were prohibited from receiving TANF benefits for five years unless the state in which they resided chose to provide and pay for those benefits on its own.[39]

These and other provisions of the PRWORA reflect what some have called the "New Paternalism."[40] The act subtly communicates a strong distrust of—if not disdain for—impoverished lone mothers even as it spells out measures to control them. In abolishing families' entitlement to aid and enforcing time limits on income assistance, PRWORA in effect suggests that lone mothers would otherwise be happy living on welfare indefinitely. By mandating work and by encouraging sanctions for lone mothers who fail to meet work requirements or other TANF rules, PRWORA implies that lone mothers are lazy and need to be coerced out of idleness. In allowing states to impose family caps, PRWORA suggests that left alone, lone mothers are prone to immoral out-of-wedlock behavior leading to the birth of illegitimate children. In sharply restricting legal immigrants' access to aid, PRWORA implies that poor immigrants are drawn to the United States by its generous welfare benefits and, once here, they and their families become leeches on the backs of taxpayers. Provisions of the PRWORA promise solutions to such problematic attitudes and behaviors on the part of impoverished lone mothers. Yet social scientists who have studied AFDC and its recipients have been able to find little more than occasional anecdotal evidence to confirm the existence of these attitudes and behaviors. Hence, most social scientists treat them as welfare myths.[41]

Recent debates around how to fine-tune the PRWORA have offered new opportunities to reinforce such welfare myths. President George W. Bush's administration (2001–present) proposed an increase in TANF work requirements from thirty to forty hours per week, implying once again that lone mothers receiving income assistance are slackers who need to be coerced into pulling their own weight. His administration also called for a portion of federal TANF funding to be used by states to implement programs promoting marriage.[42] The Bush administration presented marriage as a cure for lone mothers' poverty, even as U.S. Census statistics indicate that two-parent families make up an increasing proportion of the nation's growing population of the working poor.[43] The Bush administration's proposal subtly reinforces the notion that mothers who become or remain unmarried are mired in poverty because they have made bad lifestyle choices—simply another way of saying lone mothers are personally responsible for their plight.

Key Factors Shaping U.S. Welfare Policy

No single factor is wholly responsible for shaping U.S. welfare policy from its roots in mothers' pensions to its current manifestation in the form of temporary assistance for needy families. Scholars of welfare policy history have often seen fit to stress different factors, and there does not seem to be any real consensus. However, it is clear from much of this scholarship that U.S. welfare policy did not arise or evolve in a social vacuum. In particular, U.S. welfare policy has reflected and, in many ways, has reinforced society-wide systems of class, gender, and racial inequality. It is true that over time these systems of inequality have undergone changes, yet they seem to have always played a significant role as organizing agents, influencing the institutional as well as the interpersonal treatment and life chances of virtually every member of U.S. society. The omnipresence and significance of class, gender, and racial systems of inequality make it difficult to imagine how any U.S. welfare policy could have developed independently of them. Scholars who largely ignore or dismiss their impact as having little importance clearly are taking liberties with reality.

Class Inequality

The United States has always been characterized by a gross maldistribution of wealth and income, key indicators of class inequality. Scholars who view U.S. society's system of class inequality as a key factor shaping welfare policy have generally viewed this policy as constrained by the economic self-interests of the nation's affluent capitalist class.[44] Those who own and control the nation's means of production not only are among the most affluent members of U.S. society, but they also have a great deal more political clout at top levels of government than the poor do. Their clout is achieved through directly participating in appointed or elected positions, providing campaign contributions to political incumbents and selected challengers, and funding institutions—from foundations to policy organizations—that help to generate and disseminate ideologies supportive of capitalist class interests. Members of the capitalist class have been largely successful in protecting their access to low-cost labor and in controlling the degree to which they are exposed to personal and corporate taxation.

Even low welfare benefits, never mind more generous ones that would lift families up to or above the poverty line, can pose a challenge to capitalist class interests. The availability of income assistance to working-age adults may weaken employers' control over low-wage workers, whereas the cost of providing such assistance poses the threat of higher tax rates. Higher wages and taxes can cut into profits. Hence, from the perspective of scholars who emphasize the importance of class interests in shaping welfare policy, the antipathy of the capitalist class toward welfare is a byproduct of the logic of the economic system from which they disproportionately benefit. It is also a reflection of a dominant class ideology that stresses competitive individualism, often expressed by the maxim, "Anyone can make it in America if they really try." The meager and begrudgingly granted income assistance provided under U.S. welfare policy over the years reflects this antipathy and capitalists' success in making their ideology a component of broader public opinion.

The classic work, *Regulating the Poor*, by Frances Fox Piven and Richard A. Cloward, provides a version of the class-influence point of view that also addresses some of the dynamics of U.S. welfare policy.[45] In these authors' opinion, welfare policy cannot be understood apart from the capitalist class's need to maintain control over its most economically deprived class subordinates. Historically, Piven and Cloward argue that U.S. welfare policy has served two major functions: (1) to stifle protest on the part of the unemployed and others living in poverty, and (2) to provide low-wage workers with reason to put up with employers' often harsh and exploitive work norms.

When widespread unrest among those at the bottom of the U.S. system of class inequality threatened to erupt during the Great Depression, and threatened to do so again in the 1960s, the welfare rolls were expanded to help pacify the poor and stabilize the situation. On the other hand, when it has not been needed for such purposes, welfare has been made more difficult to access and the rolls have been held steady or reduced. Tightening up on welfare has in turn contributed to the regulation of labor, according to Piven and Cloward. In the absence of economic and political crises that may mobilize the poor, welfare benefits are made available to only the most extremely impoverished. In return for income assistance—at a level barely allowing a family to subsist—recipients are forced to suffer degrading public stigmatization and often humiliating treatment by welfare officials. The message to low-wage workers is, "This could easily be you," a message Piven and Cloward believe low-wage workers take to heart as they struggle to stoically endure the treatment they receive in the workplace.[46]

Clearly, a welfare policy that rather consistently responds to the economic vested interests of the most affluent class over and above the subsistence needs of the least affluent fails the test of respecting economic human rights. As chapter 1 demonstrated, many present-day political elites argue that poverty is best addressed by allowing the free market to work at job and income creation and by getting government assistance programs out of the picture. Yet respecting economic human rights virtually requires significant government involvement, if only to protect those—especially lone mothers and their children—who the vagaries of the market leave vulnerable to chronic impoverishment.

Class inequality is not the only key factor that has shaped U.S. welfare policy. An overemphasis on the system of class inequality typically means that other important factors, such as gender inequality, are given short shrift. As seen in this chapter, women have long been the focus of U.S. welfare policy. From mothers' pensions to TANF, welfare has primarily been directed at lone mothers; hence, it is important to address the question of the relationship between this policy and gender that, much like class, has served as an organizing agent in U.S. society.

Gender Inequality

While feminist movements aimed at ensuring that women are treated equally with men have scored major breakthroughs in the United States in recent decades, male dominance continues to be readily detectable at the top levels of U.S. society's major institutions.[47] Even today, few women hold command positions in the corporate economy, positions in which crucial decisions are made that affect the existence of jobs and their location, levels of pay and benefits, and the degree of emphasis placed on nondiscriminatory treatment in hiring and promotion. Women are similarly absent from top posts at the national level of governance. The disproportionate presence of men in key decision-making positions—from Congress, to the presidency, to the U.S. Supreme Court—has long meant that problems and issues of particular concern to women have received little attention or have been given low priority. Upping this priority has required decades of political struggle on the part of women.

Even the reforms achieved in recent years require their advocates' constant vigilance lest the reforms meet resistance, as has occurred with enforcement of affirmative action in employment and the expansion of equitable treatment of female student athletes. Meanwhile, many battles for women's rights are still ongoing. For example, political resistance has continued to block the proposed Equal Rights Amendment to the U.S. Constitution, older women remain poorly served by the Social Security retirement system, and women's reproductive rights are being increasingly contested. In the United States, women's rights are not accorded the status of fundamental human rights by law or custom; thus, women find themselves needing to continually demand recognition of their rights and press for their enforcement.

Welfare has never been treated as a "right," and from a feminist perspective, U.S. welfare policy has never been responsive to the serious problems faced by impoverished lone-mother-headed families. Throughout its history, U.S. welfare policy has largely been constructed and implemented by male-dominated political institutions and has functioned in ways that protect patriarchy and honor men's collective self-interests over and above the interests of women and their children.[48] Feminist scholars argue that meager and reluctantly proffered welfare benefits cannot be made more generous and readily available to lone-mother-headed families in need, for this would economically empower women and correspondingly would reduce their traditional dependency on males as breadwinners.[49] Women who attempt to successfully establish themselves as family heads and to live independently of men are punished with bare-subsistence-level benefits made difficult to obtain. This keeps welfare from appearing to be a viable alternative for many mothers, including those who need to escape family situations that suffer from male domination to the point of domestic violence and other forms of abuse. The failure of welfare to adequately support lone-mother-headed families undermines mothers' motivation and ability to leave their male partners and, thus, serves to buttress patriarchal social relations.

Patriarchy is served not only by the inadequate welfare benefits that are a matter of political decision-making, but also by the low pay that typically characterizes "women's work." Women have long been disproportionately concentrated in sectors of the labor market in which most other workers are women, a reflection of the patriarchal ideology holding that "biology is destiny" and that women are by nature best suited for certain limited lines of work. Women have long been overrepresented in service-sector jobs where wages are low, benefits are few, and job tenure is often insecure. The failure of welfare to adequately support families drives desperate lone mothers into such women's work, where their lack of alternatives and vulnerability to exploitation feeds into employers' drive for profits. The inability of lone mothers to adequately support their families with either welfare or women's work creates an impossible and overwhelming situation for many women, one best avoided by staying involved with a male partner.[50]

In her important work *Regulating the Lives of Women*, Mimi Abramovitz explores the historical relationship between patriarchy and U.S. welfare policy.[51] She underscores the way welfare has been used as a vehicle for sorting out the "deserving poor" from the "undeserving poor." Widowed mothers have been viewed as deserving assistance, having been left with the responsibility of lone parenting through no fault or choice of their own. In contrast, divorced, separated, abandoned, or never-married mothers who turn to welfare long have been condemned, which is in response to the moral ambiguity surrounding the source of their lone-motherhood status. Abramovitz stresses, however, that this condemnation functions to discourage women from becoming lone mothers, thus helping to shore up a patriarchal "family ethic" that calls for women to be dependents of men rather than self-reliant and autonomous individuals.[52]

While the contemporary feminist movement has sought to address women's labor force segregation, discriminatory employment practices, and pay inequities affecting women, it has been slow to put its full weight behind welfare as a women's issue. Some attribute this to the class and racial characteristics of the movement itself, which is largely middle-class and white in composition.[53] Many of those involved in the movement may well share some of the long-standing popular negative stereotypes about welfare mothers. The feminist movement has stressed equal opportunity for women, particularly in higher education and professional employment—matters particularly salient to white middle-class women for whom work outside the home offers hope of meaningful rewards. The movement has committed itself to helping such women successfully escape the confines of the household and to explore their potential beyond gender-assigned caretaker roles. At the same time, it has offered far less support to those impoverished lone mothers who would like the right to choose between remaining at home to care for their children versus struggling to find and afford decent child care in order to take on a low-wage service job.

The contemporary feminist movement has failed to see and act upon the liberating, antipatriarchal potential of recognizing impoverished lone mothers' economic human right to an adequate standard of living and the importance of their family caretaking contributions. It has had little to say to critics of welfare who advocate demanding work requirements for impoverished lone mothers—requirements that ask mothers to put work before family responsibilities. Members of the feminist movement appear to feel that since the majority of middle-class women with children are in the work force, there is no real justification for paying impoverished mothers to "sit at home." There has been little push for programs of government support that would allow mothers, regardless of economic standing or marital status, to make their own decisions when it comes to taking on paid work versus caretaking.

Scholars who stress the role of class or gender inequality as key social factors shaping U.S. welfare policy tend to treat racial inequality as a less important or secondary matter. Depending upon the analyst, either class or gender trumps the importance of race. A growing body of scholarship, however, demonstrates that racial inequality has historically played a major role in the conception, formulation, and implementation of U.S. welfare policy and continues to do so today.

Racial Inequality

In characterizing U.S. society as a "racialized social system," sociologist Eduardo Bonilla-Silva has underscored the fact that race, much like class and gender, has served as an important organizing agent in structuring this society's social relations.[54] Scientifically speaking, biologically distinct and identifiable races simply do not exist. Race is a social construction, not an empirical reality. People are classified by race based on perceived differences in physical characteristics, such as skin color, and significant meanings are then attached to these differences.[55] In the United States, the meanings many whites have attached to race differences constitute a racist ideology—a set of ideas about white superiority that historically has been used to rationalize the oppression and exploitation of people of color.

This racist ideology not only includes the belief that separate races exist, but that basic qualitative differences exist among races. For many years it was widely held that races could be classified as biologically superior or inferior to one another. In more recent decades, the notion that there is a fundamental biological hierarchy of races has been largely supplanted by the idea that races vary in the degree to which they possess certain desirable cultural traits. Either way, a society whose members believe that a hierarchy of races exists, a hierarchy with whites at the top, cannot help but practice racism. For 400 years, racist ideology has been used to explain and to justify white racial hegemony over Native Americans, African Americans, Latino Americans, and Asian Americans.[56]

It is true that the blatant and legalized racial oppression associated with chattel slavery and Jim Crow racial apartheid no longer exists in the United States. However, social scientists have provided ample evidence that racism did not disappear from U.S. society in the wake of the 1950s and 1960s civil rights movement; many contemporary scholars believe that it merely changed in form. A new racism is said to have emerged over the last few decades to supplant the old racism of the pre-civil rights movement era.[57] This new racism includes attacks on affirmative action, subtle racial profiling, waging a war on drugs in the nation's inner cities, high rates of imprisonment and capital punishment for men of color, and—most germane to this discussion—changes in welfare policy that some have likened to a war against the poor. Expressions of racism today are often much more camouflaged and more easily deniable by whites than the blatant discrimination and legally enforced segregation character-izing much of the old racism.[58]

The new racism overlaps with vestiges of the old racism that have never been adequately addressed or eliminated. Together they limit the present-day life chances of African Americans and other people of color. Among such vestiges of the old racism are entrenched patterns of residential segregation, unequal educational opportunities, labor market stratification and workplace discrimination, income and wealth inequalities, and white-dominated political institutions.[59] All contribute to the disproportionate presence of African Americans and other people of color in the poverty population, yet ignoring these conditions, most U.S. political elites take the position that racism is no longer a significant phenomenon needing to be addressed in U.S. society.

Political elites often cite existing civil rights protections and the emergence of a stable black middle class as evidence of "the declining significance of race"[60] in the United States. In rejecting the present-day salience of racism, most elites see no need to pursue race-sensitive or race-specific social policies to address problems such as poverty. Indeed, many reject government attention to race as both socially divisive and unproductive, claiming that it encourages people of color to see themselves as helpless victims for whom others (e.g., the government, whites) are obligated to provide handouts. Claims of victimization by racism in an era when—in the view of many political elites—racism essentially no longer exists are said to be used by people of color to evade personal responsibility for their poverty and welfare dependency.

The refusal of political elites to acknowledge the significance of race is a feature of the new racism.[61] Portraying themselves as race-blind and without prejudice, political elites argue that poor people are largely responsible for their own fate. In the United States, economic opportunities are said to exist for people willing to take advantage of them by working hard. U.S. political elites think that if African Americans and other people of color are impoverished, it is not a matter of past or present racism; rather, it is an outcome of inappropriate attitudes and levels of motivation, matters political elites subtly imply are rooted in underclass values and other cultural deficits people of color need to change for themselves. Welfare reform is seen as a way of helping this change along.

In *Welfare Racism: Playing the Race Card against America's Poor*, Kenneth J. Neubeck and Noel A. Cazenave view U.S. welfare policy as racism-driven.[62] While their analysis does not seek to trump class and gender with race, they provide extensive documentation aimed at showing that the racialization of U.S. society has significantly shaped the nature of U.S. welfare policy. The history of this policy is rife with *welfare racism*, defined as "the organization of racialized public assistance attitudes, policy making, and administrative practices."[63] Examples of welfare racism were mentioned earlier in this chapter, from the early years in which people of color were systematically excluded from the welfare rolls to more recent times when dramatic changes in the color composition of the recipients have been met with ever more paternalistically controlling and restrictive eligibility requirements.

One of Neubeck and Cazenave's key conclusions relates to the functions of U.S. welfare policy for racial inequality. While welfare policy is clearly about public assistance practices, the policy itself can also be understood as a form of ideology. Neubeck and Cazenave view contemporary U.S. welfare policy as a component of the racist ideology discussed earlier.[64] Political elites have legislated policy provisions that can be defended as race-blind in that they affect all welfare recipients regardless of racial identity. But, as mentioned earlier, elites also have simultaneously framed welfare as primarily a black problem. It is by no means accidental that welfare policy provisions subtly express and reinforce racist stereotypes regarding African American women. These stereotypes—part of racist ideology since the days of slavery—depict African-American women as shiftless, irresponsible, immoral, and promiscuous.[65] Such women are accused of breeding children to gain welfare benefits and are depicted as parasites who sap the pocketbooks of hard-working (read white) taxpayers.

To deal with such imagined women, U.S. political elites have mandated that lone mothers must work in return for income assistance, have tightened up eligibility requirements for welfare benefits, have instituted time limits for aid, have eliminated entitlements to welfare, have financially penalized mothers for additional births, and have allowed the monetary value of cash benefits to progressively decline. These welfare policy provisions and practices are essentially ideological statements about the moral inferiority of the women of color at whom they are largely directed. But U.S. welfare policy is more than simply an expression of racist ideology. From Neubeck and Cazenave's perspective, the heightened Draconian turns this policy has taken since the 1960s can best be understood in the context of racially-driven backlash politics. In their view, mean-spirited changes in welfare policy were set in motion in response to the civil rights movement's successful attacks on white racial hegemony and have proceeded apace ever since.[66] Insofar as the ideological content of welfare policy serves as a subtle but constant reminder of the moral inferiority of people of color, it functions to support U.S. society's system of racial inequality.[67] White politicians' condemnation of welfare and its recipients is emblematic of the new racism, for it is little more than a way of speaking to and reproducing beliefs in white superiority using racialized code terms.[68]

It is common to think of racism as a phenomenon negatively affecting people of color—its direct or indirect targets—and to think of whites as racism's beneficiaries. But racism can harm whites as well.[69] Neubeck and Cazenave's analysis found that welfare racism has harmful effects on impoverished white lone-mother-headed families. Whites' general hostility to welfare, which is kept alive by racist stereotypes, results in welfare eligibility provisions that are restrictive, punitive, and controlling as well as benefits that are grossly inadequate to meet families' subsistence needs. But both impoverished families of color and white families needing income assistance are adversely affected by such policy provisions. Impoverished whites in effect become the victims of welfare racism along with their counterparts of color.

Lone mothers and their children have long been among the most economically deprived members of U.S. society. Within this sector of the population, lone-mother-headed families of color have been overrepresented among the poorest of the poor. Their chronic and severe impoverishment has facilitated their vulnerability to racist stereotyping and consequent mistreatment. Such mistreatment includes being subject to a welfare policy shaped by racism in its conception and supportive of U.S. society's system of racial inequality in its execution. Such a welfare policy is by definition in violation of human rights.[70] A nation cannot construct a policy that respects economic human rights on a foundation of racist stereotypes.

Current U.S. welfare policy not only falls far short of the economic human rights ideals set forth in the Universal Declaration of Human Rights, but it also exacerbates already existing unequal life chances along skin color lines.

Welfare at the Intersections of Class, Gender, and Racial Inequality

In recent years, feminist scholars have played a leadership role in demonstrating ways in which societal systems of class, gender, and racial inequality are interrelated,[71] even though each system can be discussed separately from the others, as was done here. Systems of class, gender, and racial inequality are deeply enmeshed and in many respects are interdependent.[72] This is clearly evident when examining the individual, where each person simultaneously occupies a position in and is affected by the workings of each of these systems of inequality. For impoverished lone mothers, the results can be cumulative oppression.[73]

Lone mothers who are poor experience the worst of the U.S. system of class inequality by virtue of their low incomes and lack of wealth. Class location defines their poverty-level conditions. But they are not genderless and their poverty, in part, reflects the different and discriminatory treatment that women receive in the U.S. system of gender inequality. Many lone mothers who must look to welfare to help support their families have been the victims of male sexual exploitation or domestic abuse by a male partner. The system of gender inequality often imposes few or no demands for economic support on the biological fathers of their children, leaving lone mothers with the difficult task of both caring for and providing for them on their own. This task is made extremely difficult by virtue of mothers' participation in a labor market that does not place much monetary value on women's work. However, impoverished lone mothers also are not colorless. The racial status they are assigned by the dominant white population determines mothers' positions in the U.S. system of racial inequality. When combined with the disadvantages of being poor and female, the perceived race of a lone mother can either be a help or a hindrance in her struggle to meet the daily caretaking and subsistence needs of her children. As we will see in chapter 4, other systems of inequality, such as that based on disability status and sexual orientation, can add even more burdens to impoverished lone mothers in this struggle.

This brief historical overview is intended to provide background to present-day U.S. welfare policy and the impact of recent welfare reform. chapter 3 examines some of the general outcomes of welfare reform and questions political elites' claims for its success.

3
Building Character through Adversity:
General Outcomes of Welfare Reform

The United States is an extraordinarily wealthy nation, capable of spending hundreds of billions of dollars a year on activities political elites deem to be a national priority, such as defense and homeland security. Imagine in contrast a policy of enlightened welfare reform (costing but a fraction of such huge amounts) directed at making sure the subsistence needs of impoverished lone-mother-headed families are met. Ideally, reform of the U.S. welfare system should improve such families' lives and should hasten their escape from poverty.

By and large, though, welfare reform in the United States has not done these things. The Personal Responsibility and Work Opportunity Reconciliation Act of 1996 (PRWORA) dismantled the already inadequate welfare safety net that had been in place for over sixty years. The PRWORA replaced this safety net with Temporary Assistance for Needy Families (TANF), whose welfare-to-work requirements were adopted with the argument that the best way to make lone mothers and their children self-sufficient was to push them off the welfare rolls. This self-sufficiency would, however, have to be realized in a labor market whose employment practices have long made it difficult for women to support their families on their own. On average, wages received by women are lower than they are for men. For example, the U.S. Census Bureau found that in 2003 women made only 75.5 cents for every dollar earned by men.[1] Moreover, employers of low-wage labor tend to be less than accommodating to lone mothers' caregiving obligations, viewing them as the mothers' responsibility to manage.

This chapter provides a general examination of the employment, income, and family well-being of lone mothers who have been subjected to TANF's mandatory work requirements and cash-benefit time limits. Two questions are at the heart of this chapter:

- Does TANF's mandate that lone mothers move "from welfare to work" mean they and their children thereby become economically secure?
- Does leaving the welfare rolls mean poverty is left behind as well?

For the most part, the answer to both of these questions is "no." Lone-mother-headed families have a difficult time finding and retaining employment and earning decent wages. While most mothers who leave the TANF rolls do find jobs of some sort, many ex-welfare recipients end up with neither employment nor a known source of income. Even those who are employed frequently find that their wages do not allow them to provide the food, housing, or health care they and their children require. As will be discussed later, welfare reform has adversely affected child and family well-being in various ways, even as political elites maintain a remarkable consensus that it has been a success. Unfortunately, welfare reform can hardly be viewed as a success in terms of respect for economic human rights, given that it has left so many families still struggling to meet their basic subsistence needs.

The Decline in the TANF Rolls

As mentioned in chapter 2, the federal government permitted individual states to experiment with changes in their Aid to Families with Dependent Children (AFDC) programs in the late 1980s and early 1990s, granting many states waivers to provisions of the Social Security Act of 1935. However, welfare reform was not fully ushered in until the passage of the Personal Responsibility and Work Opportunity Reconciliation Act of 1996. Bipartisan Congressional passage of this act, which was then signed by Democratic president Bill Clinton, was a watershed moment in the history of U.S. welfare policy.

The act empowered individual states to design and to run their own welfare programs with little federal oversight or control. In meeting the requirements of the PRWORA, some states were able to continue the welfare programs they had developed under federal waivers. Others initiated significantly new programs for the first time. Under Temporary Assistance for Needy Families, states had the freedom to determine what, if any, benefits would be made available to lone mothers and their children, the conditions under which families would be assisted, and the duration aid would be extended. Under the PRWORA, families did not have any legally established entitlement to receive TANF aid, no matter how great their economic need. TANF eligibility policies were left up to state governments, and cash-benefit levels varied widely. In 2003, for example, a lone mother and two children could receive a monthly maximum of $170 in Mississippi and $923 in Alaska.[2] Even the higher amount did not bring a three-person family very close to the federal poverty line in 2003.

The political rhetoric surrounding the passage of the PRWORA stressed the need to end lone mothers' so-called "welfare dependency" and to transform it into "self-sufficiency." Reducing poverty itself was not a manifest goal of the act, although advocates of welfare reform frequently argued that moving mothers from welfare to work would help welfare-dependent women develop good work habits and job skills. This, it was argued, would increase the likelihood that they would be upwardly mobile and that their earnings would help their families escape from poverty. But when all was said and done, PRWORA was really directed at reducing the size of the welfare rolls. Most advocates of the PRWORA demonstrated little concern for what ultimately happened to families that left the TANF.[3]

Since the passage of the PRWORA in 1996, political elites have regularly trumpeted the success of welfare reform. They have done so even as the numbers of people living under the federal poverty line have markedly risen, as was the case during and in the years immediately following the 2001 recession. Political elites' claims for the so-called success of the PRWORA have rested primarily on statistics indicating that the nation's TANF rolls have dropped significantly since the PRWORA was passed. In 1996, for example, the average monthly number of recipients on the welfare rolls was 12,620,620 (including 8,686,000 children). By 2001, this number had fallen to 5,464,000 (4,055,000 of whom were children).[4] In March 2003, the overall TANF rolls were down to 4,963,771, a 59.5 percent decline since the passage of the PRWORA.[5]

Conflicting Interpretations of the TANF Roll Decline

The PRWORA was initiated during a period of strong economic upswing in the United States, during which it has been common for welfare rolls to go down. It has never been possible for lone-mother-headed families to do more than barely survive on the meager cash benefits of welfare.[6] Moreover, the unwillingness of states to adapt these benefits to rising costs of living has meant that their value has progressively declined. From 1995 to

2003, for example, the monthly maximum AFDC/TANF benefits declined by 18 percent for the median state after adjusting for inflation.[7] Thus, it is understandable that lone mothers in a position to do so take advantage of improved employment opportunities to leave the welfare rolls. In becoming employed, many mothers are also able to benefit from the federal earned income tax credit (EITC), a means-tested program of refundable tax credits established in 1975. EITC supplements the incomes of eligible low-wage workers with children and millions of people rely on its benefits. The EITC has been said to raise "more families with children above the poverty line than any other government program."[8]

An exodus of lone mothers from the welfare rolls during those periods when jobs become more readily available had been the norm in the past. Yet when the welfare rolls declined dramatically during the healthy economy of the 1990s, much debate occurred over how much of this decline should be attributed to mothers' predictable work-oriented responses to the economy versus how much of the decline in the rolls stemmed from TANF's coercive welfare-to-work requirements.[9] Critics of the PRWORA emphasized that most impoverished lone mothers—at least those who were able to do so—had always been eager to trade welfare for employment. They argued that mothers did not need government coercion to leave the welfare rolls but instead left the rolls on their own initiative in response to economic opportunities. By leaving the rolls, lone mothers aspired not only to improve their families' economic circumstances through employment, but also to escape the negative stigma and degradation heaped upon so-called *welfare mothers,* a pejorative code term for women who were supposedly happy to remain dependent and to linger indefinitely on taxpayers' largesse.

Almost all critics of the PRWORA stressed the healthy state of the U.S. economy in explaining the steady decline in the TANF rolls. However, some critics suggested that the especially rapid rate of this decline was in part a function of states' practices of diversion which, encouraged by PRWORA, were aimed at keeping potential TANF recipients from joining the rolls in the first place. Almost half of the states have given TANF-eligible families a small, one-time, lump-sum payment to meet their immediate needs in lieu of admitting them to the TANF rolls. Other states have chosen to discourage new TANF applications by requiring lone mothers to produce substantial documentation showing that they have engaged in significant job-search activities or that they have exhausted all possible other opportunities for aid, including local charities and family help. Some states have engaged in both types of practices. These practices were thought to discourage many TANF-qualified impoverished families from applying for it or from completing the application process. Thus, in the view of critics of the PRWORA, the welfare rolls declined more rapidly than they otherwise would have. Critics also pointed out the PRWORA permitted states to negatively sanction lone mothers who violated even minor TANF program rules and regulations. Such sanctions often led to the temporary or even permanent removal of recipients from the rolls, further contributing to their dramatic drop.

Supporters of PRWORA viewed the decline in the welfare rolls in quite different terms. Many of the act's provisions had been based on the premise that most lone mothers were unwilling to work and preferred to laze along at home on public assistance rather than to take outside employment. From PRWORA supporters' point of view, the decline in the rolls was proof that the laziness premise was correct. Downplaying the role of increased job opportunities for lone mothers due to a healthy economy, the act's supporters argued that mothers receiving TANF, in return for which they were required to seek jobs, were rapidly becoming self-sufficient. TANF work requirements had provided the nudge lone mothers needed to go from welfare to work. An analyst at the conservative American Enterprise Institute has claimed that only 35 to 45 percent of the decline in the rolls could be accounted for by the economy. The other major reasons included welfare reform (25 to 35 percent), increased government aid to the working poor (20 to 30 percent), and erosion of the real value of cash welfare benefits (5 to 10 percent).[10]

PRWORA supporters tended to shrug off critics' concerns regarding diversion practices and sanctions, suggesting that mothers diverted from the rolls with all likelihood did not really need or deserve TANF benefits and that those sanctioned off the rolls for rule violations had acted irresponsibly and, thus, deserved such punishment. From the point of view of PRWORA supporters, the legislation was accomplishing its purpose. The PRWORA was encouraging self-sufficiency by making welfare both harder to get and temporary and by mandating that its recipients go to work.

Even as Poverty Rates Rise, TANF Rolls Continue to Fall

At the turn of the twenty-first century, the economic well-being of the previous decade abruptly ended. Over a three-year period, from 2001 to 2003, the U.S. economy experienced a bout of recession followed by a serious economic slowdown. Even as this slowdown showed limited signs of reversing in 2004, chronic unemployment and underemployment continued to plague many states and locales. Rates of new job growth were so sluggish nationally that some economists used the term *jobless recovery,* and job growth became an issue in the 2004 presidential election campaign.

In the past, whenever economic downswings occurred and jobs became harder to find, poverty rates increased. Thus, it is not surprising that between 2000 and 2003 the U.S. poverty rate rose from 11.3 to 12.5 percent. In that same time period, the number of lone-mother-headed families living below the poverty line rose from 10.9 million in 2000 to 12.4 million in 2003.[11] Based on past trends, the welfare rolls should have increased in the early 2000s in response to rising poverty. Instead, the decline in the TANF rolls that began in the 1990s continued unabated.[12] Indeed, in 2001 fourteen states experienced both rising unemployment and a decline in the TANF rolls at the same time.[13] Again, critics and supporters of the PRWORA brought quite different interpretations to bear.

From the critics' point of view, the failure of the TANF rolls to respond to worsening economic conditions and increased poverty was an indictment of the program's ability to function as a safety net for lone-mother-headed families facing hard times. It was said that the individual states' frequently complex and even intimidating TANF application processes, diversion and sanctioning practices, eligibility restrictions, strict time limits for income assistance, and denial of benefits to many immigrants were keeping lone-mother-headed families off the welfare rolls at a time when they were least able to help themselves. Critics of the PRWORA argued that unlike AFDC, whose rolls expanded with economic downturns, states' TANF programs left many needy families adrift and struggling to meet basic subsistence needs.[14]

On the other hand, supporters of the PRWORA held the view that the failure of the rolls to rise during the economic downturn was a sign that TANF's work requirements, time limits for assistance, and other features aimed at producing self-sufficiency were having the desired impact. The act's supporters argued that lone mothers were now more likely to turn to work than welfare to support their families, were becoming more integrated into the labor force, were developing a stronger work ethic, and were gaining job experience that helped them to remain employed even during economic downturns. In the words of the U.S. Department of Health and Human Services' top welfare official, Assistant Secretary Wade Horn, TANF had "become relatively 'recession-proof.'"[15]

Supporters of the PRWORA have been careful, however, not to draw attention to the fact that TANF cash benefits serve fewer and fewer of the lone-mother-headed families whose level of impoverishment qualifies them to receive assistance. Because many families are failing to receive TANF's cash benefits as well as benefits from other government programs for which they may be eligible, the nation's poverty rate is higher than it otherwise would be.[16] The stereotype equating being impoverished with being on welfare is not based in reality, especially today. One study found that mothers poor enough to qualify for cash welfare benefits were far more likely to receive such benefits in the early 1990s than in the years immediately following passage of the PRWORA.[17] Data from the U.S. Department of Health and Human Services show that in 1996 almost 80 percent of the families who were sufficiently impoverished to qualify for TANF's monthly cash assistance received it. By 2000 this figure had dropped to about 50 percent of qualified families, and analysts predicted that data would show this downward trend continuing during the recession and economic downturn of the early 2000s.[18] Indeed, data from the U.S. Census Bureau showed that "cash welfare benefits did less to reduce poverty in 2002 than in any year since at least 1989."[19]

In 2003, the U.S. Department of Health and Human Services issued a press release in which Assistant Secretary Horn described a further drop in the TANF rolls during 2002 and on into early 2003 as "encouraging."[20] At about the same time this statement was being made, the U.S. Bureau of the Census released data showing that a significant increase in child poverty had taken place in 2002.[21] Between 2000 and 2002, not only did the nation's overall poverty rate rise, but the numbers of adults and children experiencing severe poverty (i.e., incomes under 50 percent of the federal poverty line) also increased by almost 1.5 million.[22] That political elites would consider declining TANF rolls an indicator of welfare reform's success when this decline occurred simultaneously with increases in lone-mother-headed families' impoverishment simply underscores the fact that welfare reform is not about mitigating poverty. Political elites are largely indifferent to data showing that lone mothers' movement from welfare to work has for the most part earned them little more than membership in the nation's growing pool of working poor. Indeed, the percentage of impoverished children living in families in which a lone mother was working rose from 25 percent in 1996 to almost 38 percent in 2000.[23]

From Welfare to What?

In 2002, almost two-thirds of all impoverished families with children contained at least one family member in the labor force. Clearly, parental employment does not mean in and of itself that families can escape poverty. This is the case whether families are headed by one or two adults, although poverty rates are highest for families headed by lone mothers. In order to provide for their families, lone mothers must balance family caregiver responsibilities with those of work. Caregiving demands often make it difficult for mothers to be employed full time or to hold on to jobs that have irregular or changing work schedules. At the same time, employers frequently have little tolerance for workers who are late or absent because of home duties. Yet mothers whose dire economic circumstances have forced them to turn to TANF for income assistance must put work outside the home before family caregiving in order to remain eligible to receive welfare benefits. For lone mothers, balancing both caregiving and workplace responsibilities presents a heavy challenge, but even handling this challenge successfully does not necessarily lead to economic security and an escape from poverty for their families.

From the passage of the PRWORA in 1996 to the recession of 2001, a strong labor market made it somewhat easier for lone mothers who were subject to TANF's work requirements to find jobs. Most states incorporated a "Work First" approach into their TANF programs, which required mothers to take almost any available job, regardless of its wages or (lack of) benefits. Programs premised on a Work First philosophy emphasized engaging mothers in work activity over encouraging them to pursue further education or training and were favored by the states as the fastest and most effective means of moving mothers off the welfare rolls. If states needed any other incentive, they faced the possibility of reduced federal assistance for their TANF programs if the proportion of welfare recipients engaging in work activity fell short of standards laid out under the PRWORA.

While political elites have pointed to the dramatic decline in the TANF rolls in touting the success of the PRWORA, they have been very selective in discussing experiences of those who have left the TANF rolls—and for good reason. Many lone mothers do not make a successful transition from welfare to work or to self-sufficiency through employment. Studies undertaken in the first few years after implementation of TANF found that even in a strong labor market only half to two-thirds of lone mothers were holding down some type of job a year or two after becoming "welfare leavers."[24] These studies also showed that many employed welfare leavers were working less than full time and that most were in low-wage jobs. Even those who were working full time frequently earned wages that did not allow their families to rise above the federal poverty line. And this was the case for those who left TANF in a period of economic upswing.

When a recession hit in 2001 and the economy entered a downturn, the real fragility of welfare leavers' post-TANF employment status was revealed. A study conducted prior to the economic downturn in 1999 surveying former TANF recipients found that 49.9 percent of those who had left the TANF rolls from 1997 to 1999 ("early leavers") were employed and were no longer receiving TANF, compared to only 42.2 percent in 2002, when the survey was conducted of recipients who had left the TANF rolls in the 2000 to 2002 period ("recent leavers").[25] Given the worsening state of the economy from 2001 on, the more recent welfare leavers—like other impoverished lone mothers not receiving TANF—clearly had much more difficulty finding or holding onto jobs. As a report from the Economic Policy Institute succinctly put it, "Because of the weak job market, low-income single mothers are having a much harder time finding work than they did in the first four years of welfare reform [1996–2000]. The unemployment rate for low-income single mothers has risen more than the overall rate; their real incomes—low to begin with—have fallen."[26]

What happened to other TANF leavers? Another major category consists of those unemployed but still eligible for TANF benefits, subsequently returning to the welfare rolls. By 1999, 20.4 percent of early leavers had returned to TANF, in contrast to the 25.5 percent of the more recent leavers surveyed in 2002. Another major category of welfare leavers, termed *disconnected leavers,* consists of recipients neither employed nor receiving TANF or other government cash benefits; this group increased from 9.8 percent of early welfare leavers surveyed in 1999 to 13.8 percent of recent leavers in 2002.[27] They may have lost TANF benefits due to program eligibility time limits or sanctions or had other reasons for not returning to the TANF rolls. Disconnected leavers are impoverished lone mothers and children who have disappeared off the welfare policy radar screen and have no known source of income. They are surviving by means that are simply unknown.

Earlier an allusion was made to low wages earned by lone mothers who have left TANF and become employed. A survey of the 49.9 percent of early TANF leavers employed in 1999 revealed that they were receiving a median wage of $7.72 per hour. Only one-third of them were in jobs providing employer health insurance. Two-thirds were working full time (defined as 35 or more hours per week), over a quarter had irregular or nighttime work schedules, and about 10 percent held multiple jobs. Again, this was in 1999, during a period of economic upswing. As mentioned already, a smaller percentage of more recent welfare leavers were found to be employed in the 2002 survey. However, the more recent leavers' median hourly wage and other job characteristics were not significantly different from those of the early leavers.[28]

Women leaving the TANF rolls for employment are likely to find themselves in jobs where the pay is low, benefits are often limited or nonexistent, and schedules are often awkward or inconvenient. In addition, job security and upward mobility frequently are issues, since many low-wage jobs are seasonal or temporary and opportunities for job growth or promotions are often absent. But in times of economic downturn, even such less-than-desirable jobs may be hard to attain. Los Angeles County is a case in point. An analysis of its welfare-to-work program found that the employment rate for program participants declined from 43 percent in 1998 to 34 percent in 2001. Only 52 percent of the welfare-to-work program participants who entered the labor force between 1998 and 2001 had any employment earnings in the latter year. Among parents who had been in the welfare-to-work program the longest, thus considered an indicator of a chronically high level of need, average annual earnings in 2001 were only $5,391. All told, "Three-fourths of the people who participate in Los Angeles County's massive welfare-to-work program can't find jobs good enough to keep their families out of poverty."[29]

When economic security and escaping poverty are the standards of measurement, the plight of most impoverished lone-mother-headed families who must move from welfare to work is dismal in both good and bad economic times. Beyond a shortage of decent-paying jobs, especially when the economy falters, what other problems do lone mothers mandated to move from welfare to work face?

Barriers to Moving from Welfare to Work

During the economic upswing of the 1990s, rates of employment increased for all lone mothers, not just for welfare leavers.[30] Lone mothers who left TANF most quickly in its first years were aided not only by a strong labor market but also in the fact that they possessed fewer barriers to finding and maintaining employment than TANF recipients less successful in this regard. Barriers to employment contribute to the depressed economic state of many lone mothers before, during, and after their enrollment in TANF. Some types of barriers are no doubt especially significant whenever the economy slows, unemployment rises, and employers find themselves able to exercise greater discretion in selecting new employees.

A number of studies conclusively point to a set of common barriers to employment for lone-mother-headed families receiving TANF.[31] Many mothers on the TANF rolls are physically or mentally impaired such that they cannot work at all, are able to work very little, or are greatly limited in the types of work they are able to do. In some cases, impairment is the result of physical or emotional harm stemming from violent treatment or sexual abuse, often by a family member or by a lone mother's current or former partner. In some instances, the health and employability of mothers are adversely affected by dependency on alcohol or other drugs. Their children's physical and mental health problems may likewise be barriers to employment for many lone mothers, who often do not have people on whom they can rely for everyday or emergency caretaking duties.

Even if they do not suffer impaired health, it is not unusual for lone mothers on the TANF rolls to lack high school diplomas or equivalents, credentials often used for initial screening of job applicants. Many mothers also have learned few practical job skills and often have a limited record of past work experiences to bring to prospective employers. Thus, they are frequently at a serious disadvantage in the hiring process, especially in settings where few job openings are available, local unemployment rates are high, and competition for even low-wage, unskilled jobs is intense.[32] Lone mothers in many cases have learning disabilities.[33] Learning disabilities and limited literacy can inhibit lone mothers' performance capabilities when it comes to on-the-job training, making it difficult to hold onto a newly found job.

TANF recipients often lack or have limited proficiency in English, which can hamper their job-search capabilities and can limit their ability to communicate with supervisors, fellow workers, or customers. Communication is a barrier to employment not only for many lone mothers who are legal immigrants and naturalized citizens, but also for some native-born lone mothers. Recall the high rates of unemployment and low annual earnings of participants in the massive welfare-to-work program of Los Angeles County, which contains many impoverished families of Latino origin. One study found that 41 percent of the county's 1999 TANF caseload had limited English proficiency,[34] surely contributing to the high rates of unemployment of lone mothers who must meet welfare-to-work requirements.

Other barriers to employment include lack of safe, stable, and affordable housing, as well as a lack of transportation. Some impoverished lone-mother-headed families are homeless, whereas many others find themselves forced into frequent unplanned moves. Experiencing and resolving family housing problems can make it difficult for lone mothers to be at work when required or to be prepared mentally and physically to deal with work demands. Likewise, a lack of adequate transportation often inhibits mothers' job-search activities. Even when public transportation proves to be affordable, it may be very time consuming to use, making searching for a job, commuting to and from work, and accessing child-care services extremely difficult for lone mothers.

Many impoverished lone mothers and their families experience multiple barriers to employment, not just one or another of the aforementioned barriers. The more barriers experienced, the less likely lone mothers are to be employed. Facing more than one barrier increases not only the likelihood that lone mothers will be unable to find or maintain employment, but also the probability that they and their children will be subject to negative sanctions for violation of TANF program rules and regulations. Mental or physical health impairments, episodes of domestic violence, and substance abuse problems may lead to missed appointments with caseworkers; reading deficiencies or the lack of English language proficiency may lead to improper completion of TANF program forms or missed paperwork deadlines—all rule violations that may call forth negative sanctions on TANF recipients. Barriers to lone mothers' employment also often function to interfere with their understanding of TANF program policies. For example, a 2002 survey of welfare recipients found that almost 40 percent did not fully understand their TANF time limits. Those with two or more barriers to employment, along with Spanish-speaking recipients, were particularly likely to lack adequate information.[35] Many TANF recipients thus find themselves unprepared when suddenly their benefits end.

Lone mothers who have left the TANF rolls, yet whose families have no known source of income, tend to have more barriers to employment than those who become employed. Earlier it was noted that the percentage of disconnected welfare leavers neither employed nor receiving government cash assistance rose from 9.8 in 1999 to 13.8 percent (one in seven leavers) in 2002. A 2002 survey comparing employed welfare leavers to disconnected welfare leavers found that the disconnected leavers were "significantly more likely to be in poor health (41.3 percent compared with 25.0 percent) and less likely to have completed high school or a GED (22.3 percent compared with 54.7 percent). In addition, 44.2 percent of disconnected former recipients have not worked in the past three years. More than half (57.3 percent) face more than one of these barriers, compared with 17.0 percent of working welfare leavers."[36]

Not surprisingly, disconnected leavers have suffered more than others from serious economic hardships. In comparison to employed welfare leavers, disconnected leavers are, for example, more likely to have difficulties making mortgage, rent, and utilities payments and to have problems affording sufficient food.[37] But it is clear that many, if not most, former TANF recipients face economic hardships, whether or not they secure employment. In 1999, almost half of families who had recently left the welfare rolls for full-time, year-round employment had experienced one or more critical hardships threatening their health and well-being, such as "going without food, shelter, or necessary medical care."[38] This was, of course, before welfare leavers' conditions were rendered even more difficult by the recession and the economic downturn of the early 2000s. During this period of economic malaise, the unemployment rate for lone mothers in general increased more than did the unemployment rate for other parents or for all adults, going from 7.5 percent in 2000 to 10.2 percent in 2003.[39] Many low-wage sectors in which former TANF recipients were most likely to become employed, such as retail trade, manufacturing, and temporary help services, were affected particularly negatively, making jobs more scarce and slowing wage growth.[40]

Coping With Hardships Accompanying Welfare Reform

Studying the hardships that go along with welfare reform is crucial in assessing the impact of the decline of the welfare rolls. If TANF leavers are not scrutinized, it might be too easy to join political elites and assume that welfare reform is successful based merely on the sharp drop in the welfare rolls since the PRWORA was passed in 1996. Asking what life is like for TANF leavers undercuts any such knee-jerk proclamations of success, for evidence shows that most TANF leavers and their families remain impoverished and facing hardships that represent the denial of basic economic human rights to food, health care, and housing.

Welfare Reform, Food Insecurity, and Hunger

Food is not a human right in the United States, reflected in official statistics. A household is food secure, according to the U.S. Department of Agriculture, when it has "access, at all times, to enough food for an active, healthy life for all household members."[41] A 2002 survey by the U.S. Bureau of the Census found that 12.1 million households containing thirty-five million people—11 percent of the U.S. population—were "food insecure."[42] In that same year, food hardship to the point of hunger existed in 3.8 million of the 12.1 million food-insecure households. Food insecurity, even where hunger is not present, threatens the ability of millions of adults and children to thrive and to achieve their full human potential.

While the national level of food insecurity stood at 11 percent of all U.S. households in 2002, food insecurity is particularly a problem for impoverished families. In 2002, among households with children under the age of 18 with incomes below 130 percent of the federal poverty line, the rate of food insecurity was 42 percent; 11 percent of households with children experienced food insecurity with hunger. Households with children headed by lone mothers were especially likely to experience food insecurity. In 2002, 47 percent of poor lone-mother-headed households experienced food insecurity, compared with 36 percent of poor married-couple-headed households with children. Over 13 percent of lone-mother-headed households suffered food insecurity with hunger, compared with 11 percent of households headed by married couples.[43] As the Food Research and Action Center has pointed out, "While starvation seldom occurs in this country, children and adults do go hungry and chronic mild malnutrition does occur when financial resources are low. The mental and physical changes that accompany inadequate food intakes can have harmful effects on learning, development, productivity, physical and psychological health, and family life."[44]

Families living below 130 percent of the poverty line are generally eligible for the federal government's Food Stamp Program, a needs-tested program intended to increase the ability of low-income households to purchase food and to eat nutritiously. In 1996, however, the PRWORA reduced food stamp benefits and also denied benefits to most legal residents of the United States who were not citizens, although some eligibility restrictions on legal residents were eased by the U.S. Congress in 2002. Unlike TANF, food stamps have remained a benefit to which most poor people are entitled under federal law, so long as they can meet income requirements. Benefits are minimal. In most instances, monthly benefits for a three-person household were worth $371 in 2004,[45] which is about $1.37 per meal, per person, on a daily basis.

As mentioned earlier, a sharp drop has taken place in the welfare rolls. As the rolls declined between 1995 and 2002, the percentage of the nation's poor children who lived in families receiving AFDC/TANF cash benefits fell by almost half, from 61.5 percent to 33.4 percent.[46] This decline in the welfare rolls was accompanied by an unexpected and sharp decline in the participation of poor families in the Food Stamp Program, though the percentage drop was not as dramatic as that which occurred in the TANF rolls. Among poor children, the percentage living in families receiving food stamps fell from 95 percent in 1995 to 75 percent in 2001. This decline did not show evidence of reversing until 2002, when the percentage moved to 80 percent. Reduced benefits for those who received food stamps also took a toll on poor families. In 1995, food stamps accounted for 25 percent of disposable income for the poorest fifth of lone-mother-headed households. By 2000, this had dropped to 19 percent of disposable income.[47]

As individual states implemented welfare reform policies, many impoverished lone-mother-headed families failed to participate in a food-assistance program providing benefits to which they were entitled. The results of increased nonparticipation in food stamps has contributed to the high percentage of poor families the U.S. Bureau of the Census annually categorizes as "food insecure" even to the point of hunger. Why, until very recently, have increasing numbers of families eligible for food stamps—in this instance lone mothers with children—not been receiving them?

A number of factors, some directly connected to welfare reform, are thought to have led many impoverished lone mothers to forgo food stamps.[48] Some lone mothers, aware of their families' eligibility for aid, have rejected it out of a desire to avoid the humiliation heaped upon those who are allegedly "welfare dependent," thus being a slothful drain on taxpayers. In other cases, mothers who have been diverted from or sanctioned off TANF or who have run out of cash benefits due to TANF time limits, have frequently not been told by welfare office staff that they and their families remain entitled to food stamps. Instead, they have been left to assume that ineligibility for TANF means ineligibility for food stamps as well. In other instances, employed lone mothers do not understand that they are income eligible, erroneously believing that their meager wages are too high to receive food stamps. Still others find the food stamp application process and eligibility criteria, both of which differ from those of TANF, overly difficult or confusing.

The chronic food insecurity experienced by a high percentage of lone-mother-headed families in the wake of welfare reform helped to energize national and state-level anti-hunger groups. Such groups successfully put pressure on federal and state governments to fund outreach activities intended to increase participation of low-income people in the Food Stamp Program. In the early 2000s, outreach did grow, and individual states made efforts to better connect those eligible—including welfare leavers—to receive food stamps. Consequently, by 2003 "a stunning reversal" had occurred in the food stamp caseload decline that took place in the wake of the passage of the PRWORA.[49] Despite this reversal in declining Food Stamp Program participation in the early 2000s, food insecurity among low-income families, disproportionately headed by lone mothers, has led to their ever-increasing utilization of soup kitchens and food pantries. Each year the demand for assistance goes up. A 2003 survey of emergency food services in twenty-five major U.S. cities found that 59 percent of those seeking food were members of families with children or their parents. Demand for food outraced supplies, and 15 percent of families' requests for assistance had to go unmet.[50]

Welfare Reform and Health Care

Just as food is not a human right in the United States, neither is health care. The United States is the only developed nation in the world that does not have some type of national health care system to meet the needs of its citizens. Instead, it has a "pay as you go" system in which those who can afford health care get it and those who cannot afford it often must delay treatment or go without. Since health care is a marketable commodity and not a right possessed by all, the distribution of good health and access to care follow along the lines of economic inequality.

When surveyed, 81 percent of adults living in affluent households (defined as having an income of $75,000 or more per year) report they are in excellent or good health, and only 3 percent describe their health as just fair or poor. In nonaffluent households (having an income below $20,000 per year), only 47 percent of adults have such a positive self-assessment, while 23 percent assess their health as fair or poor.[51] In addition, poor people are less likely than the nonpoor to report having a usual source of health care. This, together with their higher incidence of health problems, means that people living in poverty end up spending many more days on average being treated in hospitals than do the nonpoor.[52]

Much has been made in recent years about the number of people in the United States lacking any type of health insurance, as health care costs skyrocket. Official statistics reveal that vast numbers of adults and children at risk of growing ill or being injured are without insurance that could help pay for the costs of treatment. According to the U.S. Census Bureau, forty-five million people, or 15 percent of the U.S. population, in 2003 had no health insurance at all, through either employment or a government program. Millions more had insurance only for some part of that year. Low-income people, whose self-assessments show their health status to be much less favorable than the affluent, are also far less likely than the affluent to have health insurance. In 2003, 24 percent of households with incomes below $25,000 lacked insurance, compared to only 8 percent of households with incomes of $75,000 and over. Whereas over 11 percent of all children in the United States lacked health insurance coverage that year, 19 percent of children in poverty lacked coverage.[53]

In 2003, most people in the United States—85 percent of the U.S. population, or 243 million people—had at least some type of health insurance. Over twice as many had employment-provided as opposed to government-subsidized coverage. The strong link in the United States between employment and health insurance is highly problematic for low-income people. Many adults are low income because the only jobs they are able to find—when they find jobs at all—pay low wages. And low-wage jobs, whether part or full time, generally do not come with health insurance benefits, or they may require employee contributions that are unaffordable to low-wage earners. In addition, government programs, such as Medicare (for the elderly) and Medicaid (for the very poor), cover only certain segments of the population.

For low-wage workers, purchasing private health insurance is not an affordable option. Because health insurance costs keep rising, even workers in better-paying positions find themselves unable to afford privately purchased insurance policies, which can cost many thousands of dollars a year. This situation has serious implications for lone-mother-headed families affected by TANF's welfare-to-work policy. Families impoverished to the point where they are eligible for TANF benefits usually are also eligible for Medicaid benefits that will pay most of their health care costs. Indeed, the prospect of losing Medicaid benefits for their children without having a suitable replacement has long led lone mothers to anguish over the trade-off between reliance on welfare and their hope to leave it as quickly as possible. Under the current policy, eligibility for Medicaid benefits for most mothers disappears soon after mothers leave TANF for employment; ironically, most employed welfare leavers end up in low-wage jobs without employer-provided health insurance.

The Kaiser Commission on Medicaid and the Uninsured examined the health insurance status of women who had left TANF in 1997 or after and who had not returned to the welfare rolls by 1999. The commission found that 41 percent were uninsured. Another 39 percent relied on Medicaid, while only 20 percent had health insurance through an employer. Their children were slightly better off when it came to health insurance coverage, primarily because many states have instituted very stringent Medicaid eligibility requirements for low-income adults, often reserving benefits for those with incomes well below the federal poverty line. The commission found that 22 percent of the children of welfare leavers were uninsured, which is about half the uninsured rate for mothers. While only 19 percent of the children of leavers were covered by their mother's employer, Medicaid provided coverage for over 59 percent.[54]

The picture emerging from this and other studies is extremely disturbing. According to the Kaiser Commission, "Over half (54 percent) of women who leave welfare report at least one health problem (fair/poor health, health condition that limits work, or poor mental health)... Losing health insurance after leaving welfare is associated with less access to health care services and lower use of health care, especially preventive health care... The lack of health insurance coverage among welfare leavers is an important impediment to successful transitions from welfare to work."[55]

Welfare Reform and Housing Hardship

In the same way that no one has a right to food or health care in the United States, there likewise is no right to housing. Housing affordability for low-income people is a national issue that has yet to be adequately addressed. Meanwhile, as costs of housing continue to rise, low-income families find it more and more difficult to pay rent while meeting costs associated with other necessities, such as food and health care.

The National Low Income Housing Coalition periodically issues reports documenting the monetary gap between the incomes of low-wage workers and typical rental costs. According to its calculations, in 2003 in order to avoid paying more than 30 percent of income on rent, a full-time worker would have needed to earn a "national housing wage" of $15.21 per hour to afford the average two-bedroom apartment. The federal minimum wage in 2003 was only $5.15 per hour, and the figure that year for most states having their own minimum wage standards was not radically higher. In examining housing costs and prevailing minimum wages in the nation's metropolitan statistical areas (MSAs), the coalition found that 66 percent of MSAs have housing wages at least twice—and often three or four times—that of minimum wages.[56] These are averages, and they mask the level of difficulty that families with extremely low incomes have in finding safe and decent housing at a rent they can afford.

It is difficult to understand how people can be homeless in one of the most affluent nations in the world. Unfortunately, homelessness has been an especially chronic problem in the United States since at least the 1980s. Since the late 1990s, the U.S. Conference of Mayors has issued reports on homelessness in cities across the United States. In its 2003 survey of twenty-five U.S. cities, homelessness in twenty-three of the cities was attributed primarily to a lack of affordable housing. In 84 percent of the cities, local emergency shelters had insufficient resources and had to turn away homeless families. In the cities surveyed, families with children constituted 40 percent of the homeless population.

According to the Children's Defense Fund, more than 3.6 million children live in low-income families who pay 50 percent and more of their income for rent or are in severely substandard housing. In the words of the National Low Income Housing Coalition,

> Wages have failed to keep pace with rental costs; rental costs have increased faster than costs for other basic needs… and little or no affordable housing is being built. As a result, families are living in substandard conditions, are homeless, or are making choices each day to spend money on housing and do without health care, child care, or other basic necessities… Our nation strives to be a standard-bearer for the world in fairness, compassion, and quality of life, yet overlooks this problem year after year at the cost of the safety, health, and security of millions of its citizens.[57]

Impoverished lone-mother-headed families are among those whose "safety, health, and security" are adversely affected by housing hardship, according to recent surveys. From 1997 to 2002, the proportion of noncohabiting, low-income single parents who had not been able to pay mortgage, rent, or utility bills at some time in the previous twelve months rose from 32 to over 35 percent, even as it fell from 26 to 23 percent for married low-income parents.[58] Lone mothers who are welfare leavers are clearly at high risk for housing hardship. In 1999, before the recession of 2001 and subsequent economic downturn put welfare leavers into even worse economic straits, 48 percent of welfare leavers who were working part time could not make rent or mortgage payments at some time during the year, and over 44 percent of full-time workers were in the same position. Even though few lone mothers leaving welfare and working full time were forced because of hardship to share housing with others, in 1999 12 percent of welfare leavers who worked part time were forced to do so.[59]

Special Risk Factors for Experiencing Hardships

Recent research underscored the importance of why people leave welfare when they are at risk for experiencing hardships. It has been demonstrated that serious hardships confront many lone mothers who leave the TANF rolls for employment. Yet mothers forced off the TANF rolls due to sanctions or because their eligibility has expired under state time limits are even more likely to experience hardships.

According to the Center on Budget and Policy Priorities, "time-limit leavers have lower employment rates, higher poverty rates, and higher levels of material hardship than other leavers."[60] Again, the hardships experienced include food insecurity, problems with housing and utility payments, and difficulties accessing health care. Many lone mothers who run up against time-limit policies—particularly those who face multiple barriers to employment or whose primary language is not English—have an inadequate understanding of them. Their extended length of stay on TANF until eligibility runs out signals that they are among those least capable of attaining economic self-sufficiency and are at especially high risk of suffering hardships.

As discussed earlier, lone mothers who violate TANF program rules and regulations—perhaps by missing appointments with caseworkers or by not turning in paper work on time or filling it out correctly—may suffer sanctions, which in many instances have resulted in the removal of recipients from the TANF rolls. Even those who manage to get back on may have been off the rolls for months. Those recipients most likely to be subject to such serious sanctions tend to have multiple barriers to employment, often involving problems that likewise make it difficult to understand or cope with program demands. Therefore, it is not surprising that those sanctioned off the TANF rolls are at particularly high risk of experiencing hardships as welfare leavers. For example, mothers with infants who were sanctioned off the TANF rolls are more than three times as likely to suffer hardships—from hunger to homelessness—than similar mothers remaining on the rolls.[61]

Is Welfare Reform a "Success?"

How a problem is framed and defined in the first place has a great deal to do with the solutions that logically follow. Chapter 2 showed that during the twentieth century many U.S. political elites and members of the general public viewed welfare in a highly negative light, which led to efforts to distinguish between the "deserving" and "undeserving" poor when it came to administering public assistance. As was noted in chapter 2, over time the composition of the U.S. welfare rolls shifted from so-called deserving families, predominantly headed by white widows, to allegedly undeserving families, largely headed by lone mothers who either had never married or whose marriages had dissolved and who increasingly were mothers of color. This shift in the composition of the rolls became more and more apparent as the numbers of families on the welfare rolls progressively increased. The breadth and level of public hostility toward welfare and its recipients, a hostility often fanned by political elites, likewise grew.

By the last decade of the twentieth century, U.S. welfare policy was a problem begging to be addressed. It was considered problematic not because it did so very little to reduce the high rates of poverty among lone-mother-headed families or because it failed to respect their economic human rights. Rather, U.S. welfare policy needed to be addressed because it was said to encourage welfare dependency. The means-tested entitlement to welfare benefits for lone-mother-headed families, established under the Social Security Act of 1935, was denounced by political elites as encouraging shiftlessness and births out of wedlock. Lone mothers were portrayed as addicted to welfare benefits to the point where they had little motivation to strive for economic self-sufficiency or to exercise sexual self-control. Critics of the "welfare mess" denounced welfare as a system that enabled able-bodied mothers to sit idly at home, knowing their cash benefits would increase if and when they gave birth to additional children. Welfare dependency, it was said, led to sloth, immorality, promiscuity, and ever-more "illegitimate" births—all being supported by tax dollars from hard-working wage earners.[62]

Having framed the problem as welfare policy that encouraged welfare dependency, the seemingly logical solution was to change this policy so as to reduce lone mothers' presence on the welfare rolls. First, mothers needed to be the discouraged or diverted from applying for welfare in the first place. As if the negative stigma attached to receipt of welfare was not enough of a discouragement, individual states often made the application process more bureaucratically complex and difficult to negotiate success-fully. Presumably, the hope was that eligible recipients would grow frus-trated with the process and simply would give up. Second, lone mothers who did manage to get on the welfare rolls needed be coerced out of falling into dependency by the threat of sanctions (including loss of cash benefits) for violations of welfare program rules, including mandatory work requirements. The culture of welfare offices largely abandoned family case work in favor of pursuing "labor force attachment models." States estab-lished Work First policies requiring that lone mothers take almost any available employment—no matter how dead-end the job or how low the pay—in exchange for receiving cash assistance. Eligibility for the latter was governed by strict state time limits. Nationally, the result was a rapid and dramatic reduction in the welfare rolls.[63]

Washington State provides a somewhat extreme yet instructive example of the welfare office culture that has arisen across the nation. The Welfare Rights Organizing Coalition, a state-wide grassroots organization of TANF recipients and welfare leavers, uncovered documents indicating that Wash-ington's Department of Social and Health Services (DSHS) had used par-ties and contests to motivate its workers to remove recipients from the TANF rolls. The coalition pointed to DSHS memos on caseload reduction strategies, including one titled "Diversion Tactics 101: How can I avoid opening a TANF case… Oh, let me count the ways!"[64] According to the coalition, in 2003 "one DSHS office even rang a bell in celebration each time a worker terminated a welfare case."[65] The TANF rolls in Washington dropped from 97,000 families in 1997 to 53,000 in 2000; this occurred in a state that has experienced some of the highest rates of unemployment in the nation. Despite especially severe conditions of joblessness in the early 2000s, as of early 2004, the TANF rolls had only crept back up to 55,000 families.

Welfare reform can be considered a success only if the ultimate problem to be solved is welfare receipt. The dramatic decline in the TANF rolls—almost 60 percent nationally between 1996 and 2003—is routinely touted by political elites as an empirical indicator of welfare reform's success. Yet, as has been shown, this decline in the welfare rolls has not been accompanied by a similar magnitude of decline in poverty among lone-mother-headed families. Indeed, between 2000 and 2003 while the rolls continued to drop, poverty rates for such families went up. Fewer and fewer impoverished lone-mother-headed families who were actually eligible for cash assistance were receiving it. As the U.S. welfare rolls were declining in the first years of the twenty-first century, the numbers of children living in households experiencing severe poverty—household with incomes below 50 percent of the federal poverty line—were rising. Welfare reform meant that the safety net provided by the Social Security Act of 1935 was no longer there to catch lone-mother-headed families who could not meet their subsistence needs.

One goal of advocates of welfare reform was economic self-sufficiency for impoverished lone-mother-headed families. As the data presented in this chapter show, this goal is far from being reached.[66] The families of a high percentage of lone mothers who became welfare leavers continue to live in abject poverty. This is especially the case for those families headed by mothers who have been sanctioned off the rolls or who have run into benefit eligibility time limits. But poverty is also the outcome for most of the families headed by mothers who have conscientiously followed TANF rules and have made the transition from welfare to work. Mothers typically find themselves stuck in an endless revolving door of low-wage full-time and part-time jobs and unemployment.

As demonstrated in this chapter, poverty-related hardships in the form of hunger and food insecurity, lack of health care, inability to pay rent and utilities, and sometimes even homelessness are common for welfare leavers.[67] According to the Economic Policy Institute, "The prevalence of hardships among families on and off welfare is much greater than among the overall population, even among those in poverty. By this measure, families on welfare are certainly not better off than other poor families."[68] The physical and emotional weight of such hardships makes it extremely difficult for impoverished lone mothers to achieve economic self-sufficiency, thus continuing the cycle of unremitting deprivation that they and their children seek to escape.

What happens if the problem to be addressed is reframed? What if the problem is not welfare dependency but instead the chronic impoverishment of lone-mother-headed families and the violation of their economic human rights? This alternative way of framing the problem would never lead to the type of welfare reform championed in the United States. Yet, as discussed in chapter 1, U.S. political elites are unwilling to recognize the nation's high rates of poverty as a human rights issue. The U.S. Senate has failed to ratify the International Covenant on Economic, Social, and Cultural Rights that President Jimmy Carter signed and submitted to it some thirty years ago. Recent welfare reform policies, if allowed to stand, make future Senate ratification of this treaty highly unlikely.

Nation–states that ratify the International Covenant are required to take immediate steps consistent with their resources toward the realization of such rights as "freedom from hunger" and "an adequate standard of living."[69] As one of the wealthiest nation–states on the earth, the United States has the resources to make great strides toward respecting such economic human rights.[70] It has, however, chosen not to do so.

Respecting the Diversity of Families in Need

This chapter provided an overview of the overall outcomes of welfare reform in the United States. As such, it treated impoverished lone-mother-headed families as if they are a generic category, paying little attention to the diversity of their needs or to ways in which the impacts of welfare reform on families have differed. Welfare reform has proven to be a "one-size-fits all" policy initiative, one largely ignoring some of the unique difficulties various sectors of the welfare recipient population face. In chapter 4, due attention will be given to more detailed "on the ground" violations of impoverished lone-mother-headed families' economic human rights, using their diversity as a filter and guide.

4

Varieties of Little-Noticed Suffering: Deconstructing Welfare-Reliant Families

Academics, policy analysts, political elites, and members of the mass media often speak as if impoverished families receiving welfare constitute a homogeneous population. Statements about welfare recipients are frequently couched in such broad terms as to suggest that lone mothers on the welfare rolls are similar in terms of life experiences, current circumstances, and capabilities. At times, such broad statements are tied to negative stereotypes. Yet, in reality, there is no generic "welfare mother"[1] about whom we may accurately generalize. Broad generalizations about welfare recipients, even by fair-minded people, tend to ignore the diverse characteristics of impoverished lone-mother-headed families and the varied problems and challenges with which they struggle in their efforts to escape poverty.

For example, lone-mother-headed families' experiences with welfare reform are frequently affected by such negative social forces as sexism, racial and ethnic discrimination, heterosexism, and ableism. Immigrant families often face problems accessing welfare and making the transition from welfare to work that are different from those faced by the native born. The experiences of lone-mother-headed families under welfare reform also frequently differ depending upon whether they reside in isolated rural areas or metropolitan settings. Poorly housed or homeless families face different challenges from those who are adequately housed.

But the diversity among welfare recipients extends even farther. While the vast majority of lone mothers on the welfare rolls avoid running afoul of the law, some mothers are not so fortunate. Those found guilty of violating drug laws are at risk of permanently losing eligibility for welfare benefits. In some welfare-recipient families, substance abuse and other problems result in lone mothers being absent or rendered incapable of providing parental care. Their children, still on the welfare rolls, are being reared by grandmothers or other relatives. In an increasing number of lone-mother and relative-headed households, the only ones eligible for welfare benefits are the children.

As this chapter will reveal, the violation of economic human rights that welfare reform represents is often accompanied by the lack of respect for other human rights possessed by impoverished mothers and children. The chapter begins by examining the plight of lone mothers who turn to welfare as part of an effort to free themselves from domestic violence and its aftermath. How has welfare reform impacted the segment of the welfare rolls subjected to domestic violence?

Welfare Reform and Patriarchal Values: Domestic Violence and Marriage Promotion

> …Kalia, a 19-year-old mother of a 1-year-old, showed up battered and bruised at a welfare office in Oakland, California. She told her caseworker she needed to go on welfare as she struggled to break out of an abusive relationship. Although the caseworker had the option to grant Kalia a domestic violence waiver that would relax the full-time work requirements, she did not do so… Instead, it took three years before another caseworker told Kalia that she had been entitled to a waiver and special services for victims of domestic abuse.[2]

The unequal treatment of women in the United States has declined over the past forty years, largely as a result of the successes achieved by the civil rights and feminist movements. Yet despite antidiscrimination legislation and affirmative action policies, women continue to lag behind men economically and politically, and the United States retains many of the social features of a patriarchal or male-dominated society. One of the manifestations of this male dominance is domestic violence and abuse directed by men at their female partners. There is no way to know the precise incidence of domestic violence, but it is widely believed to affect millions of women. Each year, an estimated 1.5 million women are assaulted by an intimate partner, and some 800,000 go for medical treatment as a result of this violence.[3] Although in general women are less likely than men to be victims of violent crimes, women are far more likely than men to be victims of violence by an intimate partner. Indeed, some 30 percent of all murders of women are committed by their husbands or boyfriends.

The likelihood of experiencing such violence appears to be linked to women's economic status. According to the National Domestic Violence Hotline, 26 percent of women with incomes of $50,000 or more report having been physically abused by spouses or boyfriends over the course of their lifetimes, in comparison to 37 percent of women with incomes of $16,000 or less.[4] The rates for domestic violence reported by women receiving welfare are very high.[5] As many as 60 percent of lone mothers on the welfare rolls report experiencing domestic violence at some point in the past, with upward of 30 percent of those on the rolls reporting such abuse within the past year.[6]

It is often extremely difficult for a woman to leave a violent male partner, if for no other reason than fear of being unable to adequately provide for her children's subsistence needs. Abject poverty can be among the first outcomes of ending a relationship in order to gain safety and to be secure from violence. Prior to the welfare reform of the 1990s, welfare served as a barely adequate but dependable economic oasis to which women in domestic violence situations could flee. A lone mother who met the needs test for income assistance was entitled to it. Recall that the Personal Responsibility and Work Opportunity Reconciliation Act of 1996 (PRWORA) not only ended this entitlement and made welfare more difficult to get, but it also put strict time limits on lone mothers' eligibility for cash benefits. The act requires that to receive benefits mothers must abandon full-time caretaking in the home in favor of outside work activity. Lone mothers are also required to report the identity of the fathers of their children to welfare officials and to cooperate in child support enforcement.

These PRWORA requirements can exacerbate the problems confronting women who turn to welfare for help in leaving domestic violence situations. First, removing lone mothers' entitlement to assistance and placing time limits on cash benefits may force women to remain in, or return to, abusive relationships for economic reasons. Rather than expose themselves and their children to impoverishment, many lone mothers try to endure the abuse. Second, requiring that mothers work outside the home in order to be eligible for benefits can put them at risk for further partner violence. Abusive men may not only feel threatened by the possibility that their female partners might achieve economic success and, thus, seek independence from them; they also often maximize control and domination over their female partners by severely restricting the women's social interaction with others and demanding that they remain in traditional female gender roles in the home. Third, requiring that lone mothers report the paternity of their children and cooperate with welfare officials in seeking child support enforcement through the courts can lead to violent retribution from biological fathers who feel they are being attacked through the legal system. Moreover, many women need to keep their whereabouts unknown for safety reasons or do not want to open up the possibility of courts granting their children's fathers shared custody or visitation rights.

Feminist groups, aware that many of the provisions of PRWORA promised to exacerbate the dangers faced by welfare recipients caught up in or escaping domestic violence situations, pressed Congress for legislation to provide them with protection. In 1996, the same year the PRWORA was passed, Congress amended it by approving the Family Violence Option. This amendment permits individual states to temporarily waive mandatory work requirements, benefit time limits, paternity identification, child support cooperation, and other PRWORA provisions in order to assist those leaving domestic violence situations. It also requires that states provide supportive services, including counseling, for welfare-recipient families who have been affected by domestic violence.

Lone mothers fleeing abusive situations without such protections and services may find it impossible to successfully make the transition from welfare to work.[7] The Work First mandatory work requirements embedded in many states' Temporary Assistance for Needy Families programs may lead to the sanctioning of lone mothers, stripping cash benefits from those who do not take and maintain employment as required. Some states' TANF programs allow lone mothers to meet work requirements by enrolling in vocational training or other job-preparation programs that are supposed to improve their employability. Dropping out of these programs can also result in negative sanctions. Yet it may be difficult, if not impossible, for lone mothers fleeing domestic violence to conform to program rules and to avoid being sanctioned. Many are unable to get the violent male partner out of their lives. Others, even after fleeing such a partner, remain physically or mentally maimed by the abuse they have suffered.

Getting the abuser out of a lone mother's life can be critical. According to the National Organization for Women (NOW) Legal Defense and Education Fund (now known as Legal Momentum),

> Abusers often try to interfere with any efforts their partners make to gain economic independence, including efforts to find work, retain employment, or continue studying. This is done in a variety of ways: by inflicting injuries and keeping women up all night

with arguments before important events such as interviews or tests; preventing her from sleeping; turning off alarm clocks; destroying homework assignments; saying negative things about her ability to succeed; destroying clothing; inflicting visible facial injuries before job interviews, or threatening to kidnap the children from school care centers... [C]onduct such as stalking, harassment, and an abuser's refusal to cooperate with childcare arrangements are all aspects of family violence that can be barriers to survivor's employment.[8]

Escaping the abuser does not end the problem, as many lone mothers must overcome the lingering effects of abuse. Mothers who are the victims of domestic violence are more likely than other lone mothers to be long-term welfare recipients, to frequently cycle on and off welfare, to be periodically unemployed, and to have a spotty employment record that often involves holding a succession of short-term jobs.[9] "Victims of domestic violence are more likely to have physical or mental health concerns—broken bones, low self-esteem, anxiety, depression, or post-traumatic stress disorder—that make it hard to find or keep a job... Domestic violence has been an 'invisible' barrier, not unlike mental illness, substance abuse, or learning disabilities."[10]

Hence, it is deeply troublesome that many women are not receiving the protections and services promised by the Family Violence Option. Almost every state has adopted it or has created its own version. However, as the story involving Kalia indicates, it is not always being implemented effectively.[11] In many instances, lone mothers fleeing domestic violence have not been receiving either waivers from the provisions of the PRWORA or the special services for which they are eligible. Mothers may not be told of the waivers or services, or they may not be willing to acknowledge or believe they have a need for them. For any of a number of reasons, often involving issues of trust and concerns with confidentiality, some mothers are simply unwilling to report details of their abuse to welfare caseworkers. On the other hand, welfare caseworkers are often ill-trained and ill-prepared to work with lone mothers coming from domestic violence situations.

The failure of welfare reform advocates to fully recognize the "invisible barrier" of domestic violence is revealed in efforts by the presidential administration of George W. Bush to use hundreds of millions of federal welfare dollars to promote marriage and to discourage divorce. Under changes proposed for the PRWORA, states would be encouraged to divert funds away from aiding impoverished lone-mother-headed families and to use these funds to promote the virtues of marriage.[12] Oklahoma has already taken the lead in using a portion of its federal welfare funds for such purposes and has been portrayed as a role model by the Bush administration.

Ironically, almost half of divorced women in Oklahoma report that domestic violence prompted the dissolution of their marriages. Fifty-seven percent of divorced lone mothers on Oklahoma's welfare rolls—presumably a target population for the Bush administration's marriage promotion proposals—report that domestic violence was a reason for their divorce.[13] In the eyes of its critics, marriage promotion is a questionable function of government and a wrongful use of taxpayer funds: better to use the funds for income assistance for lone-mother-headed families or for programs combating domestic violence. But critics also fear that marriage promotion may end up encouraging women to marry or to stay married to partners who are violent and abusive. Just as states' Work First TANF programs claim that any job is a good job, one can imagine some states embracing a "marriage first" philosophy in which any marriage is a good marriage. The danger is not only that welfare policy will continue to show a lack of respect for economic human rights, but also that adding on marriage promotion will serve to exacerbate lone mothers' vulnerability to oppression.

The GLBT Population, Reproductive Rights, and Welfare Reform

> Welfare reform is not an urgent, conscious priority for most gay people I know. Nor has it been a priority for the gay, lesbian, bisexual, and transgender [GLBT] political movement. This is a huge mistake... Poverty is a GLBT reality and its alleviation is a matter of justice.[14]

Welfare reform clearly has not been viewed as a priority issue in the gay, lesbian, bisexual, and transgender (GLBT) movement.[15] Some within the GLBT rights movement also have chastised its participants for being in denial regarding welfare reform's real and potential impact on those for whom it advocates. Suggestions have been made that this failure to address welfare reform's impact on the GLBT population may be a reflection of racial and class bias within the movement itself.[16] Whatever the reasons, to date only one national GLBT advocacy group, the National Gay and Lesbian Task Force, has issued a comprehensive analysis of the impact of welfare reform on the GLBT community.[17]

Little is known as to the actual numbers of people in the United States who are GLBT identified or practicing. Estimates for those who are gay and lesbian alone range from 3 to 10 percent of the population. It is also impossible to make statements with any confidence as to how many people living under the federal poverty line are part of the GLBT population. Some hold that, overall, gay people are especially affluent in comparison to the rest of the U.S. population. However, this is considered to be a myth, one that apparently arose in the 1980s out of the results of market surveys focusing only on the largely white male readership of gay magazines.[18] There is no reason to believe that members of the GLBT population are underrepresented among the nation's poor. While precise data are lacking, it is known that some lone mothers heading impoverished families and struggling to contend with welfare reform are members of that population.

How well does U.S. welfare policy accommodate impoverished mothers who do not readily fit into dominant heterosexual norms? Consider the following:

1. Some mothers are among the many closeted lesbians or bisexuals who, for their own or their children's well-being, pose as heterosexual women and enter into committed relationships with male partners. Should these men prove to be abusive and violent people from whom the mothers and their children are forced to flee, they may need to turn to welfare for income assistance. Like other mothers escaping domestic violence, lesbian and bisexual mothers may be at risk for retribution from former male partners unless welfare caseworkers waive welfare program requirements, such as cooperation in child support enforcement and help to secure the mothers' protection. The risk of retribution can be especially great simply because of the mothers' sexual orientation. Their former partners are typically men who have been extremely male dominant and controlling, if not expressly violent. They may feel that their very manhood has been threatened and may become enraged if they believe they have been rejected by women who prefer relationships with same-sex partners.

2. Lesbians who become lone mothers may achieve pregnancy through artificial insemination with the sperm of an anonymous donor at a fertility clinic or sperm donated by male friends or acquaintances. Often the latter are men who are gay. While the sperm donors are technically biological fathers, ordinarily neither the lone mothers nor those men who donate sperm intend that a successful pregnancy will require the fulfillment of fatherhood responsibilities in either social (parenting) or economic (support) terms. Yet lesbian mothers who refuse to identify the biological fathers of their children and otherwise fail to cooperate with child support authorities may be penalized when it comes to receiving cash welfare benefits. Welfare

reform does not readily accommodate women who fail to conceive children within the context of a heterosexual relationship.

3. *Transgender* is an umbrella term that covers people whose sense of gender identity is at odds with their physiological sex. Consequently, their social expression of gender may be ambiguous, fluid, or completely at odds with what other people expect of those who are biologically female (or male). Often misunderstood and negatively stereotyped, transgender people frequently have a great deal of difficulty becoming or staying employed. There have been reports of transgender welfare recipients being forced to leave the rolls because they could not meet mandatory work requirements due to harassment by supervisors or peers. At times, the severe degree of impoverishment they experience has forced transgender welfare recipients to seek survival on the streets. There, some find they can provide for their families' subsistence needs only by performing as sex workers.

Pro-heterosexuality and pro-marriage biases are subtly embedded in welfare reform policy, which has been of concern to the National Gay and Lesbian Task Force. They say that "[w]elfare reform is not only, or even primarily, about poverty policy. Welfare reform is also fundamentally about family policy—about promoting and privileging particular kinds of families, and about penalizing and stigmatizing others."[19] In the task force's view, the PRWORA promotes and privileges families headed by heterosexual adult partners who practice their sexual orientation only within the confines of marriage.

The PRWORA treats lone mothers, regardless of their sexual orientation, as deviants. Nowhere is the deviant label more openly bestowed than in the case of unmarried women who bear children. The rhetoric accompanying welfare reform has commonly portrayed out-of-wedlock births as an expression of immorality on the part of poor women that must rigorously be stamped out. Children who are the products of nonmarital relations are spoken of as *illegitimate,* an extremely pejorative term. Indeed, one provision of the PRWORA provides "illegitimacy bonuses" for those states demonstrating the greatest success in reducing their out-of-wedlock birth rates (while simultaneously keeping their rates of abortion down to 1995 levels). Supporters of this provision often argue that lone mothers cannot adequately perform parental responsibilities. So lone mothers are viewed as less able to provide for their children economically than two parents, and they and their families are seen as dysfunctional when it comes to effective and responsible child-rearing. Consequently, the increase in the numbers of families headed by lone mothers in recent decades is seen as a threat to the institution of the family as a whole.

The GLBT population is not explicitly mentioned in the provisions of the PRWORA; like other populations contributing to the diversity among impoverished lone mothers, the GLBT population is treated as if its unique characteristics and needs do not exist. Welfare reform as undertaken in the PRWORA is based on the premise that impoverished lone mothers are all (1) heterosexual; (2) could and should have abstained from both nonmarital sex and motherhood; and (3) are poor essentially because they are not married. The PRWORA carries the inherent message that one can avoid welfare, with all its Draconian requirements and corresponding sanctions, by engaging in appropriately moral behavior and by committing to marriage.

In effect, the PRWORA functions as an ideological attack on any woman who defies dominant heterosexual norms—regardless of her sexual orientation—when it comes to family matters. Although the legislation does not directly address the GLBT population, implicit hostility seems to exist. The marriages the PRWORA seeks to promote are not of the same sex. Indeed, within days of Congress's passage of the PRWORA, it also overwhelmingly passed the Defense of Marriage Act, which denies federal recognition to same-sex marriages and allows states to refuse to recognize such marriages should they be licensed in other states. President Clinton, a "liberal" Democrat, signed both bills. In 2004, the George W. Bush administration tried but failed to get the Republican-dominated Congress to approve a bill calling for a Constitutional amendment banning same-sex marriage. However, Bush's supporters and other opponents of same-sex marriage did succeed in getting constitutional or statutory bans adopted or on the ballot in many individual states.[20] This is the same administration that has called for changes in U.S. welfare reform policy so as to provide hundreds of millions of federal dollars to states to carry out programs of marriage promotion. Since the 1980s, political conservatives have been extremely successful in making the nation's political environment hostile to views and practices at variance with their position on what comprises what they consider to be family values. The passage and implementation of both the PRWORA and the Defense of Marriage Act are important markers of their success in this regard.

TANF and Lone-Mother-Headed Families with Disabilities

DD is a 42-year-old woman with two children who has been trying to find appropriate work for the past five years. She has been receiving TANF… She suffers from phlebitis, which causes severe pain without warning; her leg will become swelled and force her

to rest, and on some days she cannot get out of bed at all. Extensive standing, walking, or other physical activity exacerbates the
problem... DD is not considered exempt from TANF work
requirements... and so she has had to look for work, and attend
job readiness programs, rather than focus on a program that
would enable her to get her G.E.D. and improve her chances...
DD emphasizes that she is ready and willing to support her children, but after five years on TANF, despite her steady efforts to
find work, she still does not have an education, the networking
skills, or the medical support that would enable her to leave the
welfare rolls.[21]

As noted in chapter 3, physical and mental heath problems frequently
function as barriers to success for lone mothers, preventing them from
making a successful move from welfare to work. Few people realize just
how common disability-related workplace participation barriers are for
low-income adults in general. In 2001, survey data showed that fewer than
10 percent of the ninety-six million adults aged 25 to 55 living in families
with incomes above 200 percent of the poverty line had a physical or mental health condition that limited the kind or amount of work they could
perform. Yet of the thirty million living in low-income families with
incomes below 200 percent of the federal poverty line, 24 percent had such
a disability. The disability rate rose to over 32 percent for the twelve million
adults in families with incomes below 100 percent of the poverty line.[22] At
the lowest income levels, people report that their daily activities are limited
by disabilities to a far greater degree than do the more affluent.[23]

Survey data dramatically reveal how having a disability affects work
participation rates. Regardless of income level, adults with a disability were
less likely than the able-bodied to be employed in 2001. However, this
work participation differential was especially extreme for adults in families
with incomes below 100 percent of the federal poverty line. Among poverty-stricken adults, only 28 percent of those with disabilities reported
having worked in the previous year, as opposed to 64 percent of poor
adults without a disability.[24] Needless to say, low-income families with disabilities, particularly those with incomes below the poverty line, frequently
experience severe financial difficulties as a consequence of this lack of
employment. Their financial difficulties are intensified when they have to
deal with unavoidable costs stemming from disability treatment and care,
including higher-than-average medical expenses.

Low-income adults in general—ignoring gender and marital status—have been the topic of discussion thus far. However, in particular

lone mothers with disabilities face difficult challenges in being able to find, accept, and maintain employment that will adequately support themselves and their children; thus, it is noteworthy that the rates of disability for lone mothers are so high. Survey data gathered in 1996 after the passage of the PRWORA found that 17 percent of lone mothers in families with incomes above 200 percent of the poverty line were disabled, and 5 percent of the lone mothers in this income category had severe disabilities. But the situation for impoverished mothers was far worse. Among lone mothers poor enough to be on the TANF rolls, 38 percent had disabilities, and 25 percent of the mothers receiving TANF were severely disabled.[25] More recent data analyzed by the U.S. Government Accounting Office (GAO) have confirmed this high rate of disability among lone mothers on the welfare rolls. While the GAO analysis did not address lone mothers' relative level of disability, it revealed that 37 percent of mothers receiving TANF reported having a physical or mental impairment in both 1997 and 1999.[26]

It is important to note that the issue of disability for lone-mother-headed families does not end with mothers' own disabilities. Many families on the TANF rolls contain children with disabilities, ranging from relatively minor impairments to severe disabilities requiring highly specialized and expensive care. The GAO analysis reported that child disability was present in 15 percent of TANF families. In 8 percent of families on the TANF rolls, both a lone mother and child were reported to have physical or mental disabilities. Overall, according to the GAO, "a total of 44 percent of TANF recipients reported in both 1997 and 1999 that they either had one or more physical or mental impairments... or that they were caring for a child with such impairments."[27] The frequency of disability was far lower within the non-TANF population, where only 15 percent of adults and children were reported to have such impairments.[28]

As expected, lone mothers' disabilities, as well as those of their children, can hamper mothers' rates of work participation and ability to move from welfare to work. The GAO analysis found, for example, that lone mothers with disabilities were only half as likely to leave TANF than mothers for whom disability was not an issue, and mothers with children having disabilities were less than half as likely to exit the TANF rolls. Once having left the rolls, lone mothers with disabilities were only one-third as likely to be employed as mothers without disabilities. Whereas mothers with disabilities were consequently more in need of cash assistance immediately upon leaving the TANF rolls, the GAO analysis showed that they were 50 percent more likely than mothers without disabilities to report having no income at all in the first month after exiting TANF.[29] They also could not necessarily count on support from other government programs.

TANF is not a disability-targeted assistance program, and welfare was never intended to be a source of income for impoverished lone-mother-headed families with disabilities. The inadequacy of TANF in this regard is underscored by the temporary nature and penurious level of cash welfare benefits. Government disability-targeted programs are open to impoverished families, such as Supplemental Security Income (SSI) and Disability Insurance (DI), both administered by the U.S. Social Security Administration. These two programs provide permanent and, in many instances, somewhat more generous cash benefits as well as other services to support individuals with disabilities. However, their eligibility requirements are very strict, and the programs are primarily geared to serving individuals with very serious disabilities, including impairments that make it impossible for an individual to ever work.

Some lone-mother-headed families with disabilities have been able to exit TANF and to enter the rolls of SSI or DI, and many individual states have worked to divert or shift families to such federally financed programs in order to keep their state-level costs of serving TANF families down. Families may benefit if the cash benefits for the adult or child with the disability are permanent and they are no longer subject to TANF program requirements. Yet, notwithstanding the availability of SSI and DI, many families with disabilities continue to be on the TANF rolls, either because they are awaiting an SSI or DI eligibility decision or because they do not qualify for these disability-targeted programs. Lone mothers with disabilities may have difficulties meeting the strict SSI or DI requirements if their impairments are not considered sufficiently severe. In 1996 the federal government made it more difficult for children with disabilities to qualify for SSI; many children in impoverished families already on the SSI rolls were forced off and lost their cash benefits.[30] Congressional legislation was also passed to deny disability benefits to adults impaired by substance abuse or alcoholism—impairments previously considered forms of disability.

As noted already, lone mothers with disabilities who leave the TANF rolls are less likely than their able-bodied counterparts to be employed. Most analyses focus on their disability as the cause of unemployment; in fact, in many instances this is the proper way to view the situation. Some lone mothers are simply so disabled by their physical or mental status that going to work is not a viable option. Unfortunately, analyses of TANF leavers who have disabilities systematically fail to address the employment discrimination to which people with disabilities are so frequently subject.[31] Women are more likely than men to experience disabilities and are more likely to be the object of discriminatory treatment, either because they have or are perceived as having a disability.[32] Employment discrimination makes it that much more difficult for lone mothers with disabilities to become self-sufficient. Indeed, one study found that 73 percent of lone mothers with children under the age of 6 who have a disability live in circumstances of poverty.[33]

Limitations imposed on lone mothers by a disability, discriminatory treatment by employers, and mothers' needs to make sure their children with disabilities receive adequate care all can make it difficult for them to meet TANF program requirements, including work requirements. For example, many mothers find it difficult to locate or to afford adequate child care for children with disabilities, particularly when their children need care during mothers' nondaytime or irregular working hours or when the children have special care requirements. It is not unusual for mothers to be unexpectedly forced to stay home or to leave work to assure their children receive the needed care. A real question arises as to the degree to which families with disabilities are being supported and accommodated by individual states' one-size-fits-all Work First programs. What do mothers in such families do in the face of pressures to take a job—any job—and to keep it or risk termination of their TANF benefits?[34] In many cases, the needs of those with disabilities trump the demands of employers, and mothers get into trouble or even lose their jobs. In addition, lone mothers with disabilities or who have children with disabilities are more likely than other mothers on the TANF rolls to be subject to sanctions for failure to meet welfare program requirements, including work requirements.[35] And, as seen already, they are also less likely to be employed once they have exited the rolls.

Welfare Reform and the Rural Lone-Mother-Headed Family

In 2002, Carletta Connor lost her ride to her job as a medical technician several miles from her home in rural Mexico, Missouri. A few days later her babysitter announced she was moving. With no available public transportation and no one to take care of her four children, all under the age of 13, Connor, 44, could not keep her job. With no reliable child support to rely on, Connor had cycled on and off welfare for years and now found herself again turning to the government for assistance... This time, however, after a year, she hit the federally mandated five-year lifetime limit for receiving cash benefits... Connor and her kids now subsist on food stamps and sporadic child support payments... "It's a struggle every day," said Connor with a sigh. "When you get up you're looking forward to really nothing."[36]

The debates around welfare reform that preceded the passage of the PRWORA exhibited a clear urban bias.[37] Critics of welfare, from policy analysts to political elites, often focused the debate around the need to end welfare dependency among members of the so-called *underclass,* a term often used in the process of demonizing African Americans living in poverty in the nation's central cities. The debates devoted very little attention to the ways welfare reform might affect poor people residing in the nation's nonmetropolitan or rural areas. As the implementation of the PRWORA has proceeded, it has become very clear that "place" matters. Responding to the demands posed by welfare reform carries some unique and particularly difficult challenges for impoverished lone-mother-headed families who live far from metropolitan areas.[38]

Most of the 35.9 million people living in poverty in the United States in 2003 lived in metropolitan areas consisting of central cities and their suburbs. That year the overall poverty rate was 12.1 percent for metropolitan areas, where 28.4 million people had incomes under the federal poverty line. Central cities had the highest poverty rate, at 17.5 percent (14.6 million people). The rate for more heavily populated suburbs was substantially lower, at 9.1 percent (13.8 million people). In contrast, 7.5 million people—a fifth of the nation's poor—resided in geographic areas termed *nonmetropolitan,* often used interchangeably with *rural.* In 2003 the overall poverty rate for nonmetropolitan areas of the United States was 14.2 percent, or 2 percent higher than for the nation's metropolitan areas.[39]

Nonmetropolitan areas are actually highly diverse both socially and economically, and by no means do all nonmetropolitan areas in the United States have high or uniform rates of poverty. However, some 382 of the nation's counties have had a poverty rate of 20 percent or more in every decennial census from 1960 to 2000; 95 percent of these persistently poor counties are in nonmetropolitan areas. Of the 484 counties with poverty rates of 20 percent or higher in 2000, more than three-quarters have been that way for decades. In general, nonmetropolitan counties most remote from (i.e., not adjacent to) either small or large metropolitan areas have the highest likelihood of being persistently poor.[40] Such highly rural counties are heavily concentrated in the South, whose overall poverty rate of 14.1 percent is the highest of any major geographic region.[41] Many persistently poor counties are located in Appalachia, the Black Belt and Mississippi Delta, and the Rio Grande Valley, while other counties are the sites of Native American reservations of the Southwest and the Great Plains.[42]

A federal government analysis of 48 states found that an average of 293,000 families residing in rural counties received TANF cash benefits in 2003 and that rural families comprised 14 percent of all TANF cases that

year. The rate of decline in the welfare rolls after the passage of the PRWORA is the same for metropolitan and nonmetropolitan areas.[43] Similar trends can be observed regarding the post-PRWORA increase in the percentage of impoverished lone mothers with earnings.[44] These general statistics, however, mask the fact that welfare reform may be making financial conditions much worse for many lone-mother-headed families in rural areas, particularly areas that are isolated and that have in recent decades been chronically economically depressed.

The healthy national economy of the 1990s had less of an uplifting impact on rural areas, meaning, for example, lower rates of job growth than in metropolitan settings. As observers of the 1990s put it, "America's recent economic boom has left a poorer menu of job options for rural than urban families, and unemployment, underemployment, and poverty levels remain higher in rural than in urban places."[45] The recession, and the economic slowdown of the early 2000s that followed, dealt a blow to many local nonmetropolitan economies that were not really thriving in the first place.

In rural areas, the structure of the local economy often seriously limits job availability even in so-called good times. Availability of both the numbers of and types of jobs is likely to be more limited than in metropolitan areas, if for no other reason than low population density usually signifies far fewer and a narrower range of employers. In some rural communities the economy lacks diversity and there are but a handful of principal workplaces. The health of the local economy rises and falls with their success or failure. Job seekers in rural settings may feel fortunate to have jobs at all, finding themselves in no position to complain about low pay, limited or irregular hours, lack of benefits, and less-than-desirable working conditions. Welfare reform's mandatory work requirements and cash-benefit time limits virtually force lone mothers into taking such jobs. Thus, while the movement of lone mothers from welfare to work has led to an increased percentage having earnings, in rural areas their earnings from work are on average less than those of similar mothers in urban settings. Average earnings are said to be 25 to 30 percent lower for workers in rural areas.[46]

Because job availability is such an issue in many nonmetropolitan areas, attaining and maintaining economic self-sufficiency can be an impossible task for lone mothers. In some instances, all mothers can find in the formal labor market are seasonal jobs. The wages paid may be sufficient to support a family only when combined with receipt of cash welfare benefits when unemployed. Yet with maximum five-year lifetime limits on welfare receipt mandated by the PRWORA, and with time limits being even more restrictive in some states, long-term reliance on a combination of seasonal work and welfare is no longer possible for many rural lone-mother-headed families.[47] In rural settings, insufficient numbers of full-time, year-round jobs are available providing wages high enough to enable lone-mother-headed families to rise above the federal poverty line. And little or no upward mobility is likely from the types of jobs lone mothers are able to obtain. Not surprisingly, of the lone mothers in rural areas who are working, a third of them are members of the nation's working poor.[48]

Meeting the mandatory work requirements of welfare reform becomes impossible when lone mothers do not have transportation or find it hard to access supportive services (e.g., child care, health care) that are necessary if they hope to successfully maintain employment.[49] In metropolitan areas, for example, mass public transportation (trains, trolleys, buses, etc.) is generally available, even if it is not always convenient to use or easily affordable for poor people. But the more remote a community is from a metropolitan area, the less likely its residents are to have access to any system of public transportation. Bus service, for example, may not exist outside larger towns such as county seats and may operate only on limited daytime-hour schedules. Regardless of whether they reside in metropolitan or nonmetropolitan areas, lone mothers living in poverty frequently find the costs of owning and maintaining a reliable car beyond their means. Perhaps half of the nation's rural poor do not own a car.[50] Car insurance is expensive, and drivers who have had licenses suspended or revoked for unpaid fines often cannot afford to make the payments for reinstatement. Lack of public or private transportation thus serves as a barrier to employment to a greater degree for rural-dwelling lone mothers than for those living in central cities or their suburbs.

Supportive services for lone mothers residing in nonmetropolitan areas may be more difficult to get to because of transportation difficulties, as well as few and far between. Toddler and child-care centers and after-school care programs are often a rarity in rural areas, making such care harder for mothers to arrange. Obviously, this care is generally not found on nights and weekends when many lone mothers may have to work. Lacking affordable, flexible child care, mothers are usually highly dependent upon friends, neighbors, or family members, all of whom may or may not be reliable.

The support services needed from health-care providers may also be problematic. In rural areas, primary care physicians, dentists, and health-care facilities are often far more distant and fewer in number than in metropolitan areas. Medical specialists and mental health services may be nonexistent in rural settings. Getting to appointments can require traveling or transporting children long distances, meaning mothers may have to miss work. Likewise, educational and training facilities are often scarce, limiting opportunities for lone mothers to improve or to learn new skills that could assist them in the job market. Finally, welfare office facilities are often centralized in distant towns or county seats. A lone mother's ability to get to appointments with caseworkers for benefit eligibility checks or counseling can be hampered by distance, while welfare offices' operating hours may conflict with those of a mother's employer. Failure to show up for scheduled appointments or to gain important information relevant to eligibility may lead to sanctions and to the loss of cash benefits.

The lack of available jobs in the formal labor market, the low wages most jobs pay, and the inadequacy of supportive services for working mothers together have fostered alternative forms of industriousness on the part of impoverished lone mothers. Such mothers have long been performing extensive work in the informal economy in order to supplement or even as a substitute for cash welfare benefits. Given the inadequacy of these benefits, informal work has often been absolutely critical to lone-mother-headed families' subsistence; in some cases, it has provided the bulk of families' incomes.

In the informal economy, work is frequently performed "under the table"—returns for mothers' labor may come in the form of cash, goods, or in-kind services. Child and elder care, sewing, hair styling, gardening, field work, spiritual guidance, alternative healing, and trading in used goods are examples of informal work. Welfare reform's mandatory work requirements do not recognize such activities as permissible work, and TANF policies generally make mothers seek out and take on regular employment or risk losing their cash welfare benefits. If lone mothers do take jobs in the formal labor market—assuming jobs are available—they likely find themselves with little spare time to participate in and to gain the benefits of the informal economy. In rural areas, many lone mothers have found themselves choosing to forgo cash welfare benefits, even at the risk of increased hardship, in favor of possibly more lucrative rewards from work in the informal sector.[51]

Lone Mothers and Family Homelessness

I work as a home health aide and have to get up at 4:45 in the morning to be at work by 6:30 three days a week. I'm also trying to finish a program to get my associates degree in nursing, and find an apartment so I can get out of the homeless shelter where I live. I'm looking for a place, but it's hard to find anything. I only make $200 a week, and most two bedrooms are $700 a month. I tried to find a studio, but most landlords don't want kids in a studio... We have to turn in forms that list where we looked for housing each week, and we have to have twelve, no matter what. If the landlord doesn't return your call, it doesn't count.... It's so degrading. You know, besides being homeless, we have other issues and should be treated with respect... You know, anybody could end up in this predicament—it's not because we made bad choices. That's the way life is. Some people are lucky, and some are not. And a pat on the back would be so much better than constantly putting us down.[52]

It would be wrong to claim that welfare reform in and of itself is a principal cause of widespread homelessness in the United States, but it has definitely contributed to the problem. Cash welfare benefits alone are not enough to ensure that a lone-mother-headed family can afford housing. Median benefits for a mother and two children are but a third of the federal poverty line.[53] Moreover, the employment of lone mothers receiving welfare is clearly not turning out to be a solution to homelessness. States' welfare-to-work policies have left many lone mothers to fend for themselves in the low-wage labor market, where they are often at high risk of unemployment. The risk of homelessness is high for adult wage earners whose incomes are low, whether they are lone mothers or not.[54] According to the National Coalition for the Homeless, 44 percent of those experiencing homelessness are employed.[55]

The value of the average U.S. worker's annual earnings has eroded in recent decades, taking place simultaneously with rising housing costs. Today, no full-time worker earning the federal minimum wage of $5.15 per hour, whose real value has fallen by 25 percent since 1975, can afford the average fair-market rent on a one- or two-bedroom apartment. The National Low Income Housing Coalition calculates that a worker would have to have hourly earnings nearly three times that wage in order to afford such an apartment, which is an impossible dream for many.[56] Few lone mothers who have left the welfare rolls in recent years have acquired jobs paying over $15 per hour.

The federal government defines *affordable housing* as consuming no more than 30 percent of a household's income. As housing costs have risen, however, more and more people have been forced to spend an increasing percentage of their incomes on housing, particularly those living in low-income households. According to the U.S. Department of Housing and Urban Development, over five million U.S. renting households with incomes below 50 percent of their local area median—households lacking any government housing assistance—pay over 50 percent of

their income for housing or live in severely substandard housing.[57] Many of these households contain families with children. In such economically bereft settings, rent and utility costs often drain away money needed for food, clothing, transportation, child care, or medical expenses. A sudden job loss or an unforeseen medical expense that prevents rent payment can easily channel such families into homelessness.

It is estimated that as many as 3.5 million people, including 1.5 million children, experience homelessness annually.[58] Approximately 40 percent of the homeless are families with children, and some 67 percent of homeless families are headed by a single parent, typically a lone mother. Many homeless children are very young: 42 percent are under five years of age.[59] In the early 1980s, family homelessness was likely to be a one-time affair and to be generated by a calamitous event, such as a fire or a serious housing hazard. Today, homelessness among families with children is far more likely to be poverty generated. In the last decade or so, family homelessness has undergone an unprecedented increase,[60] some of which is directly linked to welfare reform.

While data on shelter usage are of only limited help in understanding the full extent of the nation's homelessness problem, annual reports by the U.S. Conference of Mayors over the past several years have underscored the fact that homeless families have been appearing with increasing frequency at urban emergency shelters.[61] Families are often turned away from shelters in cities that are already filled to capacity. In rural areas, where a good deal of family homelessness can be found, few shelters even exist. Families live out of cars or else huddle in tents, campers, or make-shift structures.

Most of the homeless in cities are not found in shelters. Homeless people typically strive to avoid emergency shelters unless going there is an absolute necessity, viewing them as extremely stressful, unclean, unsafe, lacking privacy, and operated with little respect for human dignity. Many homeless families who lack stable, permanent residences have family or friends with whom they can temporarily double or even triple up. Though this may mean living under crowded and stressful conditions and may often require shifting from home to home, at least such families are temporarily occupying apartments or houses. Others huddle crowdedly in cheap hotels or motels. The least fortunate families live exposed on the nation's streets.

According to the National Coalition for the Homeless, many families who have lost or experienced cutbacks in their cash welfare benefits are unable to afford housing.[62] They are not likely to receive help from government housing programs, which serve only a small proportion of all poor households meeting eligibility requirements, including households headed by impoverished lone-mothers. There are long backlogs and waiting lists—extending even for years—for government housing assistance.[63] "As a result of loss of benefits, low wages, and unstable employment, many families leaving welfare struggle to get medical care, food, and housing… [H]ousing is rarely affordable for families leaving welfare for low wages, yet subsidized housing is so limited that fewer than one in four TANF families nationwide lives in public housing or receives a housing voucher to help them rent a private unit. For most families leaving the rolls, housing subsidies are not an option."[64]

In the absence of government housing assistance, many lone-mother-headed families who have left the TANF rolls find themselves homeless. Studies in various states show rates of homelessness among welfare-leaver families as high as 7 percent.[65] Moreover, families may be forced to rely upon emergency shelters or other inadequate housing arrangements for far longer than would otherwise be necessary. Research in New York City found that "family homelessness is exploding."[66] The typical homeless parent in the city is a lone mother, twenty-seven years of age, with two children. She is likely to be unemployed and receiving welfare and to have experienced a public-assistance benefit cut in the previous year.[67] In the mid-1990s, families remained in New York City's emergency shelters for five months on average before finding permanent housing. Now, due to higher housing costs and a shortage of government housing assistance, the average is nearly twelve months.[68] Because families are increasingly remaining in city shelters longer, others who also need shelter space are more likely than in the past to be turned away and forced to find other alternatives.

Lack of government housing assistance—either in the form of access to public housing or vouchers that help renters pay the costs of private housing—can be viewed as a barrier impeding the ability of lone mothers to conform to states' welfare-to-work programs. The difficulties lone mothers leaving the TANF rolls for employment often have in paying for housing already has been discussed. In the same vein, having housing problems can also undermine mothers' ability to be employed, either while on or after having left the rolls.

For example, the high costs of rent and utilities can overwhelm mothers' ability to afford the transportation and child care they need to obtain or to maintain employment. Likewise, lone mothers who lack permanent housing, who must move frequently, and who are constantly preoccupied with fending off family homelessness, may find it impossible to work regularly and to adhere to an employer's schedule. Similarly, lone mothers admitted to shelters may in turn be required to demonstrate that they have met a daily or weekly quota of housing search attempts, mandatory activities that, when added to their parenting responsibilities, can hamper mothers' search for or ability to maintain employment. In all these situations, lone mothers risk failing to meet TANF program work requirements and sanctions that include the loss of some or all cash welfare benefits. Work First TANF policies are at times implemented with little regard for impoverished lone mothers' often tenuous housing situations.[69] There is also no guarantee of housing assistance, even if mothers conform to all of the rules and become welfare-to-work success stories.

The threat of being homeless and the difficulty of finding safe, affordable housing alone are highly stressful experiences for lone mothers; however, other factors can exacerbate this stress. Many lone mothers who have fled situations of domestic violence must deal with homelessness even as they contend with being physically or psychologically impaired. Mothers know that family homelessness frequently leads to the permanent removal of children to foster homes by child welfare officials and have good reason to fear the forced breakup of their families.[70] Homeless shelters are typically a desperate last resort for most homeless families. If mothers are forced to bring their families to shelters, rules requiring that older male children be housed in separate facilities may mean at least a temporary family breakup. In addition, mothers often face a futile battle in trying to enroll, to reenroll, and to keep their school-age children in school. Children are likely to fall behind because of frequent and often disruptive household moves, and mothers may have no option but to house children with family members or friends to facilitate their school attendance. Not only the mothers, but also their children, are more likely than those who are adequately housed to suffer from chronic ill health conditions or disabilities. Such conditions may be made worse when families cannot afford nutritious food and proper medical care. Homeless children are prone to developmental problems, learning disabilities, and emotional or behavioral difficulties, all of which can have serious consequences if not dealt with early. For lone mothers, homelessness is often accompanied by anxiety disorders or serious depression and, for some, suicide attempts.[71]

Research has begun to document some of the benefits to families from government housing assistance, such as housing subsidies. Unlike homeless families not receiving housing assistance, families who do receive assistance not only achieve housing stability but also tend to maintain it. Moreover, lone mothers who leave the TANF rolls with housing assistance have somewhat higher rates of employment and higher incomes than leavers lacking such assistance. Housing assistance may free up some family income that would otherwise have gone to rent, making it available to help support mothers' ability to maintain their employment. The receipt of housing assistance does not, however, mean that welfare-leaver families are without significant economic hardships; they are still subject to disadvantaged lifestyles reflecting lone mothers' meager earnings and lack of benefits in their low-wage jobs.[72]

Child-Only TANF Cases on the Rise

> Margaret King, 64, a retired telephone operator with custody of two of her five grandchildren, said that when her daughter lost welfare benefits, the daughter had to depend more on her children's mentally ill, drug-abusing father... [A]fter the family was evicted from their Queens apartment and placed in a temporary shelter in the Bronx, the mother became desperate to keep her welfare-to-work job... She left her three children with their father at the shelter for lack of a baby sitter, and the youngest, a brain-damaged toddler, cut himself badly on an open can while the father was sleeping off a drinking binge. The mother, who has already turned over her two older children to their grandmother, was charged with neglect and is now at risk of losing the others to foster care. "She was always a good mother," the grandmother said. "She had no choice, and the system didn't help her."[73]

Historically, the overwhelming majority of welfare recipients have been lone mothers and their children. Although the discussion in this chapter has primarily focused on the often-ignored diversity that exists among such families, it is crucial not to ignore a significant development accompanying welfare reform. As the numbers of lone mothers on the TANF rolls have dramatically fallen, the numbers of "child-only" TANF cases has increased. Child-only cases involve households (or, more technically, TANF "assistance units") in which the sole persons receiving cash welfare benefits are children. In 1990, children were the only cash-benefit recipients in fewer than 12 percent of AFDC (now TANF) households. By 2002, the proportion of child-only TANF-recipient households had risen to 39 percent.[74]

In many child-only TANF households, lone mothers are present. In some instances, lone mothers whose disabilities prevent them from working are on the SSI rolls, but their children remain eligible for TANF cash benefits. In other cases, the mothers are legal or illegal immigrants barred from receiving benefits under the PRWORA, but with children born in the United States who are TANF eligible. In still other (but comparatively few) instances, mothers have been deemed ineligible for cash benefits due to sanctions or because they have exhausted benefit time limits, but their state's welfare policy permits children's welfare benefits to continue. Taken together, child-only TANF cases in which children are being reared by their mothers constitute less than half of all child-only cases. In over 50 percent, the children are being cared for by someone other than a parent, usually a relative (such as a grandparent) who has no legal responsibility to support them.[75]

A New Jersey study offers some further insight into the diverse characteristics of lone-mother-headed households in which only the children receive TANF.[76] In New Jersey the child-only TANF population grew from 17 percent of the state's TANF cases in 1995 to 33 percent in 2001. Poverty-related hunger and other hardships were common among these children and their families.

1. In 25 percent of the New Jersey child-only cases, the children receiving TANF were living with a parent with a disability who was receiving SSI. Many times these parents were lone mothers who had been on the TANF rolls. Their disability-linked inability to work to support their families made them eligible to transfer over to SSI. While SSI cash benefits are generally higher than those under TANF programs, most of these families lived below the federal poverty line. They also had surprisingly high rates of food insecurity (over half reported having had problems getting food in the previous year).

2. Another 10 percent of the New Jersey child-only cases involved families headed by parents who were legal or illegal immigrants and, thus, who were not eligible for TANF benefits even though their U.S.-born children were. In many instances the parents were lone mothers who had difficulties with employment due to lack of education and job skills, as well as limited English proficiency. Their very low incomes made these families especially vulnerable to housing hardships, with one in four having to double or triple up with other families in severely overcrowded conditions. Many immigrant lone mothers had mental health problems, but the vast majority lacked any health insurance.

3. Most of the TANF child-only cases in New Jersey, as is true nationally, involved families headed by adults other than the children's parents. Over 60 percent involved caretakers—primarily grandparents—who were rearing their young relatives with the help of TANF cash benefits. Because the children were being cared for by adults who had no legal obligation to do so, the income and assets of kin caretakers did not bear

on TANF child-only benefit eligibility. On average, nonparent-headed families in which only the children were on the TANF rolls were somewhat better off economically and experienced fewer hardships than other TANF-recipient households in New Jersey.[77]

The role played by nonparental kin who function as surrogate parents for impoverished children has drawn increasing attention as the numbers of lone mothers on the TANF rolls has fallen. According to the Center for Law and Social Policy, 5.4 million children were living in households headed by relatives in 2000, and 2.2 million of these children were living in relative-headed households without a parent present.[78] Over 60 percent of the latter were headed by relatives with low incomes, and many of these households experienced food insecurity and housing hardships.[79] Approximately 510,000 children receiving TANF lived in relative-headed households, and most (450,000) of these children received child-only benefits.[80] It should also be noted that in most relative-headed households in which TANF-eligible children reside, the children receive no TANF assistance. In some cases the relatives do not want to suffer the stigma associated with welfare, and in other cases they either do not know the children are eligible or have been rejected for assistance out of error.[81]

Nationally, grandparents are coming to play an ever more important role in child-rearing, particularly for children living in poverty. When the PWRORA was passed in 1996, an estimated 1.4 million children were living apart from their parents in households headed by grandparents, up by 52 percent from 1990. In 1996, almost half of grandparent-headed households were headed by two grandparents, while another near-half were grandmother-headed (only 6 percent contained a grandfather alone). Children living in grandmother-headed households are especially likely to be poor in comparison to children living with both grandparents or with other kin. Indeed, in 1996, 57 percent of child-rearing grandmothers had incomes below the federal poverty line and only a third were employed in any given month.[82] More recent research suggests that grandparents serving as caregivers often struggle more with insufficient incomes than do other kin caretakers who are more likely to be working and that many grandparent-headed households have problems with food and housing hardships as well as with health issues.[83]

Some grandparents have legal custody of their grandchildren, which in turn obligates them to provide full-time care. Much more frequently, however, the caregiving relationship is informally established, with the grandchildren simply sent to live with grandparents temporarily or permanently. Permanent care by grandparents has been on the increase "as a result of divorce, substance abuse, child abuse and/or neglect, abandonment, teenage pregnancy, death, HIV/AIDS, unemployment, incarceration, and mental health problems."[84] Impoverished mothers have long looked to kin for help in desperate times. Barriers to employment, along with an inability to conform to mandatory work requirements of TANF, cause many lone mothers such financial stress that they are forced to turn over their children to kinship care.

Providing permanent care for one or more grandchildren can be a serious financial burden for grandparents who are unprepared and financially ill-situated. Most grandparents can at best financially plan for their own late-life needs, and few anticipate having to once again deal with the monetary costs and resource demands involved in parenting young children. Not all grandparent-headed households engaging in care of grandchildren are poor but, as already indicated, many are low income if not impoverished, particularly those headed by grandmothers. Adding the costs of child-rearing to household budgets—specifically to the already-strained budgets of elders on a low and relatively fixed income—can make access to government financial assistance crucial.

But the burdens of kinship care are not entirely or at times even predominantly financial. The burdens and stresses of parenting once again can create or can exacerbate mental or physical health problems for those who left the parenting role long ago.[85] The demands placed on grandparents can be huge. For example, caring for grandchildren often carries many of the life problems of the dissolved lone-mother-headed family into grandparents' households. Lone mothers' inability to parent and the circumstances leading to having to give up their children to grandparents may be accompanied by negative fallout. This can include disruptive and upsetting changes in the nature and quality of the relationships between grandparents and their own children, as when lone mothers must relinquish parenting due to chronic substance abuse or incarceration. The fallout may likewise extend to problems involving the grandchildren with which grandparents must somehow cope. Not only are the grandchildren suffering the trauma of separation from their own mothers, but also their life circumstances up to that point—often highly stressful and sometimes involving abuse or neglect—can leave them with serious emotional or behavioral problems. In effect, grandparents often inherit others' traumas and their effects. At the same time, attending to time-consuming and intensive child-care responsibilities often alters and restricts grandparents' own lifestyles and relationships with family and friends. Such child-care responsibilities can isolate and exhaust grandparents at the very time when they need a supportive social network.[86]

Historically, both cash assistance and other benefits were largely provided to needy caretaking grandparents or other caretaking relatives by the precursor to TANF, Aid to Families with Dependent Children. Both caretaking grandparents and their grandchildren could be assisted financially under AFDC when lone mothers were not available to parent. The terms of assistance changed radically, however, with welfare reform. Under the PRWORA, if grandparents receive TANF cash benefits as members of the household "assistance unit," they must (with some limited federal and individual state exemptions) conform to regular TANF program rules, including mandatory work requirements, strict cash-benefit time limits, and mandatory cooperation with child-support enforcement efforts directed at their grandchildren's fathers. The grandparents enrolled in TANF may also be subject to sanctions, including loss of some or all of the household's cash benefits, for violating TANF program rules.

For a variety of reasons—including health or stamina problems, child-care issues, or caretaking responsibilities for others besides their grandchildren—many financially needy grandparents cannot meet TANF work requirements. Some also believe that being forced into helping welfare authorities enforce child-support collections could destabilize family relationships and informal custody arrangements or even could pose dangers to themselves or their grandchildren. TANF program rules thus often work against many grandparents' enrollment, even though they are eligible and in serious financial need. When the grandchildren for whom they are caring receive child-only benefits, TANF work requirements and maximum-benefit time limits do not apply, nor must grandparents get involved in child-support enforcement. However, since in most instances the amount of cash benefits going to TANF households is based on the number of people receiving benefits, households containing child-only cases receive less assistance than if the grandparent caretakers had been included in the assistance unit.[87]

In 2000, individual states' child-only payments ranged from $68 to $514 per month for a single child (benefit rates decline for additional children), with a national average of $238.[88] For low-income grandparent-headed households on relatively fixed incomes, child-only benefits do little to offset the financial burdens of child-rearing and many elders find themselves unexpectedly drawing upon retirement savings or searching for ways to earn money long after they have left the labor force. In short, households in which impoverished children are being cared for by nonparental kin are actually less well served by TANF than they were under AFDC. TANF program rules were clearly not crafted by political elites with the basic subsistence needs of caretaking kin in mind, and these rules have had undesirable consequences for families.[89]

loss of TANF benefits includes not only the lifetime loss of cash benefits, but also whatever employment-related services individual states provide to those on their TANF rolls.[95]

Loss of TANF benefits and food stamps occur for those convicted of drug-related felonies. In addition, under federal housing policy, lone mothers convicted of any criminal offense, however minor or long-ago, can be denied access to public housing. Local public housing authorities can choose to exclude ex-offenders for life, irrespective of their rehabilitation or changed personal or family situations. This federal policy was designed to allow public housing authorities to exclude potentially dangerous tenants and thus to protect the safety of residents. However, researchers have found that the policy is frequently being administered in ways that are "needlessly over-broad" and highly exclusionary.[96] Thus, not only does federal policy toward lone mothers found guilty of violating drug laws undermine many mothers' ability to support and feed their families, by allowing mothers found guilty of virtually any criminal offense to be banned from public housing, federal policy also contributes to homelessness.

Lone mothers convicted of crimes and imprisoned must endure separation from their families and may even lose custody of their children as a result of their incarceration. Each year, some 60,000 women are convicted of felony drug offenses—many of them are lone mothers with minor children. Most of these children enter kinship care arrangements. Upon their release from prison, mothers are in need of help if they are to successfully reunite with their children and to take on responsibility for their care. Lone mothers must be able to find adequate housing, to pay rent, and to provide their families with food, clothing, and health care. Employment may be difficult for them to find immediately, especially considering that they have a criminal record, but their subsistence needs begin upon release from prison. Job-hunting requires an income in order to pay for phone calls, suitable clothing, transportation, and child care. Having no money and no welfare benefits or food stamps places lone mothers released from prison in an untenable position.

As one study put it, "In a vicious circle, losing public benefits is likely to make it harder for parents with criminal records to stay clean and sober, avoid abusive relationships, take care of their children, and resist engaging in criminal activity."[97] To make it even more complicated, lone mothers released from prison may face conflicting demands from different quarters. If convicted of nondrug offenses and eligible for TANF, they will have to meet its mandatory work, child-support enforcement, and other requirements. Mothers may have court-ordered probation or parole conditions that also must be met, such as enrollment in vocational education

programs. The circumstances surrounding their conviction and imprisonment may require meeting the demands of child welfare authorities for
counseling or other rehabilitation services in order to gain or retain custody of their children. Agencies often do not coordinate their demands or
even know they may be mutually contradictory. Meeting the demands of
one agency may mean failing to meet the demands of another, and lone
mothers are often put at risk of losing welfare benefits, returning to
prison, or losing custody of their children.[98]

Lone mothers forced to rely on TANF typically are humiliated by the
stigma associated with being a welfare mother and are depressed by their
impoverished plight. However, it can be even a greater psychological blow
for impoverished mothers to be permanently banned from TANF and
other government programs that serve low-income people. Such a ban
symbolizes absolute rejection by civil society. They are refused help in getting back on their feet and establishing productive roles for themselves as
parents and workers, even as other mothers are being granted these public
benefits. Exclusion from TANF functions as an additional and unremitting
punishment for lone mothers who have violated the law, a punishment
that goes well beyond the dues they have already paid under the criminal
justice system.

Discriminatory Treatment of Lone-Mother-Headed Families of Color

> People of color routinely encounter insults and disrespect as they
> seek to navigate the various programs that make up the welfare
> system. Women are subject to sexual inquisitions in welfare
> offices and sexual harassment at their assigned work activities.
> People whose first language is not English encounter a serious
> language barrier when they have contact with the welfare sys-
> tem… Eligible immigrants and refugees are often told to go back
> where they came from when they try to get help for themselves or
> their U.S. citizen children.[99]

At first glance, U.S. welfare policy appears to be race-blind, having little
to do with race, racism, or racial and ethnic inequalities in the United
States. Scholars, however, have documented a long history of discrimination in the conceptualization, formulation, and implementation of U.S.
welfare policy,[100] which has continued through contemporary welfare
reform under the PRWORA.[101] Welfare reform's impact has been disproportionately adverse for impoverished lone-mother-headed families of

color, including many immigrant families who have come from Latin America, the Caribbean, and Asia.[102]

Earlier, chapter 2 described ways in which racism and racist stereotypes historically shaped the nature of welfare policy in the United States, particularly when it came to the treatment of African Americans. Examples were given of discriminatory practices resulting in the direct or indirect exclusion of many eligible people of color from the welfare rolls. Today, for the most part the racial and ethnic discrimination that occurs is often more subtle than in the past, but it is no less insidious in its overall effects. The PRWORA has given individual states license to treat their impoverished lone-mother-headed families more or less harshly in designing their TANF programs; this degree of harshness often follows skin color lines.

For example, a study comparing states' TANF programs found differences highly correlated with the racial and ethnic composition of states' welfare recipients. States having a higher proportion of African-American and Latino recipients tended to treat welfare recipients more harshly than other states and were more likely to impose harsh sanctions when lone mothers violated TANF program rules, including removal of some or all of recipient families' cash benefits. The states containing proportionately more recipients of color tended to have the shortest maximum time limits for receiving TANF cash benefits and were also more likely to impose family caps on cash benefits, resulting in very minimal or no additional income assistance going to families on the TANF rolls to which an additional child was born.[103]

In 2002, six years after the passage of the PRWORA, the U.S. Commission on Civil Rights issued a scathing indictment of the mistreatment of the civil rights of impoverished families of color under welfare reform.[104] Its report was built upon a growing number of studies documenting "disparities in access to and utilization of services" along racial and ethnic lines and "discrimination in the delivery of welfare benefits."[105] The outrage being expressed by activist groups concerned with such discrimination found expression in the Commission on Civil Rights' report. In addition, such groups persuaded sympathetic legislators to introduce bills into the House of Representatives and, later, into the Senate that were specifically aimed at protecting the civil rights of welfare recipients. These bills, introduced in 2002 and 2003, would have addressed some of the commission's concerns regarding racial equity and fairness in TANF administration by the individual states.[106] However, they gained no support from the administration of President George W. Bush or his allies in the largely Republican-dominated Congress. Such political elites were far more interested in pressing for an increase in the mandatory work requirements of the PRWORA and in promoting marriage as an antipoverty measure.

This failure of Congress and the president to act has left the following types of problems unaddressed:[107]

1. Impoverished lone-mother-headed families are disproportionately of color. In most states, programs have been developed to divert families from joining the TANF rolls by, for example, keeping cash benefits low, establishing strict eligibility requirements, restricting public outreach and information on benefits and services, and making enrollment bureaucratically difficult or a humiliating process. Even when applied by TANF caseworkers in a nondiscriminatory manner (which is not always the case), the disproportionate number of TANF-eligible families of color means that diversion programs have a disparate impact along skin color lines. Far more families of color are eligible for TANF than end up receiving it.[108]

2. The PRWORA erroneously assumed that a level racial playing field existed in the U.S. labor market. Its mandatory work requirements are blind to the racial and ethnic discrimination on the part of employers that makes it particularly difficult for lone mothers of color to find jobs, remain employed, and stay off the TANF rolls. White families have been leaving the rolls at higher rates than families of color, in part due to the greater success of white lone mothers in the labor market.[109]

3. States' Work First TANF policies force mothers to take any job open to them. Due in part to discrimination by employers and employment agencies and by discriminatory referral practices by TANF caseworkers, the jobs mothers of color are required to accept tend not only to be the most poorly paid but also among the least stable (e.g., temporary, subject to layoff). Failure to meet mandatory work requirements can result in sanctions, and mothers of color lose TANF benefits for this reason more frequently than do white mothers. If they are able to reestablish their eligibility, many of the mothers of color who are sanctioned off apply to reenter the TANF rolls. However, their families are likely to suffer increased hardships in the interim.[110]

4. As they are often the poorest of the poor, lone-mother-headed families of color tend to have the most numerous barriers to employment. On average they are forced to rely on TANF for much longer than white families. This, together with the reentry of many families of color to the TANF rolls sanctioned off for noncompliance with

program rules, has resulted in their becoming a growing majority of the nation's TANF recipients. White families who leave the TANF rolls are most likely to have lost their TANF eligibility as a consequence of employment-related income. Families of color are more likely to leave due to sanctions or because they have hit maximum-benefit time limits.[111]

5. In some TANF programs, white lone mothers are more likely than mothers of color to be provided with job-readiness skills, transportation assistance, child-care subsidies, and other benefits or services supportive of work. They are also more likely to receive encouragement to continue their academic educations, to participate in enrichment programs, or to receive tutoring.[112]

6. Lone mothers of color are more likely than white mothers to work at unpaid jobs, generally known as *workfare,* in order to meet mandatory work requirements and to receive TANF cash benefits. Such workfare jobs usually involve very low-skilled forms of service work and, as such, are rarely routes to paid employment at livable wages for mothers who reach their maximum time limits and lose their benefits.[113]

7. In some settings, white women are more likely than eligible women of color to receive TANF benefits for unborn children. This differential treatment means that white mothers may be better able to care for themselves and thus may be less likely to suffer problematic pregnancies or to bear children with birth defects.[114]

8. There is evidence that mothers of color are more likely than white mothers to be subjected to preemployment tests for drug use or criminal background checks and to be required to work undesirable schedules or difficult-to-manage shifts.[115]

9. TANF program staff and their largely English-language written materials frequently fail to meet the needs of language minorities with limited English proficiency. Such language minorities are disproportionately people of color, both immigrant and native born. (Immigrants in general are discussed in the following section.) Lacking English, they often have difficulty determining their eligibility for the TANF rolls and for available benefits and services. Once on the rolls, language minorities frequently fail to comprehend TANF program rules, have difficulty meeting mandatory work requirements, and end up being sanctioned for noncompliance.[116]

10. Following the implementation of TANF significant overall decreases were observed in the numbers of impoverished families enrolled in government-funded Medicaid (health care) and food stamp

(antihunger) programs. The PRWORA ended entitlement to cash welfare benefits, but due to states' administrative blunders and TANF caseworker errors, many eligible families also were dropped from these two means-tested entitlement programs or were given no reason to believe they were entitled to them. Impoverished families of color are especially subject to health problems and food insecurity. They have been disproportionately harmed by this alarming failure to recognize the entitlements of all eligible for Medicaid and food stamps, a failure state and federal officials have only recently begun to remedy.[117]

These and other adverse impacts of welfare reform disproportionately affecting impoverished families of color led to the coining and increasingly widespread use of the term *welfare racism*.[118] Clearly, racism and racial inequality are intimately tied to the continued failure of U.S. welfare policy to address poverty.

Welfare Reform's Impact on Impoverished Immigrants

"I'm stuck and it's frustrating," said Thao Nguyen, 35, an unemployed single mother of three children, ages 10, 9, and 5. "I don't know what my future will be. I can't afford to leave my children and work and I don't have the skills I need to make a better living." Nguyen, whose mother was Vietnamese and whose absent father was a U.S. soldier, was raised in poverty in Vietnam and never attended school... Nguyen married after immigrating, but her husband—and the father of her three children—left her about five years ago... "I just can't buy anything and I have to be real frugal," Nguyen said, adding that she devotes her time to raising her children and making sure they keep up with school work "so they don't become like me." With no job skills, illiterate in Vietnamese and unable to understand English, Nguyen relies on her 10-year-old to navigate the daily world... "I was hoping to get help when I really need it the most, but I was cut off from it instead."[119]

The United States is often characterized as a nation of immigrants. The overwhelming majority of U.S. residents can trace their family ancestries to other nations. In recent decades, millions of new immigrants have come to the United States, and they have been coming at an increasing rate. While 7.8 million immigrants were legally admitted into the United States from 1961 to 1980, more than twice as many—18.6 million—were admitted in the two decades following. In 2001 and 2002, this higher rate of admittance continued.[120] In addition to legally admitted immigrants, the U.S. Department of Homeland Security estimates that another 7 million immigrants may be in the United States without authorization. Over two-thirds of illegal immigrants are believed to be from Mexico.[121]

Immigrants legally admitted to the United States in recent decades differ from immigrants of the more distant past in that a far smaller percentage of the former are white-skinned Europeans. Recent immigrants have disproportionately been people of color, most of whom were born in Latin America, the Caribbean, or Asia.[122] These newer immigrants have, however, come to the United States for much the same reasons as their earlier counterparts. Most immigrants are joining family members who are already here or have come seeking employment opportunities. Others are admitted as refugees or asylum seekers or enter the United States under the auspices of special federal immigration programs. Thao Nguyen, whose voice is heard at the beginning of this section, came to the United States under a special program for Vietnamese children fathered and left behind by U.S. servicemen.

Some adult immigrants arrive in the United States with strong educational credentials, a record of work experience, English language proficiency, and skills that are in demand. By and large, such immigrants are able to integrate into the economic mainstream. Many others do not possess such advantageous "human capital" and find themselves struggling to gain a foothold in this mainstream. Even though more immigrant than nonimmigrant families contain adults in the labor force, on average, families headed by noncitizens are more likely to be low income or living in poverty than families headed by native-born adults—a reflection of the disproportionate representation of adult immigrants in low-wage jobs. Consequently, immigrant families are more likely than others to require economic assistance to meet their basic subsistence needs.[123]

Adults and children who are in the United States illegally have never been eligible for welfare benefits, even before welfare reform. Immigrant families who were legally admitted to the United States and who met eligibility criteria could receive benefits under Aid to Families with Dependent Children; eligibility for welfare benefits did not require citizenship. Prior to recent welfare reform, noncitizens who were in the United States legally, along with naturalized and native-born citizens, could all access AFDC. The PRWORA introduced radical changes into U.S. welfare policy when it came to immigrant eligibility. For the first time, most legal immigrants who were not citizens were declared ineligible for all federally funded assistance programs, including welfare.[124]

The PRWORA permitted individual states to exclude from TANF legal immigrants who had arrived in the United States on or before August 22, 1996, the date the PRWORA was passed. With some exceptions, these "preenactment" immigrants became ineligible not only for TANF but also for other federally financed programs, such as Social Security Income and food stamps.[125] Under the PRWORA, if states wished to provide TANF benefits to legal immigrants, the federal government would share their costs, just as it shared the costs of states' TANF benefits for naturalized or native-born citizens. Given this financial incentive, almost all states immediately opted to retain TANF benefits for preenactment immigrants. Although Congress ultimately revised the act's outright exclusion of almost all preenactment immigrants from SSI and food stamps (e.g., allowing assistance to children, people with disabilities, and the aged), heavy restrictions on preenactment immigrant eligibility for these and other programs remain in force.

The PRWORA also imposed important restrictions on "postenactment" immigrants, i.e., those who arrived legally in the United States after August 22, 1996.[126] This population would grow, but in 1996 it naturally was numerically much smaller than that of preenactment immigrants. Eligibility for SSI and food stamps was denied most postenactment immigrants, barring them from benefits unless and until they became naturalized citizens. Most postenactment immigrants were also made ineligible for TANF benefits—both cash and noncash benefits and services, including those supporting employment—until they had been in the United States for five years. The PRWORA permitted the states to offer TANF benefits to such immigrants during this five-year period, but states doing so would receive no financial help from the federal government. Rather than incur the costs, fewer than half of the states chose to offer the benefits.

These and other changes affecting immigrants under the PRWORA, such as more stringent income requirements for their sponsors, have made it extremely difficult for immigrants to combat impoverishment and to avoid the heavy toll its hardships take on families.[127] Why were legal immigrants targeted for such unprecedented discriminatory treatment? In the 1990s, anti-immigrant rhetoric, reflecting both xenophobia and racism, emerged as an important facet of national politics. Congressional welfare reformers' treatment of legal immigrants under the PRWORA was heavily influenced by the discourse surrounding California's anti-immigrant Proposition 187, a ballot measure approved by 59 percent of voters. The proposition, ultimately declared unconstitutional by federal courts, proposed ending access to tax-supported public services (e.g., emergency medical care, children's public schooling) that California had been providing to many illegal immigrants residing in the state. Most people targeted by Proposition 187 were undocumented Mexican workers and their family members, many of whom were noncitizens and had been living and working in the state for years.

Proponents of Proposition 187 argued that illegal immigrants were overwhelming the state's ability to provide services and were overburdening California taxpayers. Their influx had to be sharply restricted, if not halted, and denying them access to state services would help do this. Anti-immigrant rhetoric by proponents of Proposition 187 reverberated well beyond California. Many political elites elsewhere around the nation, including members of Congress, took notice of the public's apparent receptivity to such sentiments. In turn, they stirred and exploited the belief that too many immigrants were coming to the United States solely to take advantage of its so-called generous welfare programs. Even though no evidence existed to support this claim, many political elites argued that if access to the welfare rolls were tightened up, fewer immigrants of "lower quality"—meaning immigrants they believed were intent on becoming "public charges"—would enter the United States.[128]

Besides holding to the belief that the United States had become a "welfare magnet" for poor people from other nations, some political elites argued that public expenditures on benefits and services to support immigrants outweighed their contributions to the U.S. economy. This idea fit with the stereotypical notion that the goal of immigrants was welfare dependency, not self-sufficiency. Once again, no real evidence could be found to support such claims. But as with the welfare magnet stereotype, proponents were not much affected by lack of evidence in support of their arguments. In their view, by cutting back noncitizens' access to welfare, indolent immigrants would be made to increase their participation in and contributions to the economy or else would be forced to migrate back to their nations of origin.

Such beliefs and arguments became central to a bipartisan effort that emerged in Congress aimed at cutting federal and state welfare expenditures by making it more difficult for noncitizens to gain income assistance. When the PRWORA was voted on in 1996, members of Congress claimed that the law could save the federal government over $50 billion in welfare expenditures by 2002, $26 billion (44 percent) of which would come from decreasing benefits for legal immigrants.[129] This claim was made despite the fact that legal immigrants comprised only 15 percent of welfare recipients in 1996. For various reasons, this magnitude of savings was not achieved, but the intent of the immigrant provisions of the PRWORA clearly went beyond projected cost savings.

Introducing Congressional legislation designed to adjust the numbers and characteristics of those coming to the United States would likely attract a good deal of unwanted political controversy. Both immigrants and native-born citizens could be expected to contest a major shift in federal immigration policy, particularly if it seemed to be a veiled but discriminatory form of population control. Instead, Congress used the PRWORA as a surrogate for legislation that would straightforwardly change U.S. immigration policy, drawing support for its immigrant provisions from both anti-immigrant sentiments and the more general public antipathy toward welfare and its recipients. The anti-immigrant sentiments informing the PRWORA were also consistent with those informing other bills passed in Congress in 1996 that restricted the rights of noncitizens to remain in residence, the ability of illegal immigrants to gain legal status, and opportunities for immigrants to appeal the government's treatment of them.

There is no sign that the immigrant provisions of the PRWORA deterred immigrants from seeking admittance to the United States or that the provisions drove noncitizens to leave, but there is evidence that the well-being of immigrant families has been adversely affected as a consequence of the PRWORA.[130] The Center on Budget and Policy Priorities has reported that "the percentage of legal noncitizens participating in each of the major means-tested federal programs—Medicaid, Food Stamps, TANF, and SSI—has *declined* significantly since 1996"[131] (italics in original). The percentage of immigrant-headed families in which at least one person received TANF benefits fell 60 percent, from almost 6 percent in 1996 to just over 2 percent in 2001.[132] This dramatic decline in immigrant families receiving TANF benefits was not caused by rising family incomes or categorical loss of eligibility for TANF, which had largely been restored by the states for preenactment legal immigrants who far outnumbered the postenactment legal immigrant population following the passage of the PRWORA.

The rapid decline seems to have had more to do with other legislation Congress passed that same year. In part, such legislation was a response to the 1993 bombing of New York City's World Trade Center by international terrorists. New laws restricting noncitizens' rights to residence and the ability of illegal immigrants to attain a legal status, along with limitations on immigrants' rights to judicial appeal, provoked anxiety and fear. Many immigrants became concerned with trying to avoid doing anything that would draw government attention. Many legal immigrants believed, albeit erroneously, that applying for government assistance could adversely affect their ability to be granted citizenship or even to stay in the country. In addition, changes in the rules for eligibility also often left not only immigrants but also welfare caseworkers confused. Due to caseworker errors, administrative foul-ups, and misinformation, many immigrants either ceased participation in assistance programs in which they had been enrolled or did not apply at all. The post-PRWORA rate of decline in immigrants' federal program participation clearly exceeded that of citizens who were eligible for such programs.[133]

The decline in the participation of legal immigrants who are eligible for TANF and other assistance programs serving low-income families has left immigrant children in a particularly vulnerable situation. One in five children in the United States is an immigrant's child. If *low-income families* are defined as having an income below 200 percent of the federal poverty line, over half of children living in immigrant families can be categorized as such, compared to 37 percent of children in nonimmigrant families. One in four low-income children is an immigrant's child.[134] In comparison to children in low-income families with parents born in the United States, children of immigrants are likely to live in poorer families, to have health problems, to be in families having trouble affording food, to be in families struggling to pay rent, and to live under crowded housing conditions.[135]

Children of immigrant parents are less likely than children of native-born parents to be in families who are accessing programs of government assistance directed at such hardships, including TANF.[136] Many of these low-income children are U.S. citizens, born in the United States to legal or illegal immigrants. The immigration status of family members is often "mixed," and immigrant families frequently are comprised of legal and illegal immigrants and naturalized or native-born citizens. If they are U.S. citizens, children in low-income immigrant families are eligible for TANF and other government programs. However, the fear or confusion causing noncitizen adults in immigrant families to pull back from participation has affected family heads' willingness to apply for government programs for their citizen children. For example, families in which one or more members—adults or children—is in the United States illegally may fear that involvement with TANF will result in discovery and family breakup by forced deportations. It is for such reasons that eligible low-income U.S. citizen children in immigrant families are less likely to receive TANF benefits than children in low-income citizen families.[137]

In discussing the diversity of the TANF population, the attention here has largely been focused on lone-mother-headed families. While many low-income immigrant families are headed by lone mothers, immigrant families are far more likely than native-born families to have two parents present in the household. Moreover, immigrant families are much more likely to have at least one working adult in the household. Clearly, promotion of marriage and work by the PRWORA as the route to self-sufficiency rings hollow in the face of the poverty-related hardships experienced by immigrant families headed by adults already married and working. Many immigrant parents do the right thing only to find themselves unable to escape impoverishment.

The Work First philosophy of most TANF programs, in which opportunities to learn new skills and to gain English language proficiency have largely been replaced by demands to take the first job offered, clearly does not help immigrant families. Families headed by adults who have few skills or meaningful work experience or who lack English language proficiency tend to stay on the TANF rolls the longest. Immigrant family heads are more likely than their native-born counterparts to be pushed off the rolls by TANF program time limits, only to be left ill-equipped to gain self-sufficiency.

Reforming the Welfare of Native Americans

> As the leader of the White Mountain Apache Tribe, which has an unemployment rate of at least 35%, [the PRWORA] gives me grave concern. In my opinion, it is a perfect reflection of the perception that the dominant society has of the welfare community. That is, those who are on welfare are perfectly capable of working, and at the snap of the fingers could enter the workforce. Of course, how people find jobs when no jobs are available is an issue not addressed in the legislation… The White Mountain Apache Tribe did not create welfare, the federal government did. So if it's the federal government's intent to dismantle welfare, then it should provide opportunities for welfare recipients rather than throwing them out on the street.[138]

There are approximately 2.5 million Native American (American Indians and Alaska natives) in the United States, many of whom suffer extreme impoverishment. The federal poverty rate for Native Americans averaged over 23 percent between 2001 and 2003. As in the 1990s, this three-year average was about twice that of the U.S. population as a whole and was almost three times the average rate for whites.[139] The economic deprivations contemporary Native Americans suffer are the legacy of generations of social, economic, and political oppression and exclusion by the majority white population and its institutions, a dynamic that in many respects continues to this day.[140]

AFDC came to serve as an important means of survival for many Native Americans, given the extreme poverty in which their families so often found themselves. It served, for example, as the primary source of income for many families living on reservations. AFDC offered impoverished Native American families at least a minimal contribution to their basic subsistence—and one they could call upon as long as it was needed. The benefits went to families regardless of whether they lived on or off tribal reservations. Native American reservations have long been centers of concentrated deprivation, the first Americans' version of isolated black ghettos and places where high rates of severe poverty are the norm. Chronic unemployment and underemployment, low educational levels, hunger and food insecurity, physical and mental health problems, inadequate housing, substance abuse, out-of-wedlock births, domestic violence, marital dissolution, and other poverty-linked phenomena are serious issues on many reservations.

The PRWORA changed the ground rules for impoverished Native Americans, just as it did for other poor families, but with some important added twists. Once AFDC was abolished, Native Americans became eligible to apply for TANF. In return for TANF benefits, Native American families were made subject to state TANF program rules, which include the usual mandatory work requirements, sanctioning policies, and maximum-benefit time limits. However, in recognition of the employment difficulties facing many who reside on reservations, the PRWORA provided an exception to TANF time limits for Native Americans. On reservations or Alaska native villages with populations of 1,000 or more, where the unemployment rate is above 50 percent, adult recipients are exempt from time limits.[141]

Most Native Americans on the TANF rolls, including those residing on reservations, participate in their own state's TANF program. As state TANF rolls have undergone their dramatic decline under welfare reform, the total numbers of Native Americans being served has declined as well. But the movement of Native Americans off states' TANF rolls has often been slow, difficult, and uneven. In states where they reside in large numbers (e.g., North Dakota, South Dakota, Montana), Native American families have come to comprise an increasing and highly disproportionate share of the TANF rolls.[142] In more and more instances, Native Americans are reaching their state's maximum benefit time limits without finding the stable and adequately paid employment that could allow their families hope for an escape from poverty.[143]

In an important departure from the treatment of other sectors of the poverty population, the PRWORA allows federally recognized tribes (or tribal consortia) to seek approval from the U.S. Department of Health and Human Services to administer their own TANF programs. Under the

PRWORA, over 330 tribes in the nation's forty-eight contiguous states, along with thirteen Alaskan native groups, could seek approval to do so. As of mid-2002, thirty-six tribal plans serving some 24,000 families had received federal approval. These approved plans involved 174 tribes and Alaska native villages in fifteen states and were believed to encompass well over a third of Native American families participating in TANF.[144]

Under the PRWORA, tribal TANF programs are permitted somewhat more flexibility than state TANF programs when it comes to matters like determining the definition of *work*, setting eligibility standards, and establishing maximum time limits for receipt of benefits. The PRWORA allows tribal plans to be more lenient when it comes to benefit time limits. Also, tribal TANF programs differ from those of individual states in having greater freedom to define participation in educational certificate, diploma, or degree programs as work. Participation in programs aimed at rehabilitation for alcohol and other drug abuse can also qualify as work activities. Tribal programs can also extend the definition of work to include some activities deemed culturally appropriate, such as hunting-and-gathering tasks or the production of crafts.

Despite this programmatic genuflection toward an especially poverty-stricken sector of the U.S. population, the impact of welfare reform has been at odds with the needs of Native Americans from the start. Native American lone mothers residing on reservations confront especially difficult barriers to employment due, in part, to the lack of jobs on or near many reservations. Consequently, many have found it impossible to successfully make the move from welfare to work.

One of the few systematic studies of the impact of welfare reform on Native Americans focused on 445 current or former welfare-recipient families with children on three of the twenty-one Native American reservations in Arizona.[145] The overwhelming majority were headed by lone mothers. Only a third of the adult TANF recipients had gone as far as graduating from high school, and nearly half had never worked at a regular job with pay. Only 13 percent reported having recent employment income (averaging $432 per month and wages at $6.70 per hour). Twenty percent were taking classes or were involved in on-the-job training.

Twenty-six percent of the adult TANF recipients said their children had gone to school or to bed hungry in the previous three months, and 49 percent said there was a point in those three months during which they had insufficient money to buy food. Twenty-two percent said that their household's electricity was turned off for failure to pay their bills. The vast majority of the welfare-recipient mothers had children under thirteen years of age. Yet only two of the 445 families in this study had ever used a formal child-care program; they either cared for their children themselves or depended upon other relatives and friends. Only 29 percent of the recipients lived in households owning an automobile. Over half who had wanted to go to the doctor in the previous three months had been unable to do so because of lack of transportation.

Three obstacles to Native American lone mothers' achieving self-sufficiency through work repeatedly arise: (1) insufficient child-care resources; (2) lack of transportation; and (3) lack of jobs.[146] Child care is a problem not only because child-care centers on or near reservations are in short supply, but also because many Native American mothers are distrustful of the quality and cultural appropriateness of the care provided by formal programs. Public transportation is generally unavailable on reservations, and rates of automobile ownership are low. Coupled with the long distances that often must be traveled, a lack of access to transportation leaves many lone-mother-headed families isolated and unable to get to doctors' offices, grocery stores, and places of employment. Indeed, on many reservations this isolation is compounded by the absence of modern communications facilities, such as basic telephone and other telecommunications services.

Perhaps the greatest obstacle, however, to mothers moving from welfare to work is the lack of jobs to move to.[147] Many tribal TANF plans stress job training and vocational education and permit participation in diploma and degree programs to count as work. The latter type of investment in the human capital of Native American lone mothers is necessary and highly important and generally is unavailable to lone mothers enrolled in non-tribal, state-run TANF programs. However, in the case of Native American reservations this Education First approach also reflects the fact that the typical Work First approach cannot succeed when there are no jobs to be had. As a study by the U.S. General Accounting Office concludes, "Job scarcity in Indian Country is an overwhelming barrier to the success of employment and job training programs."[148]

Critics of the mismatch between the PRWORA and reservation conditions have rejected the notion that job creation in and of itself can provide a solution to the plight of Native American TANF recipients. In many instances, federally-financed programs of various types have created more jobs on reservations, but this has mostly taken the form of government-subsidized public employment, which on many reservations is almost the only employment available. Government-subsidized employment falls far short of meeting the huge unemployment problems found on many reservations and is vulnerable to politically-driven decisions and budgetary cutbacks occurring in distant government agencies. Critics have called for greater investment in tribal infrastructure and in tribal-controlled endeavors that promise to produce sustained economic growth. Economic growth must rest upon tribal-owned and other business enterprises located on and near reservations—not on public employment. Such enterprises are seen as critical to the creation of the large amount of unsubsidized employment that will be needed if the current state of deep impoverishment on many reservations is ever to be overcome. One of the more probing analyses of the impact of welfare reform on reservations asserts, "[W]ithout an economic growth strategy—that is, without jobs—welfare reform in Indian Country will fail. Either it will drive significant numbers of tribal citizens further into poverty as they lose support and find no alternatives, or it will force large numbers of them to leave their homelands in search of employment, undermining tribal communities and embittering Indian peoples. Neither outcome is acceptable to Indian nations; neither outcome should be acceptable to the United States."[149]

While many Native Americans have left their tribal homelands in search of economic opportunities in U.S. cities, particularly since World War II, migration is not the preferred solution to economic problems for those living on reservations. Migration often means leaving supportive kinship and friendship networks behind, as well as geographical locales to which Native Americans have deep historical and cultural attachments. Moreover, not all who leave their homelands find the economic security for which they sacrificed reservation life, although the level of poverty of reservation leavers tends to be less severe than of those who remain. Researchers have found that many Native Americans migrating from their reservations harbor hopes of returning and would do so readily if the harsh economic conditions and lack of educational and employment opportunities that led to their leaving were to change.[150]

One Size Does Not Fit All

Welfare reform clearly was undertaken by U.S. political elites with a mythical generic recipient in mind. This mythical recipient appears to have been conjured up to conform to a broadly conservative ideology heavily informed by class biases, racist stereotypes, and (hetero)sexist views. The PRWORA is a one-size-fits-all approach to social policy that ignores the extremely diverse characteristics and experiences of this nation's impoverished lone-mother-headed families. Instead of providing these families with an adequate standard of living and helping mothers to fulfill the role of parent and caregiver within an environment of economic security, welfare reform does neither of these things. As social policy, the provisions of the PRWORA are inappropriate to the diverse needs of the women and children it purports to be serving.[151]

The many shortcomings of the PRWORA should not be at all surprising, given that few of the conservative policy analysts and mostly white, male, affluent political elites who formulated its provisions can truthfully claim to have ever had much contact with families living in poverty. Many have been outspokenly committed to stereotypes about the poor that have little or no grounding in reality, and few have allowed themselves to be swayed by readily available facts running counter to their views. Holding up a mythical generic recipient made it possible for political elites to maintain strikingly contemptuous depictions of welfare and those who must rely upon it. "Welfare mothers" were almost unique in that they—unlike just about every other sector of the U.S. population—could be categorically demeaned without violating most people's norms of political correctness. Many members of Congress communicated their scorn for these allegedly lazy and immoral women both by their public discourse around the PRWORA and by passing this legislation with practically no prior hearings to which any impoverished mothers were invited to testify.[152]

As chapter 3 showed, welfare reform has had little overall effect on reducing the amount of poverty that exists in the United States. Supporters of the PRWORA, however, do not take that fact as a criticism. Instead, they correctly point out that this legislation was never intended to be an antipoverty program. Rather, the PRWORA was simply intended to move lone mothers from welfare to work and to reduce the size of the welfare rolls, and its supporters claim success on both counts. But by not directly addressing and substantially reducing the high poverty rates for lone-mother-headed families prior to, during, and after they leave the TANF rolls, the United States has put itself at odds with economic human rights. Most other affluent nations do far more than the United States to address the economic human rights of lone-mother-headed families, as the next chapter will clearly show.

5

Combating Family Poverty: How Other Affluent Nations Are More Successful and Why This Is So

As we have seen, U.S. welfare policy has never fully provided for the subsistence needs of impoverished lone-mother-headed families, and it still does not do so today. Indeed, U.S. welfare policy has functioned in ways that have left many eligible families without any public assistance at all. The Personal Responsibility and Work Opportunity Reconciliation Act of 1996 effectively abolished the weak income safety net on which at least some of the nation's neediest families had been able to rely. In adopting this legislation, U.S. political elites proceeded as if economic human rights simply did not exist. Indeed, in the years of debate over welfare reform preceding passage of the act, the human rights of the poor were never the subject of White House statements or Congressional debate. As chapter 1 demonstrated, U.S. political elites do not accept the notion that poverty is a violation of economic human rights or that those whose human rights are being violated include impoverished families in the United States.

Chapter 1 pointed out that 151 nations have ratified the International Covenant on Economic, Social, and Cultural Rights, but that the United States has chosen not to do so. This important UN treaty establishes the right of all people to "an adequate standard of living... including adequate food, clothing and housing, and to the continuous improvement of living conditions." It recognizes "the fundamental human right of everyone to be free from hunger" as well as "the right of everyone to the enjoyment of the highest attainable standard of physical and mental health."[1] Given the U.S. government's treatment of impoverished lone-mother-headed families, discussed in chapter 3 and chapter 4, the United States would have to make major changes in welfare policy in order to conform to the economic human rights provisions of the International Covenant.

As the present chapter will outline, the U.S. government defines *poverty* very narrowly and in absolute dollar terms. Many antipoverty advocates believe the definition obscures and understates the magnitude of economic deprivation and insecurity that actually exists. When poverty is measured using standards commonly employed in making cross-national comparisons, the U.S. poverty rate is strikingly higher than many other affluent nations. It is, of course, true that nations differ in the policies they pursue to mitigate poverty. None of the 151 nations that have ratified the International Covenant can legitimately claim to have fully met their obligations to respect the economic human rights of all of their people. Yet a number of the world's more affluent nations have worked much harder and have come closer to meeting this challenge than has the United States. Important disparities are present between the United States and other affluent nations when it comes to policies that effectively address the needs of impoverished families.

This chapter addresses ways in which the United States is a comparative outlier among affluent nations in terms of policies expressing respect for economic human rights. The chapter also offers an examination of some of the policies other nations have in place that contribute to their relatively greater success in reducing poverty among lone-mother-headed families and that help to reduce the social exclusion from the larger community and its institutions often experienced by the impoverished. These include income transfer policies, such as child allowances, child-support assurance, unemployment insurance, and social assistance. However, equally important to poverty reduction among such families are policies that assist working mothers, such as subsidized child care, health care, maternity and parental leave, and the regulation of working time and pay.

Also discussed in this chapter is the spirited debate occurring in Europe over the desirability of implementing in European nations a universal basic income, which, sufficient for subsistence, would be paid in an equal amount to all citizens regardless of age or economic status. Political elites in the United States have certainly never considered the desirability of providing everyone with a universal basic income—an idea even many people in Europe reject as utopian and problematic for a variety of reasons. But in the recent past, U.S. political elites have considered proposals to provide a means-tested guaranteed minimum income to impoverished families. Ultimately, however, they not only rejected these proposals, but also ended up going on to eliminate impoverished families' entitlement to even the most meager welfare assistance. The U.S. public has gone along with these policy decisions and the chapter will close by delving into why people in the United States appear willing to tolerate the existence of poverty much more so than do people in other affluent nations.

The next section begins by examining some issues pertaining to the ways in which the United States defines and measures *poverty.*

The Evolution of Antipoverty Policy in the United States

Previous chapters have made reference to the federal poverty line and the percentage of the U.S. population said to live in circumstances of poverty because of incomes that fall below the line. Prior to the early 1960s, the U.S. government did not have an official definition of poverty and did not systematically collect data on the extent to which poverty existed in the United States.[2] Even the extremely visible and seemingly intractable economic deprivation suffered by millions during the 1930s Great Depression did little to change that situation. World War II pulled the United States out of the Depression and the nation entered a period of economic stability and growth in the postwar years. With joblessness reduced and the most visible manifestations of widespread poverty in a state of decline, U.S. political elites saw little need to be overly concerned with the remaining chronic conditions of poverty.

Once the Cold War gathered momentum in the 1950s, however, U.S. political elites' relative indifference to domestic poverty began to erode. Among other things, the Soviet Union and its allies sharply criticized the positive economic self-image the United States was projecting around the world as capitalist propaganda. Socialist nations sought to draw international attention to the gross economic inequalities existing in the United States and the poverty conditions U.S. political elites had largely chosen to ignore. In truth, according to its socialist critics, the United States was a textbook example of how capitalism's purported success inevitably meant the enrichment of the capitalist class through the systematic impoverishment of the working class. In Cold War politics, U.S. political elites could only view the continued existence of widespread poverty in the United States as a liability when it came to demonstrating the inherent merits of capitalism over socialism.

Political elites' concern with the image of the United States abroad was also heightened by postwar international condemnation of the nation's climate of racial oppression and the extremely severe poverty conditions among people of color to which this climate obviously contributed. As was discussed in chapter 1, the United States helped to create and then voted for the UN adoption of the Universal Declaration of Human Rights in 1948. Yet the U.S. government's failure to effectively dismantle institutionalized racial apartheid raised questions in many other nations as to the seriousness with which the United States actually took human rights. The struggles of the U.S. civil rights movement were closely followed and received support from people around the world. The U.S. government's glacial movements toward ending legalized racial segregation and its tolerance of Southern states' denial of African-American voting rights was pointedly attacked by the nation's Cold War adversaries as evidence of U.S. hypocrisy when it came to respect for human rights. White racial hegemony, and the ways in which it helped to shape the distribution of poverty in the United States along skin color lines, had become an international embarrassment for U.S. political elites.[3]

Beyond international considerations, U.S. political elites' propensity to cast a blind eye toward domestic poverty was also undermined by the public dismay expressed in response to media depictions of poverty conditions and the misery of those experiencing them. Michael Harrington's 1962 book, *The Other America*, which focused upon the vast numbers of "invisible poor" residing in both rural regions and central city areas, generated an extraordinary amount of public discussion.[4] It is commonly believed that Harrington's book had an important impact on the thinking of President John F. Kennedy (1960–1963), who, having already been taken aback by the poverty he observed when campaigning in Appalachia, began pressing his administration to think of ways to address such conditions.

Kennedy died before he was able to see a national antipoverty agenda initiated. However, almost immediately after Kennedy's death, his successor, President Lyndon B. Johnson (1963–1969) followed through on that agenda by declaring a War on Poverty in 1964. In order to reliably target and effectively administer the federal programs being launched under the umbrella of this "war," U.S. political elites and their policy analysts needed accurate and detailed statistical data on the extent of poverty in the United States and on its geographic and demographic distribution. Somewhat fortuitously, in 1963–1964 U.S. Social Security Administration economist Mollie Orshansky was busy developing a statistical measure of domestic poverty. Even though political elites' support for the War on Poverty had largely dribbled to a halt by the mid-1970s, Orshansky's income-based poverty line—with minor modifications over time—is still being used by the U.S. government.[5]

The U.S. Federal Poverty Line and Its Limitations

Orshansky based her measure of poverty on the results of a 1955 U.S. Department of Agriculture survey, which found that the typical U.S. family of three spent one-third of its after-tax income on food. Orshansky defined a family of three as living below the federal poverty line (i.e., living in poverty) if its after-tax income was less than three times what it cost for such a family to eat at a minimally adequate nutritional level. This minimum level corresponded with what U.S. Agriculture Department dieticians called the "economy food plan," the lowest-costing among four alternative family food plans said to provide a nutritional diet. In actuality, government dieticians considered the economy food plan appropriate only for a family's emergency or temporary use. Under Orshansky's poverty line formula, the absolute dollar income amount marking the federal poverty line varied depending upon such factors as family size and the number of children in the family under age 18. But it is clear that as defined, the federal poverty line was set at an income level that would hardly provide an adequate standard of living.

The U.S. Bureau of the Census currently uses a somewhat modified version of Orshansky's formula in its annual national survey aimed at gathering data on poverty. The census bureau bases its family poverty statistics, however, on the amount of income a family receives before, rather than after, taxes. Its definition of income includes money from all sources, such as employment, Temporary Assistance for Needy Families, and Social Security Income. However, it excludes noncash government benefits some low-income families receive (e.g., public housing, food stamps, Medicaid). Using the consumer price index, the census bureau adjusts poverty-line thresholds annually to reflect inflation. Thus, in 1996, the year the Personal Responsibility and Work Opportunity Reconciliation Act was passed, a family consisting of a lone mother and two children was labeled as poor if its income was under the federal poverty line of $12,641. In 2004, such a family was considered poor if its income was under $15,219.[6]

Antipoverty advocates have been highly critical of the way poverty is defined and measured. Many question the wisdom of continuing to base the federal poverty line on the assumption that food constitutes a third of a typical family's living costs. That might have been true in 1955, but now, low-income families are faced with high prices for basic necessities other than food—and an increasing proportion of family budgets must go toward nonfood expenditures. Food costs have not increased at anywhere near the same rate as housing or health-care costs in recent years. In addition, child care, clothing, and transportation expenses can constitute significant expenses for low-income parents who work outside the home. According to the Food Marketing Institute, food costs were just over 10 percent of family income in 2003.[7] Other estimates suggest that food now represents one-fifth or one-sixth of a typical family's expenditures. Indeed, many of the millions of low-income families experiencing food insecurity do so precisely because so much of their income must go to rent, utilities, or medical bills.

Other criticisms of the federal poverty line focus on the extremely low-dollar threshold or income cutoff at which it is set, inevitably masking the degree to which economic insecurity exists above that line. This threshold is still based upon Mollie Orshansky's original food-expenditure-based poverty-line formula. Clearly, the incomes of families living at or below the poverty line do not allow for even a minimally adequate standard of living. But families with incomes just above the poverty line also suffer economic problems. Labeled by the government as the "near poor," those with incomes between 100 and 200 percent of the federal poverty line often experience economic stress and insecurity, if not absolute deprivation.[8]

Many middle-class families enjoy consumption beyond their basic needs as a matter of course. In contrast, near-poor families not only often struggle to meet their basic needs, but also are at constant risk of falling below the poverty line. Many families who manage to struggle out of poverty get no further than membership in the near poor. Some then experience downward mobility back into poverty when economic setbacks strike. A significant blow to family income, such as the loss of a wage earner, is often all that is required for a near-poor family to plummet back into poverty.[9] Near-poor lone-mother-headed families are especially vulnerable to such downward mobility and generally do not have to fall very far to find themselves under the poverty line.

Critics also point out that the federal poverty line, while adjusted in accordance with inflation, family size, and number of children under 18, applies uniformly across the entire United States. The poverty line ignores important sources of variability in low-income families' expenditures that are linked to where they reside. It is well known that the costs of housing, food, clothing, transportation, health care, and other necessities vary by geographic area. Families with identical incomes may experience quite different degrees of deprivation, depending upon how much their necessities cost. A lone-mother-headed family of three with an income below the 2004 federal poverty line of $15,219 will find decent housing much more affordable in a small town in rural Alabama than a family with the same poverty-line income searching for housing in metropolitan Boston or the San Francisco Bay Area.

A family's place of residence also matters in terms of taxation and its effects on disposable income. Although the federal poverty line is based upon before-tax income and is uniform across states, state and local systems of taxation differ in how they affect after-tax incomes of low-income families. For example, families with before-tax incomes that place them below the poverty line are affected differently depending upon the extent to which the state in which they reside levies personal income taxes versus sales taxes to generate revenue. Low-income families typically spend all of their disposable incomes, having little or no surplus to save after paying for basic necessities. In states with sales taxes, a higher percentage of their incomes is taxed than that of affluent families, who have surplus funds to save or profitably invest. Likewise, after-tax incomes of low-income families with working parents are often supplemented by a state-level earned income tax credit (EITC). However, not all individual states provide such credits and low-income families without working parents do not qualify for either individual state programs or the federal EITC.

In the eyes of many antipoverty advocates, the federal poverty line significantly understates and obscures the numbers of people in the United States who have serious difficulty obtaining or maintaining an adequate standard of living. Efforts to highlight the limitations of the federal poverty line as a measure of economic need have resulted in the creation of other measures, some of which antipoverty advocates in the United States are finding useful. In particular, the *self-sufficiency standard*, developed by Wider Opportunities for Women and University of Washington professor Diana Pearce, has drawn a great deal of attention.[10] The standard is particularly useful in assessing the level of income a lone mother leaving the welfare rolls must have to provide her family with an adequate standard of living.

The Self-Sufficiency Standard

Supporters of the self-sufficiency standard, developed to counter some of the limitations of the federal poverty line mentioned in the previous section, believe it provides a far more realistic picture of what it takes for a family to maintain an adequate standard of living. It is a calculation of just how much income working adults must receive to meet the basic needs of their households without having to rely on outside subsidies or assistance of any kind. According to the standard, a self-sufficient household is one whose standard of living is adequate in the sense that its basic subsistence needs are met. It is able to meet its members' basic needs without government assistance (e.g., housing subsidies, Medicaid, food stamps, subsidized child care) and, likewise, does not need to rely upon informal or private sources of financial aid or goods and services provided by relatives, friends, charities, or faith-based groups.

The absolute dollar amount of the self-sufficiency standard can vary in accordance with costs of living in a particular geographic region and locale, family size and composition, and the ages of children. The standard assumes that adults in the household, whether married or single, are employed and working full time, and their incomes are assumed to be sufficient to pay marketplace prices for the goods and services required to meet their family's basic needs. The standard is calculated to take into account the fact that costs of housing, food, health care, and other major budget items not only differ from place to place, but often increase at different rates. It also allows for the inclusion of special expenses—like workplace clothing, transportation to and from work, and child care—confronted by working parents. Costs of child care can have a marked impact on the calculation of the standard for households with young children, particularly of preschool age. Finally, the standard is calculated to include the net economic effect of taxes (income, sales, payroll) and available tax credits on households.

To illustrate, consider the self-sufficiency standard developed in 2004 for the state of Pennsylvania. A lone-mother-headed family containing a preschooler and a school-age child, living in the most expensive area of Pennsylvania, Bucks County, would have needed an income of $46,499 in 2004 in order to meet its basic needs without any government or private or informal assistance. Even in the least expensive area of the state—Forest County—the family would need an income of $23,552.[11] When these figures are compared to the federal poverty line in 2004, set at $15,219 for a family of one adult and two children under 18, the poverty line came to only 32 percent of the self-sufficiency standard for Bucks County and 65 percent of the standard for Forest County.

Even residing in the least expensive county in Pennsylvania, a lone mother with two small children who was leaving welfare would have to generate a household income well above that of workers being paid at minimum wage. Minimum wage income for such a family in Pennsylvania was $13,770 in 2004 (taking taxes and tax credits for which the lone mother was eligible into account). As chapter 3 and chapter 4 revealed, welfare leavers have great difficulty finding and holding down employment that provides earnings anywhere near the self-sufficiency standard.

Revising the U.S. Government's Definition of Poverty

How the federal government defines and measures poverty is unlikely to change anytime soon, even though bodies, such as the National Research Council, have advocated for fundamental revisions.[12] Any changes in this regard would have to be approved by the White House Office of Management and Budget. Presidential administrations are unlikely to approve revisions to how poverty is defined and measured if this means an increase in the apparent statistical size of the U.S. poverty population.

The level at which the federal poverty line is drawn is really a political decision rather than a scientific one. Raising the poverty line above its currently low dollar amount could lead to a significant increase in the apparent numbers of impoverished families in the United States, providing political ammunition to the many groups (see chapter 6) highly critical of the growing economic inequalities and the chronic poverty conditions to which U.S. political elites seem largely indifferent. One way political elites have been able to avoid acknowledging poverty as a serious social problem in the United States is by framing its definition in ways that downplay the numbers of people affected by it.

In recent years, some political elites have proposed that the value of noncash government benefits, such as Medicaid, be included in the calculation of low-income families' incomes for the purposes of poverty measurement. Including noncash benefits in the calculation of incomes without revising the current definition and way of measuring poverty would reduce the apparent size of the poverty population and would make poverty seem even less in need of attention by political elites than it currently is. In the case of Medicaid, if an eligible lone mother or child was treated for illness or injury, the family's income could be viewed as having increased. Under this odd logic, the more serious a family's medical needs, the higher its income could appear.

Resistance to changing the definition and measurement of poverty is also a product of bureaucratic inertia. Many federal and state agencies rely on existing poverty statistics in formulating their budgets and programs. The federal poverty line, or some multiplier of it, is often used in determining families' eligibility for receipt of government assistance. From a bureaucratic viewpoint, changes in the calculation of poverty statistics and thresholds are not necessarily welcome, given that such changes would have consequences for a wide range of government operations and at multiple governmental levels.

Poverty in Affluent Nations: Where the United States Stands

The federal poverty line defines poverty in *absolute* terms. It is drawn at a certain dollar amount and is then used to distinguish between the numbers of "poor" and "not poor." As has been discussed, the self-sufficiency standard avoids many of the limitations of the federal poverty line and is considered far more realistic in addressing the size of incomes today's households must receive to meet their basic needs without assistance. Yet by calculating a dollar amount that distinguishes the "self-sufficient" from the "not self-sufficient," the standard is similarly an absolute measure.

Neither of these two approaches addresses *relative* poverty. The latter places more emphasis on a nation's pattern of income inequality than on the absolute minimum amount of income people in a particular nation must have to meet their basic needs.[13] A measure of relative poverty might ask, for example, what percentage of the population (or what percentage of families, or lone-mother-headed families, or children) has incomes significantly below the national median. Those with incomes significantly below this median would be defined as poor relative to others. The dollar amount marking the relative poverty line is not fixed, as in the case of absolute measures of poverty, but rises with an increase in a nation's overall standard of living.

The most comprehensive database for examining both absolute and relative poverty cross-nationally is the Luxembourg Income Study (LIS).[14] Begun in 1983, LIS is a cooperative international research project that now has income data archived from twenty-nine nations, most of which are European. However, the project also has several non-European participants: the United States, Canada, Mexico, and Taiwan. The LIS database, which includes decades of information in the case of some nations, is derived from household income surveys. LIS has developed methods to harmonize and standardize these data to make cross-national comparisons possible. LIS is highly regarded by scholars around the world as a useful body of data for studying poverty in a cross-national context.

How the U.S. Compares on Measures of Absolute and Relative Poverty

The United States is one of the most affluent nations in the world. Its population has the highest average income among all industrialized nations in the LIS database, with the exception of Luxembourg. Yet scholars working with LIS data also report that "the United States has one of the highest poverty rates of all the countries participating in LIS, whether poverty is measured using comparable absolute or relative standards for determining who is poor."[15]

One study compared absolute poverty rates cross-nationally using a standardized version of the U.S. poverty line and 1990s data on eleven affluent LIS nations (all Western European except the United States, Canada, and Australia). The United States did not fare well in comparison to most of these other nations. While it ranked second (after Luxembourg) among the eleven nations in terms of average per capita income, the United States came in third (after Australia and the United Kingdom) in the percentage of its population with incomes below the poverty line.[16] The phrase "poverty amidst plenty" is clearly accurate when depicting absolute poverty in the United States.[17]

Nations differ from one another in their population's overall affluence, often measured by their average per capita income. This can be deceiving, however, because it obscures the degree to which incomes are unequally distributed within the population. One must ask how a nation's overall affluence is internally shared. To what degree are some people income deprived even as others are much more affluent? Nations with high average per capita incomes do not necessarily distribute income more equally than less affluent nations. The United States is a case in point in this regard.

The concept of relative poverty speaks to the extent to which income is distributed unequally in a given nation and can be defined in different ways. Frequently, cross-national studies of relative poverty adopt a poverty threshold of 50 percent of national median income. People with incomes below this threshold are considered poor. At 50 percent of the national income median, the relative poverty threshold is higher than the U.S. federal poverty line. In the 1990s, the federal poverty line was only about 40 percent of the U.S. national median income, a percentage that has since fallen. Some European scholars and policy analysts believe that even putting the poverty threshold at 50 percent of the national median is unnecessarily restrictive and have argued that it should be set at 60 percent.[18] As is the case with absolute poverty measures, deciding where the relative poverty line should be drawn can be politically important. A 60-percent instead of a 50-percent threshold would mean that far more members of a population are designated relatively poor, which could have significant implications for government policies and programs.

How does the United States look in comparison to other affluent nations when it comes to relative poverty? One study of nineteen LIS nations, using data from the early to mid-1990s, addressed this question with the most widely used cross-national measure of relative poverty: the percent of a nation's population with incomes below 50 percent of the national median. Researchers also analyzed the LIS data using an alternative and lower poverty threshold of 40 percent of the national median, a measure closer to the mid-1990s U.S. poverty line. Using this more conservative measure, the average overall poverty rate for the nineteen nations was slightly less than 5 percent. Eleven of the nations had relative poverty rates below that average. In contrast, the United States had the highest relative poverty rate, almost 11 percent. When 50 percent of the national median was used to analyze relative poverty rates, the United States still ranked number one by having the highest fraction of its population living below the relative poverty threshold.[19] The researchers concluded that "more poor people in the United States suffer from extreme relative poverty than is the case for other high-income countries."[20]

Poverty among Lone-Mother-Headed Families

Having high absolute and relative poverty rates in comparison to other affluent nations alone is alarming, but how does the United States compare with other nations when it comes to poverty among lone-mother-headed families? Viewed cross-nationally, is there an inverse correlation between lone mothers' labor-force participation and their impoverished situations? More specifically, do nations with high labor-force participation of lone mothers have lower rates of poverty among lone-mother-headed families? This last question is of particular relevance when it comes to the United States, since advocates of welfare reform praise the contribution it has made to increasing employment among so-called welfare-dependent lone mothers.

Before addressing these questions, two trends should be considered briefly. First, in recent decades a marked increase has occurred in the number and percentage of families headed by lone mothers, not only in the United States but in other affluent nations as well. A study encompassing the United States, Canada, Japan, and nine Western European nations found that all of these nations experienced increases in the proportion of households headed by lone mothers between 1980 and 2001.[21] Families with children can be lone-mother-headed for a variety of reasons: divorce, childbirth outside of marriage or cohabitation, or (less commonly) widowhood. The United States experienced a high rate of births to unwed females between 1980 and 2001 and, compared to other nations, had especially high rates of birth among unwed teenagers. Unmarried mothers in the United States were far less likely to cohabit with their children's male biological parent than in most European nations. Finally, the United States had high divorce rates involving couples with children. In comparison to the other eleven nations studied, between 1980 and 2001 the United States had the highest proportion of lone-mother-headed households with children under the age of 18 as a percentage of all households with children.[22]

A second major trend in recent decades has been the increase in labor-force participation among women in affluent nations. Rising costs of living, combined with declining or stagnating real wages and bouts of unemployment, have made it impossible for many men to adequately support their families on their own; employment by the spouse outside the home has increasingly become a matter of economic necessity. Shifts in attitudes among women and men regarding work outside the home have made employed mothers, including mothers of small children, increasingly common.[23] In the case of lone mothers, who often bear principal responsibility for their families' support, employment can be imperative. In a study of work activity in fifteen European Union nations, 71 percent of lone mothers aged 25 to 49 were working at least one hour per week outside the home in 2001. Although rates of lone mothers' labor-force participation and the number of working hours they averaged per week varied among nations, only 15 percent of lone mothers in the European Union stated that their main activity was full-time housework or looking after children or other persons, compared to 21 percent of all women in the same 25 to 49 age group who engaged in such full-time activity in the home.[24]

In a study of the United States and nine Western European nations, the United States had higher rates of employment among lone mothers than almost all of its affluent European counterparts.[25] Lone mothers in the United States have high rates of employment, even though they receive little government help in balancing family responsibilities with employment. Other nations, many of them in Europe, are much more supportive in this regard.[26] High rates of employment alone do not produce low poverty rates among lone-mother-headed families, however. In the United States, high rates of labor-force participation among lone mothers are offset by their low wages: "[A]ccording to the Luxembourg Income Study (LIS), in the mid-1990s more than 45 percent of U.S. single mothers were poor; by comparison, single mothers' poverty rates were 13 percent in France and around 5 percent in Sweden and Finland... [C]ompared with their Western counterparts, U.S. women and single mothers are among the most likely to earn poverty-level wages. When working full-time (at least 35 hours a week)... more than 40 percent of U.S. single mothers earn wages too low to free their families from poverty. In other western nations... working full time pulls the vast majority of women (including single mothers) and their families above the poverty line."[27]

Data from LIS nations indicate that children in lone-mother-headed families generally tend to be overrepresented in lower-income groups. But in LIS nations besides the United States (again, whose employment rates for lone mothers are high) being labeled *low income* is less likely to mean living in poverty—especially severe poverty. Researchers have analyzed the percentage of children in fifteen LIS nations whose lone-mother-headed families fell into the low-income category, defined as having incomes in the lowest third of the national income distribution. Within this broad low-income category, the United States not only had the highest overall child poverty rate among the LIS nations studied, it also had the highest percentage of extremely or severely poor children.[28] The high level of labor-force participation of lone mothers in the United States has not brought its child poverty rates down to the levels of most other affluent nations.

A Note on *Relative* versus *Absolute Poverty*

Relative poverty has been referred to thus far as an expression of the degree of economic inequality within a nation. It is imperative to stress that relative poverty is not simply a subjective condition or state of mind. Those who are dismissive of poverty in the United States sometimes argue that the U.S. poor have little to complain about. They should, it is said, consider their situation relative to the "real" poverty experienced by people in Africa, Asia, or Latin America. The concept of poverty, however, is based upon the premise that a state of economic deprivation exists—deprivation that can prove harmful. Such is the case whether poverty is defined in absolute or relative terms.

Absolute poverty refers to the absence of the income people must have to meet their basic subsistence needs. But relative poverty likewise has serious consequences for those experiencing it. As Amartya Sen stated, "[R]elative deprivation in terms of *incomes* can yield *absolute* deprivation in terms of *capabilities.* Being relatively poor in a rich country can be a great capability handicap, even when one's income is high in terms of world standards. In a generally opulent country, more income is needed to buy enough commodities to achieve the same social functioning"[29] (italics in original). Contemporary analysts have increasingly emphasized ways the deprivation associated with poverty is social as well as economic. This section ends with a brief quote characterizing some of the social deprivation that can accompany poverty: "[P]eople cannot carry out the roles, participate in the activities, or maintain the social relations that are definitive of mainstream members of society if their resources (over some period of time) fall short of a 'certain minimum.'… [Relative] poverty is the condition of being excluded from the life made possible by the customary level of consumption."[30]

This topic will be revisited in a later discussion of European concerns as to how poverty can contribute to the social exclusion of low-income people from the larger community and its institutions.

How Other Affluent Nations Fight Poverty

A 2005 article titled "It's Better to Be Poor in Norway than in the U.S." underscored that the material living standard of many people in the United States is among the highest of all nations. Using Norway as a point of reference, the article noted that of the 62 percent of residents in each country with the highest incomes, those in the United States are better off. Indeed, those in the top and middle income levels in the United States tend to have more purchasing power than their counterparts in other affluent nations. Nevertheless, this article also disclosed a less familiar fact: An examination of poverty conditions in thirty prosperous nations found that, in relative poverty terms, people who are poor in the United States "are poorer than almost anywhere else in the developed world."[31]

To illustrate, the poorest 18 percent of Canadians fare better economically in purchasing power than the poorest 18 percent of U.S. residents. Similar statements can be made about the poorest 12 percent of Swedes, Finns, and the Dutch; the poorest 15 percent of Germans; and the poorest 20 percent of Belgians. Norway's poorest 38 percent have more purchasing power than the poorest 38 percent in the United States.[32] For children in lone-mother-headed families, the likelihood of being poor, as well as the meaning of *poor* itself, depends on the nation in which one resides.[33]

It is evident that other nations are much more attuned and responsive to their obligation to respect economic human rights than the United States. Unlike the United States, virtually every other affluent nation has ratified the International Covenant on Economic, Social, and Cultural Rights as well as treaties with important economic human rights provisions such as the Convention on the Rights of the Child and the Convention on the Elimination of All Forms of Discrimination Against Women. Numerous member-nations of the Council of Europe, a multinational political organization with human rights goals, have signed the European Social Charter.[34] This treaty protects such economic human rights as "the right to work, the right to fair remuneration, the right to protection of health, the right to social security, the right to social and medical assistance, and the right to benefit from social welfare services."[35] Their compliance with the social charter is monitored by an elected European Committee on Social Rights, and nations signing this treaty must provide ways for various rights violations to be remedied. In comparison to the United States, other affluent nations have made important strides toward adopting an economic human rights approach in thinking about helping families meet their basic subsistence needs and escape absolute poverty, thinking that is reflected in many of their policies.

Many of the world's most affluent nations have two important types of policies in place to help families avoid being mired in severe poverty. First, many nations have developed systematic and reliable income transfer policies that assist families whether they are mother-headed or not. Income transfers can take the form of either direct cash assistance or tax benefits. However, as significant as income transfer policies are to the mitigation of poverty in most affluent nations, many nations also pursue another type of policy strategy relevant to poverty reduction by providing free or subsidized services, such as child and health care, that enhance the ability of families to function.[36] Such services, along with other family-friendly government actions (e.g., laws governing pay, working hours, and leave policies) provide crucial support for the many lone mothers who must mesh parenting with full- or part-time participation in the labor force.[37]

When combined with policies making it easier for parents in the labor force to balance work with family responsibilities, income transfers appear to offer the greatest promise of poverty reduction for lone-mother-headed families. "The countries most successful in reducing poverty among single mothers encourage them to pool income from a variety of sources. Examples of various 'policy packages' that accomplish this include employment supports, such as child care, that provide single mothers with access to paid work; welfare benefits, such as child allowances, that all parents receive; and cash and near-cash subsidies."[38] The policy packages of nations, however, are frequently complex and their details vary. This section briefly describes some of the basic policy elements appearing with some frequency.[39]

Some Income Transfer Policies that Help to Mitigate Poverty

Income transfers in the form of cash and tax benefits boost the economic levels of low-income families by providing them with more economic stability and purchasing power than they would otherwise have. Low-income families are able to consume more of the goods and services available to those higher in the economic mainstream. In effect, by reducing economic inequality within a nation, income transfers can help to make its poor objectively better off as well as relatively less deprived in comparison to others. In many instances, a nation's package of income transfers is highly instrumental in moving families out of poverty.

The United States and other affluent nations differ in the degree to which their governments act to assist low-income families through an income transfer approach. In many European nations, for example, the income transfers that help to mitigate poverty are, at the very least, considered a right of citizenship if not an absolute economic human right. The U.S. government, on the other hand, takes the position that poverty can and should be addressed with minimal government intervention. Impoverished people in the United States are not considered entitled to government help. Poverty, it is said, can best be mitigated by encouraging individuals to take advantage of opportunities in the economic marketplace. The U.S. government limits income transfers and instead tries to make the road out of poverty a matter of individuals' personal responsibility. The solution to poverty is allowed to rest with the relationship that individuals establish with the free market.[40] Clearly, the reliance of the United States on the market as a solution to lone-mother-headed families' poverty is not working.

Cross-national researchers Lee Rainwater and Timothy M. Smeeding assessed the contributions government income transfers make to poverty mitigation using LIS data from fifteen nations, including the United States. They found that differences in nations' income transfer packages produce marked differences in poverty rates for lone-mother-headed families. In commenting on how children in such families are affected, Rainwater and Smeeding stated, "In most of these countries a solid majority of children in single-mother families would be poor if their families received only income from the market… [M]ost single-mother families cannot depend on market income alone to rescue them from poverty or near-poverty. Social transfers are an integral part of the income package for single mothers."[41]

In Sweden, for example, over 90 percent of the children in lone-mother-headed families who would otherwise be considered poor—based upon their families' pretransfer income—are moved out of poverty by income transfers. In Nordic nations as a whole, over 75 percent of children are moved out. The rates for other LIS nations vary, but ten out of the fifteen nations studied by Rainwater and Smeeding had child poverty reduction rates over 50 percent. The United States was at the opposite end from Sweden among the fifteen nations. Fewer than 25 percent of U.S. children in lone-mother-headed families are moved out of poverty by income transfers.[42]

On average, low-income mothers in the United States work more hours than their counterparts in other affluent nations, yet they receive the least government income support.[43] Among the more important income transfer programs found in other nations contributing to the reduction of absolute and relative poverty are child allowances, child support assurance, unemployment insurance, and social assistance.[44]

Child Allowances   Virtually every affluent nation (the United States being the exception) offers child allowances (sometimes called child benefits or family allowances) to families to assist parents in providing for their children. Child allowances provide cash benefits based on the presence and number of children in the family. Benefits vary depending upon factors such as the children's ages or the parents' employment status. In most instances child allowances are universal (not means tested) and are not subject to taxation. A sum is provided for each child, either through direct government payments or, in a few nations, as a part of a working parent's earnings. Child allowances are not a major income source for most lone-mother-headed families. They can, however, be an important supplement to other income transfers lone-mother-headed families may receive, such as child support, as well as to earnings from employment.

Child Support Assurance   Impoverished lone mothers in the United States are often in great need of child support from their children's biological fathers.[45] Unfortunately, biological fathers are sometimes unknown, impossible to locate, or resistant to making payments. Even when mothers are successful in securing payments, the amounts they receive are often low, and their receipt is frequently irregular or unreliable. Many fathers are low income and have little or nothing to provide in the way of financial support. Often they are unable to make payments because they are unemployed or in prison.

In some instances, lone mothers prefer not to seek child support out of fear of retaliation, when, for example, they have fled situations of domestic violence and do not wish to risk the possibility of having contact with their children's fathers or when they are concerned the fathers may retaliate by demanding shared custody of the children they fathered. In other instances mothers choose to forgo demanding child-support enforcement so as not to alienate fathers from somehow remaining involved in their children's lives. If impoverished lone mothers are recipients of TANF, they are asked to identify their children's biological fathers. Government child-support enforcement officials then attempt to locate the fathers, to establish their legal relationship to the children, and to collect child-support payments. While not all mothers receiving TANF are able or willing to identify their children's biological fathers, aggressive child-support enforcement by the individual states has generally been successful in increasing the percentage of biological fathers who make payments.[46] Some states' practices, however, have the effect of holding down the degree of this success.

Individual states can require all or part of fathers' child-support payments to be withheld from lone mothers to offset the benefits their families receive. Many states only pass through the first $50 of monthly support payments. When states fail to pass through the fathers' full child-support payments to lone mothers, fathers are often discouraged from making the full payments.[47] In some instances, fathers informally and surreptitiously pay child support to mothers when and if they can, avoiding states' pass-through withholdings. When fathers are unwilling to pay in secret, some lone mothers enforce covert payments by threatening to turn fathers in to child-support enforcement authorities.[48]

In the United States, reliable and adequate child-support payments can be very important to lone-mother-headed families living below the federal poverty line or just above it. These payments can help mothers provide for their families by supplementing their earnings from employment and can also enable lone mothers to get through temporary economic setbacks such as a job loss—a not-infrequent event given the types of jobs many mothers hold. The problem is that too few eligible low-income families in the United States receive child support, and often the amounts they receive are minimal in comparison with these families' income needs.

In 2001, only 36 percent of the children in poor lone-mother-headed families received child support (up from 31 percent in 1996, when provisions of welfare reform began increased enforcement efforts). On average, support payments constituted 30 percent of the total incomes of recipient families whose incomes were below the federal poverty line. Those just above the poverty line were likewise provided with relatively little support. Even though 50 percent of children in near-poor families (with incomes between 100 and 200 percent of the poverty line) received child support in 2001, the payments averaged only 15 percent of these families' incomes.[49]

Many other affluent nations take a very different approach to child-support payments, by establishing policies providing universal guaranteed child support. Their first priority is making sure adequate child support is available to lone mothers and their children; the collection of payments from absent fathers is of secondary concern. The results of such policies are highly beneficial to lone-mother-headed families. In cases where non-custodial parents are unable to pay child support, make inadequate or irregular payments, or otherwise fail to meet their child-support responsibilities, the government steps in and makes the payments.

Child-support assurance (sometimes called advanced maintenance payments) guarantees lone mothers that they will always receive at least a minimum cash payment on a regular basis. The governments in other nations attempt to get fathers to pay back the child support money they have advanced, but families are not denied child support if collection efforts are unsuccessful for whatever reason. Child-support assurance results in a much higher percentage of lone mothers receiving reliable and predictable child-support payments than they do in the United States. The level of child support received by mothers in other affluent nations varies, but it is generally an important source of income for lone-mother-headed families.

Unemployment Insurance   Welfare reform policy pushes impoverished lone mothers to make a rapid transition from welfare to work, and TANF eligibility time limits are intended to make that transition permanent. More often than not, however, lone mothers leaving TANF are forced to take low-skilled jobs that are temporary, unstable, or otherwise subject to layoffs. Unfortunately, the income protection provided by individual states' programs of unemployment insurance is meager and time-limited, and for those who become unemployed the eligibility for assistance varies from state to state.

In the United States, unemployment insurance was originally set up to serve full-time male breadwinners whose female partners were homemakers, not lone mothers attempting to balance work and family. The cash benefits provided by unemployment insurance are usually little more than 50 to 60 percent of the wages a worker received in the job that was lost, and eligibility ordinarily requires a certain base amount of past earnings. Since so many lone mothers are in low-wage jobs, they often do not achieve past-earnings eligibility; when they do, their benefits do not amount to much. Mothers forced to take short-term or part-time jobs or able to work only sporadically due to family care responsibilities may find it difficult to qualify for benefits. In most states, eligibility for unemployment benefits also requires that a worker be available for full-time employment, a requirement which many lone mothers cannot hope to meet. Finally, unemployment benefits are available for only a limited time period, even when workers remain unemployed. In short, in the United States unemployment insurance simply does not provide lone mothers with much in the way of income protection.

Only a few other nations (e.g., France, Sweden) have lone mother labor-force participation rates that approach the high rates in the United States. In many European nations this participation is much more heavily part than full time. Nonetheless, overall the level of lone mothers' labor-force participation rates in other affluent nations is quite high. In many of these nations, unemployment insurance functions in ways that serve lone mothers' income needs to a far greater extent than is typical in the United States. Other affluent nations have policies allowing most unemployed lone mothers to receive cash benefits without the kinds of eligibility restrictions and cash-benefit time limits found in the United States. Moreover, although varying among these nations, the benefit levels are frequently generous enough to serve as an important component of total family income. For example, some nations' unemployment benefits, when combined with child allowances, are sufficient to prevent many lone-mother-headed families from living in poverty.[50]

Social Assistance   The principal means-tested program of cash income assistance for lone-mother-headed families in the United States is, of course, TANF, with its eligibility restrictions and minimal income support. Under the PRWORA, individual states are permitted to offer TANF to impoverished two-parent families, but a third of the states choose not to do so. In comparison, many other affluent nations offer what is typically called *social assistance* to low-income families, whether they are lone mother-headed or not. Eligibility is usually far less restrictive and benefits are more generous than is the case for TANF. In most instances, cash assistance is simply extended to all families whose income falls below a certain government standard. The criteria included in this means test, as well as the amount of income assistance eligible families receive, vary from nation to nation.

For the most part, other affluent nations do not single out lone mothers as a problematic group of people needing special treatment or a group required to meet special behavioral requirements in return for social assistance. This more even-handed treatment of low-income families, regardless of how they are headed, helps to minimize the negative stigmatization of being labeled *welfare mothers* that has been so common in the United States. However, this is not to say that such stigmatization, or the potential for it, is not on the increase.

In recent years, the idea that cash assistance inevitably encourages sloth and dependency and that recipients of cash assistance should be made to work in return for benefits has received increased attention in some other affluent nations, including some in Western Europe.[51] This attention has been fanned by the discourse surrounding the implementation of welfare reform in the United States and its advocates' claims that welfare reform is now a proven success. To date, however, mandatory work requirements for lone mothers have not become the kind of political obsession among other affluent nations' elites that they have in the United States. New policies have been fashioned in some other nations to encourage, support, and even require greater labor-force participation on the part of lone mothers (as well as the long-term unemployed, unemployed youth, and immigrants). Such policies have not generally been introduced in the punitive and coercive spirit accompanying adoption of mandatory work requirements as a part of U.S. welfare reform. Rather, the policies have been framed as a way of integrating often-marginalized populations into the world of work, the goal being reduction of the social exclusion from the larger community and its institutions that often accompanies low-income status.

Policies That Help Lone Mothers Balance Demands of Work and Family
Overall, the level of lone mothers' labor-force participation is quite high in most affluent nations. While few such nations have rates of lone mother labor-force participation approaching the high rate in the United States, many lone mothers are working at least part time. Unlike the United States, however, other affluent nations have put many policies in place that provide a great deal of support to working mothers, including lone

mothers, U.S. welfare policy coerces lone mothers into labor-force partici-pation as a means to self-sufficiency, but does not follow through with the kinds of family-friendly policies found in other nations which help moth-ers to balance the demands of work with family responsibilities. Among the supportive policies other affluent nations provide to help working mothers are subsidized child care, free or low-cost health care, generous maternity and parental leave, and the regulation of working time and pay.

Child Care   Clearly, the shortage of safe, dependable, accessible, afford-able child care poses an important employment barrier to many lone mothers in the United States. The U.S. government's failure to adequately subsidize comprehensive child-care services leaves many employed lone mothers with significant expenses for what is often less than adequate care. It is estimated that only 14 percent of U.S. preschool children ages 3 to 5 are in publicly supported day care—more than 25 percent below that of any European nation. In Sweden and France, where mothers' labor-force participation rates are akin to the high rates in the United States, the per-centage of children in publicly subsidized day care ranges from 80 to 95 percent.[52] Readily accessible, high-quality care provided by well-trained child-care workers enhances lone mothers' willingness take on employ-ment and helps them maintain their attachment to the labor force.

Child care is not treated as a public responsibility in the United States, and employed mothers are forced to find child-care solutions on their own. In nations where it is considered a public responsibility, child care is heavily subsidized by the government and attracts child-care professionals who take pride in the high quality of care provided. Child care and con-cern with child development are often inseparable, and caregivers often combine simple care with age-appropriate educational programming. Publicly subsidized child care is freely available to parents who need it, and the quality is the same for children regardless of their mothers' marital sta-tus or income. In the United States, in contrast, mothers' child-care solu-tions largely reflect their ability to pay, and the quality of care children receive varies a great deal. Low-income lone mothers tend to rely upon private individuals for child care (e.g., family members or neighbors), who may function as little more than babysitters. More affluent mothers, on the other hand, are better able to afford to send their children to privately run day care or afternoon care programs, which often offer enriched and stim-ulating preschool or after-school experiences.

Ironically, over three decades ago the U.S. Congress voted favorably on a bill aimed at establishing a system of federally subsidized child-care cen-ters, which would have provided a range of health, education, and social services specifically aimed at enhancing child development. They would have targeted preschool children and would have given special attention to the oft-ignored needs of children from low-income families. The Comprehensive Child Development Act of 1971, had it been adopted, would have been a major step toward making child care a universal right in the United States.

President Richard M. Nixon (1969–1974) expressed support for federal child-care subsidies to help low-income mothers needing to work full time. Nixon was convinced that "...the Federal Government's role, wherever possible, should be one of assisting parents to purchase needed day care services in the private, open market, with Federal involvement in direct provision of such services kept to an absolute minimum." However, Nixon vetoed the 1971 bill, saying, "For the Federal Government to plunge headlong financially into supporting child development would commit the vast moral authority of the National Government to the side of communal approaches to child rearing over against [sic] the family-centered approach."[53]

The idea of using federal funds to make child care possible for all those who needed it would never again be seriously considered by U.S. political elites. There would be no universal right to child care in the United States, even as the vast majority of mothers—both lone mothers and those with partners—have become labor-force participants. The Nixon administration and subsequent presidential administrations instead lent support to income-tax deductions and tax credits that give eligible working parents a way to offset some of their child-care costs. Such tax breaks, although limited, can be important to lone mothers earning decent wages and able to take advantage of them. However, such breaks are of far less help to the many lone mothers who are underemployed or who need child care while they search for employment. Most importantly, these tax breaks do little to address the serious nationwide shortage of affordable, quality child care with which employed mothers must contend.

In 1996, the PRWORA authorized the Child Care and Development Fund, through which the federal government provides individual states with block grants aimed at helping working families pay for child care. These block grants allow states to provide means-tested subsidized child care to eligible low-income families, which can include families on the TANF rolls or making a transition off those rolls.[54] States have a great deal of leeway in deciding eligibility requirements for receipt of subsidized child care and the degree to which care will be subsidized. Consequently, the availability and extensiveness of these means-tested benefits vary among individual states, depending upon how broadly or narrowly they define the low-income target population to be helped with the available funds.

Meeting child-care needs is particularly difficult for impoverished lone-mother-headed families who have turned to TANF or who are struggling to survive economically after leaving the TANF rolls. Prior to welfare reform, lone mothers on the welfare rolls who were employed or were leaving the rolls for employment were generally able to count on getting at least some state assistance to help with child care. This assistance was open ended in the sense that federal funds for AFDC programs went to individual states in accordance with the changing size and requirements of their caseloads. Under the PRWORA, however, states receive only the limited money provided by the Child Care and Development Fund block grant—although states are also permitted to divert a limited percentage of their TANF program funds to child-care assistance. Unfortunately, the funds available to individual states for child care fall far short of meeting the needs of impoverished lone mothers and their children.

Over the last decade, employed lone mothers' need for child care has escalated. Welfare reform pushed this need to new heights by establishing mandatory work requirements, which mothers must meet or risk suffering sanctions that could jeopardize their TANF cash benefits. Usually meeting these requirements involves the use of child care. In addition to those on the TANF rolls, increasing numbers of lone mothers have been leaving TANF after coming up against cash-benefit time limits. The limited aid to states provided by the Child Care and Development Fund does not solve the problems TANF recipients and leavers face in finding accessible, affordable, quality child care. Thus, lack of child care is an ongoing barrier to employment for many impoverished lone mothers.

Health Care　The medical model dominating health care in the United States defines *health* as the absence of illness. Health-care providers, whose focus is on treating individuals, favor administering drugs to deal with illness. An alternative to the medical model would be defining health as present when people are capable of using their physical and mental capacities to the fullest. Conditions in a nation interfering with many people's ability to fully utilize their capacities—such as joblessness, lack of affordable and adequate housing, or food insecurity and hunger—would be considered threats to their health.[55] Treatment in this case would necessitate government intervention to end such threats. Either way health is defined, the United States falls far short of supporting the health status of all of its citizens. In comparison to many other affluent nations, life expectancy is shorter in the United States, and infant and maternal mortality rates tend to be higher. These cross-national differences are no doubt due to many factors, but two stand out.

First, in the United States health care is an increasingly expensive commodity most people must purchase in the marketplace. The majority of U.S. families have no access to government-subsidized programs providing health care, such as Medicaid. In the absence of government assistance, most U.S. families are left on their own to buy care, whether by making direct payments to health-care providers or by purchasing private health insurance. Even families fortunate enough to be eligible for government-subsidized programs or who can afford private insurance face strict coverage limitations, requiring that they pay for a portion of their care. Treating health care as a commodity would not be such a problem if income were distributed relatively equally in the United States, and if rates of absolute and relative poverty were low, but this is not the case. Costs of health care keep rising, and millions of U.S. families are finding themselves either unable to afford the health care they need or having to settle for less-than-adequate treatment.

The United States also ranks poorly in cross-national comparisons of people's health status in affluent nations because it does not consider health care to be a right. Instead, access to health care is tied to income and employment status, and the employed are highly dependent upon the willingness of their employer to share the costs of employee health-care insurance. Some forty-five million people in the United States, including nine million children, have no form of health insurance at all. In contrast, virtually every other affluent nation has created a national health-care system to provide universal care.[56] For example, Canada, Denmark, Norway, and Sweden have national programs in which health insurance is publicly administered and doctors are largely in private practice. Spain and Great Britain are among the nations maintaining national health services with publicly owned and operated hospitals and government-salaried doctors. In Germany and France, health insurance is universally provided to people by sickness funds that pay doctors and hospitals regulated and uniform rates when people receive care. These national health-care systems pose a sharp contrast to the lack of any such system in the United States.

Poor people are much more vulnerable to the risks of disease, illness, and accidents than the affluent, given the environments within and stresses under which they live. As chapter 3 demonstrated, many impoverished lone-mother-headed families in the United States are not enrolled in Medicaid or other government health-care programs. Even when they are enrolled in such programs, coverage limitations usually mean they are still faced with heavy health-care expenses. Health problems are an obstacle to many lone mothers' taking or keeping employment, whether their own health status or the health status of their children is problematic. Many lone mothers in the United States are working less than full time and for employers either not offering the option of sharing the costs of health insurance or else offering plans with very limited coverage (e.g., plans not covering the mothers' children). Because of low average wages, coupled with other expenses, many lone mothers cannot afford adequate health insurance for their families even when working full time. Lone-mother-headed families, along with other families, in other affluent nations receive universal health-care coverage, usually at little or no out-of-pocket cost. This, together with other family-friendly policies, contributes to their ability to balance work and family responsibilities.

Maternity and Other Parental Leave　The U.S. government has historically been reluctant to interfere with private employers' prerogatives to determine whether and under what conditions employees will be granted leave from their jobs. This reluctance has prevented the United States from adopting parental leave policies that would facilitate lone mothers' ability to maintain their ties to employment while attending to maternal and other family responsibilities. The Family and Medical Leave Act of 1993 is the principal parental leave law enacted in the United States. It provides eligible employees with job-protected leave for specified purposes. Employers are required to grant leave to parents who want to stay at home to care for a newborn, newly adopted, or foster child; who need to assist a child, spouse, or parent with a serious health condition; or who need time to recuperate from a serious health problem of their own.

However, the act has a number of serious limitations rendering it incapable of meeting many employees' family needs.[57] First, although it covers all public employers, it only covers private employers with fifty workers or more. Some forty-one million workers (approximately 60 percent of private-sector employees) are thus not covered by the law. Second, to be eligible for leave parents must have worked at least 1,250 hours the previous year. Third, the maximum leave employers are required to grant is only twelve weeks. Finally, and very importantly, whereas employers must continue parents' benefits during the leave, they are not required to provide wages during this time. Relatively few employers replace the wages, even in part, that are lost by taking the leave.

Lone mothers are particularly disadvantaged when it comes to benefiting from taking leave from employment under this act. The low-wage jobs in which they are disproportionately working are most likely located in places of private employment with fewer than fifty workers and, thus, are not covered by the act. Even when lone mothers' employers are covered by the act, mothers often cannot financially afford to take unpaid leave or may be forced to take a much shorter leave than that to which they are legally entitled. The lower an employed mother's education level, wages, and household income, the less likely she is to receive paid or unpaid family leave. In the United States, "workers with greater needs and fewer resources are the least likely to have job-protected leaves or cash benefits."[58]

In short, the act provides little in the way of economic security or incentives for lone mothers to take parental leave, even when they are entitled to it by law. Nor does the act help lone mothers who must meet unexpected family-related demands that do not fall under its provisions. Some individual states do supplement and expand upon the provisions of the act with their own parental leave policies. A number of states, for example, go beyond the requirements of the act by extending coverage to include workers in smaller private establishments or by supplementing the approved reasons for which eligible employees must be granted a leave. But for the most part, the fundamental limitations built into the act prevail nationally.

When it comes to parental leave policy, the United States is clearly an outlier in comparison to the much more generous and extensive policies existing in other affluent nations.[59] In many European nations, for example, mothers can take advantage of a variety of paid and unpaid, job-protected leave opportunities.[60] Paid maternity leave is nearly universal among these nations. Employers typically offer fourteen to twenty weeks of paid maternity leave, and they often require that women schedule their leaves to encompass the time period immediately before and after giving birth. Paid maternity leave gives lone mothers an opportunity to prepare for and to recover from childbirth, as well as time to bond with their newborns—all without having to worry about loss of income.

Maternity leave is often followed by other generous leave opportunities allowing mothers to keep their ties to the labor force.[61] Whether or not such postmaternity leaves are paid, as well as the level of the wage replacement provided, varies from nation to nation. But in the nations in which such leaves are available, coverage of employees is very high, and mothers make extensive use of these opportunities. Nordic nations are particularly generous in terms of leave duration and wage replacement, giving parents the right to take anywhere from one to three years of leave from employment while receiving at least two-thirds of their wages (high wage earners are usually subject to wage replacement caps).[62] In European nations, there is a growing trend toward extended child-rearing leave policies that enable parents to take time off from employment at various stages of their children's lives. Extended leave frequently allows working mothers to remain at home part or full time while providing ongoing job protection and employee benefits.

Postmaternity leaves allow employed mothers to focus more of their time on child care, especially in the preschool years, as well as to be with ill or disabled children or other family members. Many affluent nations are generous in providing paid leaves for family reasons, such as when mothers must be away from work to care for school-aged children who have suddenly taken ill. Contrasted sharply with this policy is the condition in the United States, where no provision exists for paid leave for mothers who must attend to such routine emergencies. In this nation, many lone mothers who hold down low-wage jobs and who miss work to care for a sick child risk losing their employment.

Regulation of Work Time and Compensation   The importance of accessible and affordable child care in lone mothers' efforts to balance work with family responsibilities has been discussed. It is also extremely helpful if the amount of time mothers must put into employment outside the home can be minimized. Employer practices should make it possible for lone mothers to work and still adequately care for children or other family members. Mothers who must work part time should not be subject to discrimination by employers in terms of pay and benefits. In comparison with other affluent nations, the United States takes a *laissez-faire* attitude toward such employer practices, making it much more difficult than it should be for lone mothers to be both wage earners and care providers.

Standard work weeks and overtime.   Employers in the United States use the forty-hour work week as the definition of full-time employment. In reality, many full-time employees work far more than forty hours per week, either voluntarily or in response to employer demands. The federal Fair Labor Standards Act, passed in 1938, requires that employees be given extra compensation if they work more than forty hours per week, though certain categories of employees are exempted from this provision, such as executives, managers, and professionals. While the act requires overtime pay, it does not prohibit employers from making overtime hours mandatory. Workers have no right to job protection if they refuse employers' requests to work the extra hours. Such requests are particularly problematic for low-income lone mothers. On the one hand, they are by definition in need of the extra income overtime pay can provide. On the other hand, working overtime often means additional child-care arrangements and extra child care costs, not to mention less opportunity for lone mothers to have leisure time with their children outside of work.

Other affluent nations have recognized the important benefits families experience when the number of hours working parents spend on the job each week is reduced. Most European nations do not allow employers to require full-time workers to be on the job beyond a standard work week, which ranges from thirty-five to thirty-nine hours. In most instances, employers may neither require workers to work overtime nor penalize them if they refuse to do so. France's short thirty-five-hour work week for full-time employees, made compulsory for employers in 2000, was initiated as a way of creating jobs, thus reducing unemployment among French workers. While the latter remains problematic, workers have expressed satisfaction with the shortened week in terms of the additional time it provides to be with their children and other family members.[63]

Valuing and rewarding part-time employment. In the United States, employees are considered part time if they work less than thirty-five hours per week. Federal law does not address issues of pay and benefits for part-time workers, nor does it provide them with special protections. Thus, it is common for employers to treat part-time employees as inferior to full-time workers. Part-time workers are commonly paid less per hour than full-time workers, even when they are doing the same tasks. In addition, part-time workers usually do not receive full-time workers' benefits (even on a prorated basis). They are typically denied employer health insurance, are not given paid holidays or paid vacation time, do not receive paid sick leave, and are frequently excluded from pension plans. For the most part, part-time jobs in the United States are in the most poorly paid sectors of the economy. Part-time employment is generally less secure than full-time employment and offers employees few chances for upward mobility.

Workers wanting to reduce their work hours, for whatever reason, are often seriously penalized for taking on part-time employee status.[64] Unfortunately, many lone mothers find it impossible to work forty hours per week or more while adequately attending to their parental and other family responsibilities. Some cannot take on full-time employment due to difficulties accessing or affording adequate child care. This is particularly the case for lone mothers whose children are disposed to chronic illnesses or who have disabilities requiring specialized care. Moreover, mothers are at times limited in the number of hours they can work because of their own health problems or disabilities.

Some lone mothers do take on full-time jobs, only to find they must reduce their hours—either temporarily or permanently. U.S. employers rarely allow workers to reduce their weekly working hours just below forty (e.g., to thirty-five to thirty-nine hours) and still be treated as full time.

Workers usually must drop from forty to below thirty-five hours weekly, changing their status to part time. Beyond the penalties associated with leaving full-time for part-time employee status, the costs of dropping from full- to part-time employment commonly include having to change jobs, employers, and even occupational areas.

Other affluent nations have been attentive to the harm done by employer discrimination against part-time work and have taken steps to reverse it.[65] While nations' approaches vary, many European nations, for example, prohibit the kinds of gross full-time–part-time inequities that exist in the United States. From pay to participation in pension programs, part-time workers are given employment rights similar to those of full-time employees. It is not unusual for European governments to require that employers allow workers to voluntarily change their job status from full to part time without having to leave their jobs, then to shift back later to full-time status. Beyond helping to make part-time jobs a form of high-quality work and an option available across workplace settings, employer flexibility regarding reduced hours makes it possible for many workers to adjust to changes in their nonwork situations. The positive treatment other affluent nations accord part-time work can be extremely beneficial to lone mothers and the often cyclical, sometimes unpredictable, demands family caretaking places on them.

Expanded vacation time. Full-time workers in the United States work more hours per week than their counterparts in other affluent nations. The average work week for U.S. workers is an estimated forty-seven to forty-nine hours per week when overtime is included, some ten to twelve hours more than workers in most other affluent nations. Yet in the United States workers also receive far less paid vacation time than their counterparts elsewhere. Once again, the federal government leaves the question of vacations up to employers, who are free to give workers as few weeks of annual vacation as they wish. Most workers get two weeks per year, but only by completing a year-long period of full-time employment to gain eligibility. In general, vacations are considered a privilege extended by employers, not a right.

Many U.S. workers are reluctant to take all of what little vacation time they are granted by their employers. In the present-day U.S. economy, few workers have a sense of job security, and competition among workers to get and keep jobs is often intense. Many employees experience supervisor pressures to be at work every day and are informally discouraged from taking time off. Increasingly, workers are fearful that taking vacation time could be taken as a sign of lack of commitment to the workplace and could increase their risks of becoming victims of employer layoffs or so-called reductions in force.

In the United States, eligibility for the two weeks or so of paid vacation most full-time workers receive can be lost simply by changing jobs. Eligibility may have to be reearned by a full year on the new job. In addition to those who are ineligible, millions of other U.S. workers either receive or take no vacation time at all. Lack of government concern with assuring workers vacation time erects a structural barrier for parents—including lone mothers—who wish to have more time with their children. It also increases parents' child-care costs beyond what they would otherwise be. Most European nations, in contrast, have laws guaranteeing workers—including entry-level employees—four or more weeks of paid vacation annually.[66] Such vacation laws provide working mothers, including lone mothers, valuable opportunities to spend additional time with their children and other family members.

European Governments' Concern with Social Exclusion

Since the late 1980s, nations with membership in the European Union have been showing increased willingness to entertain definitions of poverty that go beyond income deprivation and that take into account multiple dimensions of social and economic disadvantage.[67] Interest in moving beyond a narrow income-based definition of poverty has largely been spurred by European scholars and policy analysts, who have argued that income deprivation is also often accompanied by damage due to social exclusion.[68] The term *social exclusion* carries many different meanings and to date there is no one meaning on which scholars and policy analysts are in agreement.[69] But in general, social exclusion is a way of talking about the outcome when people lack the resources they need to be full participants in the larger community and its institutions.

Research attempting to define and measure social exclusion, both within European nations and cross-nationally, is still in its early stages. Such research may raise whole new social policy issues beyond how to raise or close gross gaps between families' incomes. When defined solely in terms of income, poverty among lone mothers (and others) is a distributional problem. It is a problem that can, as has been shown here, be mitigated by income transfer policies along with policies helping to facilitate lone mothers' ability to balance work and family responsibilities. But income poverty is only one type of disadvantage with which low-income families frequently must contend. Use of the term social exclusion draws attention to a wide range of social and economic disadvantages suffered by such families, many of which are not addressed by policies that primarily affect income distribution.[70]

For example, many low-income families find themselves residing in largely economically segregated communities with others in their financial situation. This is not simply a matter of choice. Families go where they can find affordable housing. In such low-income communities, local schools are often in poor condition, public transportation is inadequate, parks and other public amenities are few and poorly maintained, access to quality health care is an issue, and there are too few local employers. Frequently, such communities are segregated not only economically but also racially and ethnically. Many harbor disproportionate numbers of impoverished immigrants and people of color. Such conditions are in many instances far worse in the United States than in most of Europe, but Europeans currently express the most concern about such communities.

Those who relate such conditions to social exclusion frequently argue that it is a more deep-seated problem than income poverty.[71] Due to social exclusion, many low-income families experience differences between themselves and others that go well beyond their relative power to consume, as important as these differences may be. They experience an involuntary disconnect and lack of integration with the larger social order. They feel they have little access to the social, political, and economic rewards this order makes available to most other people. This feeling is renewed every time they look at their surroundings and reflect on their resource-poor immediate environment or are made to feel unwelcome by the larger community and its institutions. In short, social exclusion functions to marginalize and to alienate low-income people in ways that attack their sense of human dignity. In the view of many European scholars and policy analysts, social exclusion can be a major contributor to criminal behavior, mental troubles, substance abuse, and family instability.

European scholars view social exclusion as a process, not simply a condition. Researchers are interested in determining how social exclusion originates, the various forms it takes, and how it can be reversed. Social exclusion clearly involves relationships between different groups or sectors of society. Researchers hope to identify the agents of social exclusion and to understand their actions: Who is excluding whom, how, and why? This requires examining issues of power and the ways power is used by some groups to impede others from possessing or being able to freely access the resources they need for full community participation. It also means figuring out how power relationships can be altered to facilitate the integration of the socially excluded.

European concern with social exclusion reflects a belief that governments must find ways to overcome domestic conditions that deny some people a sense of common citizenship, and thereby get in the way of national solidarity. European governments are slowly moving beyond addressing income poverty and taking up social exclusion as one of those conditions. But national solidarity need not be at the cost of individual freedom. A debate is raging in Europe over the desirability of a universal guaranteed income some argue would enhance the freedom of every individual recipient, regardless of their economic station in life.

The European Proposal for a Universal Basic Income

Despite the reduction of absolute and relative poverty by other affluent nations to levels lower than the United States, a number of European scholars, social policy analysts, and economic justice activists have expressed dissatisfaction with the current progress. Since the 1980s they have been pressing European nations to take more aggressive steps toward the elimination of poverty by implementing a universal basic income (UBI). Unlike the income transfer programs Europeans generally refer to as *social assistance* that target low-income people, the UBI would not involve a means test and would be available to individuals regardless of their economic standing. In this respect, it would be similar to the annual payments the U.S. state of Alaska makes to all residents based on proceeds from Alaskan oil.

The UBI would not be linked to an expectation that recipients will work and would be set at a level sufficient for subsistence.[72] Proponents of the UBI have organized the Basic Income European Network (BIEN), which holds that income should be a basic economic right of individuals "based on citizenship, rather than on one's relation to the production process or to one's family status."[73] As a citizenship right the UBI would be short of a human right, but it would be a right.

One of the central figures of the BIEN is Philippe Van Parijs, a French scholar whose writings on behalf of a universal basic income have contributed to ongoing international debate.[74] He views enactment of a UBI as something that ideally should occur globally, but that affluent European Union and North American nations—given their wealth, productivity, and national incomes—are in a position to implement now. In Van Parijs's view, the UBI should be in the form of a grant paid at regular intervals to all adults who are citizens or permanent residents. It would be paid unconditionally, meaning that there would be no obligations or duties expected in return. Individuals could, of course, receive income from other sources, but this would not affect receipt of the UBI grant. Van Parijs suggests that governments might wish to modify existing income transfer programs, depending upon the level at which the UBI is initially set and the needs of the particular populations such programs serve.

In Van Parijs's words, "The main argument for UBI is founded on a view of justice. Social justice, I believe, requires that our institutions be designed to best secure *real freedom* to all" [italics are his].[75] The UBI would contribute to freedom in the sense that removing any possible threat of severe economic deprivation would empower people no matter what their economic status. Absent this threat, individuals would have greater freedom to engage in tasks they wanted to carry out and could more easily pursue goals and opportunities of their own choosing. Applied to the present discussion, a UBI would make it possible for lone mothers to meet their family caretaking responsibilities while allowing them to make their own decisions about whether and how much they wished to engage in labor-force participation. Indeed, Van Parijs speaks of the gender implications of a UBI in terms of how it would empower women vis à vis the labor market: "Given the sexist division of labor in the household and the special 'caring' functions that women disproportionately bear, their labor market participation, and range of choice in jobs, is far more constrained than those of men. Both in terms of direct impact on the inter-individual distribution of income and the longer-term impact on job options, a UBI is… bound to benefit women far more than men…. It provides a modest but secure basis on which the most vulnerable can stand, as marriages collapse or administrative discretion is misused."[76]

Rips in the Shrinking U.S. Safety Net

While certainly controversial, the idea of the right to a universal basic income has been the subject of serious debate in Europe. In the present political climate it seems outlandish to think that this idea could receive similarly serious treatment in the United States. It is, however, worth noting that the U.S. government has twice considered and rejected proposals to at least provide a federally funded, means-tested guaranteed minimum income to impoverished families. President Nixon's Family Assistance Plan (1969) and President Carter's Program for Better Jobs and Income (1977) proposed what were essentially negative income tax programs. Simply put, families whose annual incomes fell below a certain threshold would have received a payment from the federal government to bring their incomes up to a guaranteed minimum. The principal welfare program providing income assistance to lone mothers and their children, then called Aid to Families with Dependent Children, would no longer have been needed. The individual states and the federal government would not have been burdened with the costs of administering the then rapidly-growing AFDC program.

While both presidents' proposals had important limitations, particularly when it came to benefit levels, they opened up the potential for all impoverished lone-mother-headed families to receive income assistance as a matter of course. The stigma of applying for and receiving welfare benefits would have been eliminated by a negative income tax, which would have operated in much the same routinized and invisible way as the popular federal Earned Income Tax Credit (EITC) program that supplements the incomes of low-paid working parents.[77]

In 2002, the federal EITC lifted a total of 2.7 million children under the age of 18 above the federal poverty line, thus serving as the most powerful federal antipoverty program in this regard. The other programs that moved notable numbers of children out of poverty in 2002 were Social Security (one million); food stamps (897,000); TANF (482,000); unemployment insurance (468,000); Supplemental Security Income (427,000); and housing assistance (426,000).[78] At the same time, however, the U.S. Census Bureau reported that over twelve million children under 18 were living in poverty in 2002, up from 11.7 million the previous year.[79] A disproportionate number of these impoverished children were in lone-mother-headed families. Clearly, the programs the U.S. government has in place are failing to make any significant impact on reducing children's impoverishment.

While U.S. income transfer programs for low-income families are clearly inadequate, the United States also lacks or inadequately funds other programs that assist such families in other affluent nations. Government support for child care, for example, is nowhere near what would be required to seriously address the caretaking needs of impoverished lone mothers who are or wish to be in the labor force. Thus, absolute poverty rates in the United States are much higher than in other nations, particularly in Western Europe, and the United States fares poorly in cross-national studies of relative poverty. High rates of child poverty persist in the United States even during periods of national economic growth and expansion. The United States seems to tolerate not only a great deal of economic inequality but also widespread poverty—including severe poverty. The question is why?

Does the U.S. Public Prefer Poverty?

The failure of the United States to adopt effective antipoverty policies has produced sharp disparities between the life chances of its lone-mother-headed families and those of similar families residing in other affluent nations. Whether to adopt policies that will mitigate poverty is a choice made by nations' political elites. In the United States, present-day political elites appear committed to national policy priorities that leave little room for initiatives aimed at poverty reduction, no less its elimination.

Are the differences between the United States and other affluent nations in this regard simply a reflection of different cultures? Are U.S. political elites merely reflecting the attitudes of the U.S. public?

This question has been addressed by Sheldon Danziger.[80] In his view, people in the United States "'prefer' a high level of poverty." It "is not very high on their agenda and they are content to live in a society that has more economic hardship than most Europeans would tolerate."[81] Danziger reasons that most people in the United States are by and large comfortable with the workings of a market economy with minimal government intervention. Most seem content to leave the impoverished with little access to high-quality health care or education. As he puts it, "Given that America is a rich country... it must be the case that Americans care less than do Europeans about the living standards of the poor."[82] Danziger views the popularity of welfare reform as consistent with his argument, and states that "poverty is still higher in America than in Europe because Americans want to increase work among the poor and give themselves tax cuts more than they want to reduce poverty."[83]

Danziger's position is that attitudes are the main reason higher poverty rates exist in the United States than in much of Europe. It is, of course, very difficult to isolate and to compare attitudes toward poverty cross-nationally. One study compared attitudinal differences using the results of public opinion polls in the United States and nine other nations, all of them Western or Eastern European nations except for Japan and Australia. Using poll data gathered in the early 1990s, this study examined the percentage of those polled who agreed that "the government should guarantee everyone a minimum standard of living." Data were available on this question for seven of the ten nations. Only 27 percent of those polled in the United States agreed with this statement. Other nations showed levels of agreement from the mid-50-percent range on up to 80 percent.[84] In this same study, researchers found that only 35 percent of those polled in the United States were in agreement with the statement that "the government should provide everyone with a guaranteed basic income." Poll data available from seven other nations found respondents much more likely to be in agreement with this statement, with 50 to 80 percent again agreeing.[85] Based on this study, it certainly appears that people in the United States are less supportive of programs providing income assistance to the poor than in other nations.

One must be extremely careful, however, in interpreting U.S. public opinion data when it comes to attitudes toward poverty. Interpretation is particularly fraught with problems in this case because of the active and highly visible demonization of the poor—particularly of welfare recipients—that took place in the United States from the 1960s through the 1990s. This demonization, which was in full force when the U.S. data for the survey just described were gathered, involved the promotion of highly negative public perceptions of impoverished lone-mother-headed families by U.S. political elites. Such perceptions helped to ease the way for welfare reform legislation that restricted eligibility for and ended entitlement to public assistance.

As discussed in chapter 2, for decades U.S. political elites' harsh attacks on welfare and demands for reform were accompanied by the mobilization of often-subtle racist stereotypes that negatively portrayed so-called welfare mothers as lazy, promiscuous, immoral, parasitical, and undeserving of assistance.[86] Danziger describes welfare reform in the United States as popular in public opinion terms, but fails to give adequate attention to the major roles political elites played in shaping the public's attitudes up to and toward it. It is difficult to know just what U.S. public opinion regarding the implementation of a government-guaranteed minimum standard of living or a guaranteed basic income would have been in the 1990s had political elites' decades-long "war against the poor" not been conducted.[87]

Finally, another factor must be part of any explanation for attitudes in the United States that seem to tolerate poverty, even severe poverty. Simply put, the United States lacks a human rights culture. U.S. political elites bear a great deal of responsibility for this, both because their human rights discourse is so limited and because it is so narrowly directed to criticisms of civil and political human rights violations in other nations. The absence of a human rights culture in the United States minimizes the likelihood that impoverished people in the United States will articulate their plight in human rights terms or that the public will know what to make of it when they do. This leaves political elites in the United States free from the obligation to respond to economic human rights violations under the principle that "if you don't acknowledge them, they don't exist."

Toward Building Respect for Human Rights in the United States

Critics of present-day U.S. welfare policy have expressed deep dismay over the way it pushes impoverished lone mothers into low-wage, dead-end jobs; provides insufficient support for child care; offers meager cash benefits that progressively decline in real value; carries punitive sanctions that can result in loss of aid; and places strict time limits on the receipt of income assistance regardless of families' economic needs. The United States has not been alone in its efforts to cut back or retrench when it comes to welfare expenditures.[88] Political elites in other nations have also sought to slow down the rate of growth of their welfare programs. Some have made policy changes that place increased demands on recipients as a condition of eligibility for receipt of benefits, particularly when it comes to work requirements.[89] While some non-U.S. scholars and political elites argue that U.S. welfare reform provides a model from which valuable lessons can be drawn, no government abroad has implemented the severe eligibility restrictions and benefit limitations implemented in the United States. U.S. welfare reform involves a regression from respect for economic human rights that is unmatched by any other affluent nation.

President Franklin D. Roosevelt's proposal for an Economic Bill of Rights, receiving increasing attention from some scholars as well as anti-poverty activists, helped to inspire provisions of the UN Universal Declaration of Human Rights as well as provisions of such important treaties as the International Covenant on Economic, Social, and Cultural Rights. Roosevelt's impact on contemporary thinking about economic rights is reflected in policies and practices of nations around the world. More so than poorer nations, affluent nations possess the resources and capabilities necessary to positively and progressively fulfill such rights. This is not happening in the United States. As a consequence, the life chances and capabilities of this nation's impoverished lone-mother-headed families are restricted to the point of severe harm.

Fortunately, a new and militant domestic economic human rights movement has begun to take root in the United States, whose goal is to end domestic poverty. This growing economic human rights movement is now joined with other progressive groups in a new organizational structure, or network, seeking to build a human rights culture in the United States. This human rights culture would recognize and respect all human rights, including economic human rights, and would hold the U.S. government accountable for remedying and preventing human rights violations. The U.S. economic human rights movement and the larger human rights network of which it is a part will be examined in the remaining chapter.

6

Establishing Respect for Economic Human Rights in the United States

Previous chapters have emphasized the failure of the United States to recognize and respect economic human rights. U.S. political elites do not view the existence of poverty in the United States or cutbacks in income assistance to the poor as human rights violations. Moreover, they have rejected the notion that government has a responsibility to initiate programs whose goal is to end poverty. Poor families' escape from poverty is considered their own personal responsibility. U.S. political elites underscored this message in 1996 by adopting welfare reform legislation that abolished impoverished lone-mother-headed families' sixty-one-year-old legal entitlement to income assistance under Aid to Families with Dependent Children.

AFDC was replaced by Temporary Assistance for Needy Families, which, as shown already, offers only the most meager, time-limited cash benefits to impoverished families who manage to gain access to the welfare rolls. The miserly treatment of families by TANF and its mandatory work requirements for lone mothers are aimed at discouraging so-called welfare dependency, which lone mothers are to replace with self-sufficiency by increasing participation and applying greater efforts in the labor market. Over the years, U.S. political elites successfully forged a causal link in the public's mind between lone mothers' supposedly deficient work ethic and their families' impoverishment. They simultaneously reinforced and addressed this imaginary link through welfare reform, while offering lone mothers little assistance in balancing work and family responsibilities. Deaf to any calls for the adoption of new antipoverty measures, U.S. political elites have been pushing federal spending priorities in other directions, even while poverty continues to be widespread. As this chapter will discuss, their spending priorities are fostering sustained and exacerbated "homeland insecurity" for millions of low-income families in the United States.

The failure of the U.S. government to take any new initiatives to address poverty, along with cutbacks in the availability of income assistance for impoverished families, have contributed to the emergence of a new movement for economic human rights in the United States. This movement is still in its early stages, yet its participants have already begun to make visible strides. Movement activists have issued formal appeals to international human rights bodies, requesting that they intervene and press the U.S. government to respect the human rights of the tens of millions of people in the United States who are impoverished. And the economic human rights movement has also begun to put pressure on individual state and local governments to bring their laws and policies in conformity with international human rights standards.

A variety of antipoverty, welfare rights, feminist, antiracist, and legal rights organizations are at the forefront of the economic human rights movement. Many have become members of a large human rights network whose interests encompass protecting not only economic human rights but also social, cultural, civil, and political human rights. As will be discussed, the goals of this recently formed network include building a domestic human rights culture in the United States, U.S. ratification of human rights treaties, incorporation of international human rights standards into U.S. domestic law and policy, and an end to human rights violations by the U.S. government both at home and abroad. The emerging economic human rights movement and this new human rights organizational network deserve the active support and involvement of all persons committed to establishing respect for human rights within the United States.

Before discussing the economic human rights movement, a brief consideration of the skewed national priorities this movement must struggle against is necessary.

Post-9/11 "Homeland Insecurity" for Impoverished Families

Defining Threats to Domestic Security

Since the tragic events of September 11, 2001—also referred to as 9/11—the U.S. government has devoted a great deal of attention to the issue of international terrorism and has allocated significant resources to detect and combat possible external threats to homeland security. People in the United States have obvious reasons to be concerned, although historically the United States has been highly fortunate in experiencing very few attacks by international terrorists. In other nations, such terrorist attacks are tragically commonplace. Sadly, however, many U.S. political elites have exploited the tragic events that took place on 9/11 for their own or their political party's purposes. International terrorists may or may not pose serious imminent threats to the United States. Yet some political elites, seemingly unconstrained by the absence of facts, have used the specter of another 9/11 to keep the public's fears of terrorist attacks alive and churning.

In response to 9/11, President George W. Bush hurriedly established a cabinet-level Department of Homeland Security in late 2001. By 2005 this federal department (created largely by merging twenty-two existing federal agencies) had 183,000 employees and a budget of almost $34 billion.[1] Its periodic color-coded terrorism alerts have functioned to remind the public of its vulnerability to attack. Beyond their exposure to periodic color-coded alerts, every time people go to a U.S. airport or view high-profile, televised public events (ranging from presidential swearing-in ceremonies in Washington, D.C., to New Year's Eve celebrations in New York City's Times Square), the omnipresence of highly visible antiterrorist security procedures provides another reminder of the possibility of such attacks. The news media routinely issue additional threat reminders, reporting on the investigation of suspected terrorists or their supporters, evacuations of major U.S. government buildings in response to "suspicious" packages or activities, and the scrambling of military jets to intercept private aircraft wandering off course in ways that could indicate a terrorist threat.

The public's heightened sense of vulnerability to international terrorist attacks was exploited during the Bush administration's 2004 presidential reelection campaign. The president and his supporters made the question of who could best protect the United States from international terrorism a central campaign issue. Republican Vice President Dick Cheney portrayed Democratic presidential challenger Senator John Kerry as "weak on terrorism" and even charged that the election of Kerry to the presidency would increase the probability of another 9/11-like terrorist attack on the United States.[2] This type of campaign tactic, which helped provide Bush with a reelection victory, may well be mobilized in future presidential campaigns. Political elites know full well that fear of an external threat—real or imaginary—leads members of the public to look to and rely upon government leadership.

The Use of Fear to Shape Budgetary Priorities

The public's fears of a future 9/11 or a similarly catastrophic domestic event have been manipulated by U.S. political elites to shape the national political climate in ways that make it difficult to challenge their legislative and budgetary priorities. Such fears also serve to distract members of the public from serious domestic problems such as poverty. Political elites' priorities currently include unprecedented levels of spending on military, intelligence, and counterterrorism activities, all rationalized as necessary to protect homeland security.

These priorities have come to prevail even as they are rendering the lives of many people in the United States less secure. Low-income families have fallen largely outside the realm of political concern and prioritizing at the national level. For example, despite the rising annual poverty rates reported by the U.S. Census Bureau at the time of the 2004 presidential campaign, the need to assist low-income families was hardly addressed. The Republicans did little more than praise reductions in the size of the TANF rolls, while calling for more stringent mandatory work requirements for TANF recipients. The limited efforts made by Democratic presidential candidate John Kerry and vice presidential candidate John Edwards to make poverty a campaign issue seemed to draw little response from their Republican opposition.

Even as U.S. political elites have escalated spending for the military, intelligence agencies, and antiterrorism activities in the post-9/11 era, they have approved major federal tax cuts. These cuts have disproportionately benefited large corporations and the wealthy and have also helped to worsen gross economic inequalities in the United States by further enriching the already very rich.[3] The federal government has thus forgone tax revenues that could have been used to help pay for domestic social programs. Meanwhile, individual states have found themselves increasingly unable to meet low-income families' needs for income assistance, affordable housing, child care, and health care. Federal aid to individual states is proving insufficient in the face of the magnitude of the needs, and state legislatures have resisted approving their own tax increases to help support such programs. Many states have instituted program cutbacks, have redefined eligibility rules, and have made it increasingly difficult for low-income families to gain state government assistance.

Large-scale federal tax reductions, U.S. political elites argue, are necessary to encourage capital investments, to promote economic growth, to decrease unemployment, and to ensure the United States is successful in contending with global economic competition. Political elites in most other affluent nations are likewise concerned with global competition, and some have made reference to the demands of globalization as a rationale for welfare cutbacks.[4] But only in the United States have political elites created a government fiscal situation that virtually locks in the probability of even further welfare program retrenchment. They have done so by drastically increasing the annual federal budget deficit to the point where programs serving the nation's poor are increasingly in jeopardy. Large-scale federal spending on antiterrorist, military, and intelligence programs, on the other hand, is generally considered sacrosanct by political elites.

One estimate put the annual federal deficit at over $400 billion for 2005 alone,[5] although improvements in the economy that year were expected to increase federal tax revenues, thus lowering that figure somewhat. Reducing the huge and growing federal deficit, many U.S. political elites now argue, will require cutting certain categories of government spending. Domestic social programs, including programs serving the poor, are an obvious target. Consequently, federal budgetary support of the cash benefits of TANF and its welfare-to-work services is extremely vulnerable to new restrictions and cutbacks. Social Security continues to receive widespread political support from millions of older workers and retirees, thwarting recent proposals by some political elites to seriously reduce its cash benefits. But impoverished lone mothers lack both power and voice in the political arena. There is no well-financed lobbying and advocacy group—such as the pro-Social Security AARP (formerly called the American Association of Retired Persons)—that can effectively challenge additional federal retrogression when it comes to funding TANF or other programs on which many low-income families must rely.

Balancing the Federal Budget on the Backs of the Poor

Political elites' lack of concern over the well-being of low-income families is readily apparent in the Bush administration's 2006 budget proposal. Presidential proposals shape the parameters within which the U.S. Congress undertakes its annual budget decisions. President Bush's $2.5 trillion 2006 budget proposal was greeted in highly positive terms by the Republican majority in the House and Senate. Their annual budget priorities did not depart very much from the parameters the Bush administration outlined.[6]

Without going into great detail, suffice it to say the Bush budget proposal for 2006 called for significant freezes and cuts in many domestic social programs, especially those serving low-income families, while increasing military spending and further reducing taxes (again, much to the benefit of the wealthy).[7] For example, the Bush administration requested $419 billion for the Department of Defense for 2006, which is $19 billion over the Defense Department's 2005 funding. In contrast, the administration requested only $16.6 billion to fund TANF—a reduction of $1.2 billion from 2005. The requested 2006 increase in Defense Department spending was greater than the entire 2006 TANF budget. The proposed cut in spending for TANF, according to the Bush administration, reflected reduced caseloads, although the Bush administration could not truthfully claim reduced levels of poverty among lone-mother-headed families.

Among the other budgetary areas designated for freezes or cuts affecting low-income families were funds for child-care assistance, food stamps, Medicaid, and housing. Meanwhile, in addition to the $419 billion requested for the Department of Defense, the Bush administration requested $41 billion for homeland security. Requests for the Department of Energy's nuclear weapons programs added on another $19.5 billion. The Bush budget for 2006 did not even include the tens of billions of additional dollars Congress would have to appropriate to cover military and infrastructure rebuilding activities in Iraq and Afghanistan. From March 2003 to mid-2005, the United States spent an estimated $200 billion on Iraq alone. Justified as part of the nation's "war against terrorism," a mere two months of U.S. spending on Iraq cost taxpayers far more than the entire 2005 federal budget for TANF. Such spending on militarism is accelerating earlier-begun tendencies to defund domestic social programs.[8]

Redefining Homeland Security to Include Ending Poverty

Homeland security has been defined by U.S. political elites in the narrowest of terms, referring primarily to the protection of people in the United States from threats emanating from abroad. There is little concern on the part of political elites with other, equally important, forms of domestic security. President Franklin D. Roosevelt, as chapter 1 revealed, had a much more nuanced and holistic sense of the meaning of *security*. In his view, the term meant "not only physical security which provides safety from attacks by aggressors" but also "economic security, social security, moral security."[9] In proposing that the United States adopt an Economic Bill of Rights to supplement the political and civil rights protected by the first ten amendments to the U.S. Constitution, Roosevelt commented that "rights spell security."[10]

Roosevelt strongly believed that everyone had the right to an adequate standard of living, including those who were unable to work: "I assert that modern society, acting through its Government, owes the definite obligation to prevent the starvation or dire want of any of its fellow men and women who try to maintain themselves but cannot."[11] He also asserted, "If, as our Constitution tells us, our Federal Government was established among other things, 'to promote the general welfare,' it is our plain duty to provide for that security upon which welfare depends... The security of the home, the security of livelihood, and the security of social insurance are, it seems to me, a minimum... of the promise that we can offer to the American people."[12] In Roosevelt's view, the security provided by government's respect for people's economic rights was as important to their democratic freedoms as political and civil rights guarantees.

Roosevelt noted that "governments can err... Better the occasional faults of a Government that lives in a spirit of charity than the consistent omissions of a Government frozen in the ice of its own indifference."[13] It is difficult to avoid concluding that the U.S. government is "frozen in the ice of its own indifference" when it comes to the well-being of impoverished lone-mother-headed families. This indifference is communicated through the harsh treatment of such families under welfare reform, where success is measured by reduced caseloads and not reduced poverty. It is communicated by federal budgetary decisions privileging militarism over programs that would help impoverished U.S. families with income support, child care, health care, housing, and food. It is communicated not only by skewed federal spending priorities but also by tax cuts for the wealthy that contribute heavily to the federal deficit and make it increasingly difficult to fund domestic social programs. Finally, the indifference is communicated by the glaring gap between the economic security and well-being of lone-mother-headed families in the United States compared to their counterparts in other affluent nations, which was examined in chapter 5.

The U.S. government clearly does not "live in a spirit of charity" when it comes to this nation's poor. The next section discusses a newly arisen movement working to bring about respect for economic human rights in the United States. Participants in this movement are not interested in stimulating charitable spirit on the part of government. Instead of calling for expressions of charitable benevolence on the part of government—which experience shows is likely to be paternalistic, conditional, and subject to arbitrary withdrawal—this movement seeks to establish poverty as a human rights violation that the U.S. government must take steps to eradicate under international law.

Attacking Poverty as a Violation of Economic Human Rights

The Kensington Welfare Rights Union

The Kensington Welfare Rights Union (KWRU) is a multiracial, grassroots antipoverty organization based in Philadelphia.[14] It was started in 1991 by five mothers angered by the treatment they were receiving under the state's welfare program and by their inability to find decent and affordable housing for their families. The mothers believed that neither they nor others should have to accept the harmful conditions found in Kensington, the deeply impoverished Philadelphia neighborhood in which they lived. The mothers formed KWRU to collectively fight these conditions and began organizing protests by poor and homeless people.

The union has since grown in numbers and in the diversity of its membership, but the organization continues to be under the leadership of persons who are poor, and in some cases homeless. Its policies are formulated by its leaders' War Council, so named in recognition of the U.S. government's "War on the Poor." KWRU is concerned that those living in poverty have largely been excluded from discussions of government policies affecting them, such as welfare reform. This exclusion has taken place despite the fact that, in the view of KWRU, the poor are in a better position than anyone else to know what must be changed to end poverty. KWRU takes the position that ending poverty will take a mass movement and that this movement must be led by poor people to be effective.

The organization has become well known for organizing large-scale, militant demonstrations and marches aimed at ending the political invisibility and silencing of the poor. KWRU has, for example, organized "Bushville" tent encampments on city lots to emphasize the similarity between the plight of impoverished families today and that of Depression-era families whose lack of jobs, incomes, or homes forced them into "Hooverville" squatter communities. In Philadelphia, the activities of KWRU have included illegal takeovers of abandoned housing units owned by the U.S. Department of Housing and Urban Development, which the organization has turned into "human rights houses" sheltering homeless families.

The organization began to articulate its antipoverty concerns within the framework of international human rights principles shortly after Congress passed federal welfare reform in 1996. Viewing poverty from the standpoint of the economic human rights provisions of the Universal Declaration of Human Rights, KWRU concluded that it was an economic human rights violation. The Universal Declaration gave KWRU a new language with which to frame its members' experiences; the notion that poor people possessed economic human rights—internationally recognized rights the U.S. government was failing to respect—gave KWRU a new sense of empowerment and a vision of a better future as it planned and undertook protest activities.

KWRU discovered that a focus on human rights can be highly unifying. Belief in the existence of universal human rights can bring together people frequently divided along the lines of identity politics or isolated from one another in the course of pursuing single-issue causes. KWRU found that its use of human rights discourse worked to further the diversity of its membership, allies, and supporters. Its numerous and highly visible protest activities in Philadelphia and elsewhere have been notably inclusive of both men and women, whites and people of color, the able-bodied and people with disabilities, children and elders, those who are straight and those who are gay, the unemployed and members of labor unions, immigrants and the native born, welfare recipients and professionals in health care, education, and law.

Over the last decade, KWRU has delivered its call for an end to poverty well beyond the Philadelphia area. Its members have traveled to cities and towns across the United States. They have given talks and lectures, have formed alliances with other groups and organizations, have encouraged people to document economic human rights violations, and have garnered support for protests and marches in which poverty is framed as a human rights issue. KWRU has cooperated in the filming of videos that document its economic human rights protests and related activities, and it has issued a detailed report on economic rights violations in the United States.[15] KWRU members have journeyed to other nations, particularly underdeveloped nations, and have participated in such international events as the 2005 World Social Forum in Brazil. The organization has found that human rights discourse is a language of solidarity, binding together people from different locations and cultures, all of whom are engaged in struggles against poverty.

The successes of KWRU in using a human rights framework in its organizing and protest activities became crucial to its decision to help to build a nationwide movement to end poverty. In 1998 KWRU convened a Poor People's Summit on Human Rights at Temple University in Philadelphia. The summit meeting attracted grassroots groups from across the United States, all intrigued by the promise they saw in using human rights principles in the struggle against poverty. The Poor People's Economic Human Rights Campaign (PPEHRC) emerged the following year out of discussions that took place at this summit, and KWRU has been the lead organization in the conduct of this campaign.[16]

The Poor People's Economic Human Rights Campaign

At the national level, the prototypical U.S. antipoverty organization often operates under the direction of well-educated salaried professionals seeking to articulate the needs of (and, in effect, speak for) the poor. Such organizations often portray government assistance to the poor as a moral obligation and argue that such assistance is a socially beneficial and ultimately cost-effective investment for taxpayers in human capital. They do not consider ending poverty in the United States to be a politically realistic goal and are generally wary of pursuing the issue of economic redistribution. Instead of calling for an overall attack on economic inequality and an end to poverty, the prototypical antipoverty organization lobbies Congress and the White House for support of existing programs, trying to hold the line against cutbacks that would adversely affect low-income people. Such organizations, though often critical of the failure of political elites to do more to address the needs of the poor, are unlikely to protest in ways that offend the sensibilities of those whose spending and policy decisions they hope to influence.

Imagine, then, the emergence of a whole different type of national antipoverty organization. The Poor People's Economic Human Rights Campaign began to take form in 1999.[17] PPEHRC is not an organization directed by salaried professionals; rather, it is more of a loose-knit social movement involving over fifty grassroots groups located across the United States. Recall that Kensington Welfare Rights Union is a lead organization in PPEHRC: It has not only played a major role in shaping its goals, structure, and activities but also is at the forefront of most of the actions of the PPEHRC. The movement's national coordinator in 2005, Cheri Honkala, a formerly homeless single mother, was also the director (and an original founder) of KWRU.

Like KWRU, the PPEHRC is led by people who are poor, with nonpoor participants asked to serve primarily as supporters, resources, and allies to the cause. The goal of the PPEHRC is simply put: to end poverty in the United States. Movement participants are not interested in simply reducing the incidence of poverty, a notion leading some to ask rhetorically, "So, which of your children would you choose to remain poor?" Nor are participants interested in seeing poverty better managed by government agencies and their programs as opposed to being abolished.

The activities of the PPEHRC are variable and often imaginative, including freedom bus tours to gather information on economic human rights violations experienced by individuals across the United States, the filing of complaints about U.S. government economic human rights violations before international bodies, and militant demonstrations against political elites' indifference to domestic poverty at the 2002 Winter Olympics in Salt Lake City, Utah, and the 2004 Republican national convention in New York City. The educational and training arm of the PPEHRC is called the University of the Poor, a web-based institution through which PPEHRC develops leadership in the movement. The university covers such topics as social movement history and effective organizing models.[18]

Rather than being fearful of offending the sensibilities of U.S. political elites, PPEHRC participants have actively sought to embarrass the U.S. government internationally for its failure to seriously address domestic poverty. Through use of the Internet and direct contacts with grassroots antipoverty organizations in other nations, the PPEHRC has opened up lines of communication that allow it to draw worldwide attention to poverty conditions within the United States. As it condemns these conditions, the PPEHRC outspokenly criticizes the U.S. government for its failure to recognize and respect economic human rights.

In early 2003, the PPEHRC issued a declaration "on the full realization of human rights in the United States."[19] The declaration cited inspiration drawn from Mahatma Gandhi's statement that "poverty is the worst form of violence," and Dr. Martin Luther King's observation that "'if a [person] doesn't have a job or an income [s]he has neither life, nor liberty, nor the possibility for the pursuit of happiness."[20] In this declaration, the PPEHRC endorsed the principles contained in the Universal Declaration of Human Rights, along with key international human rights treaties, such as the International Covenant on Economic, Social and Cultural Rights. Among the rights the PPEHRC made specific reference to in the declaration are human rights to education, health, housing, food, work, and social security, about which the PPEHRC said, "The *right to social security* guarantees an adequate livelihood, sufficient to meet all basic needs consonant with dignified life, to every member of society" [italics in original].[21]

The declaration of the PPEHRC noted that the U.S. government has abandoned the commitment to providing economic security contained in President Franklin D. Roosevelt's Economic Bill of Rights. The PPEHRC also pointed out that the U.S. government's resistance to the application of economic human rights standards has undermined such rights both at home and abroad: "[T]he United States has vigorously opposed the realization of economic and social rights, claiming that such rights are merely 'aspirational,' and that governments should not be held accountable for guaranteeing them. Using its global power and prestige to block the development of economic and social rights, the United States has undermined the dignity and well-being of countless poor persons around the world."[22]

In the declaration's Call to Action, the PPEHRC called on the U.S. government to ratify the International Covenant on Economic, Social, and Cultural Rights and to ensure that international human rights standards are adopted and implemented at all levels of government within the United States. Among the many other actions it listed as needed, the PPEHRC called for the U.S. government to restore and improve the safety net removed by 1990s welfare reform and to guarantee all people in the United States a basic minimum income allowing them to "lead a dignified life" as a matter of right.[23]

The next section discusses some of the criticisms of the U.S. government's economic human rights record recently coming from other nations and also from human rights-based groups within the United States. Then a description will be given of the unprecedented appeals of the PPEHRC to the international human rights community for relief from such economic human rights violations, among which it includes welfare reform.

Taking the U.S. Government to Task in the International Human Rights Arena

Criticisms of the U.S. Government's Economic Human Rights Record

The PPEHRC has rejected the notion that existing welfare reform policy will help end poverty. U.S. courts have deemed welfare benefits to be a privilege and not a right, and the courts do not recognize any responsibility on the part of government to uphold economic human rights.[24] The PPERHC has turned to the international community and has been bold about taking the U.S. government to task as an economic human rights violator. The actions of the PPEHRC in this regard are intended to raise public awareness of economic human rights and to put pressure on U.S. political elites to meet the nation's international human rights obligations.[25]

The appeals by the PPERHC to international human rights bodies are consistent with complaints from other nations and human rights watchdog groups that view the U.S. government's human rights commitment as shallow. Each year the U.S. Department of State issues a human rights report in which it criticizes violations reported to have taken place in over 190 nations and regions. *Country Reports on Human Rights Practices* largely reports on civil and political rights violations (economic rights violations have not been cited in the State Department's report since President Jimmy Carter's administration).[26] The State Department excludes the United States from its annual human rights report, a fact that has not gone unnoticed abroad.

Following the annual human rights report issued by the State Department in 2000, and every year since, China has issued a detailed report commenting on the human rights record of the United States.[27] Among the numerous human rights concerns China addressed in a report issued in 2005 is that the U.S. government has refused to ratify the International Covenant on Economic, Social, and Cultural Rights. The report offered detailed commentary on the high level of economic inequality in the

United States, as well as the high incidence of poverty (including child poverty), homelessness, food insecurity, and unmet health care needs. China's report also devoted a good deal of attention to discriminatory treatment and other problems experienced by people of color and women in the United States. All of these matters were presented in the report as human rights violations the United States was refusing to acknowledge, even as the U.S. government accused China and numerous other nations of being human rights violators. China's report concluded by stating, "No country in the world can claim itself as perfect and has no room for improvement in the human rights area. And no country should... view itself as the incarnation of human rights, which can reign over other countries and give orders to the others... [T]he United States should reflect on its erroneous behavior on human rights and take its own human rights problems seriously."[28] According to media reports, the criticisms of the United States in China's report were echoed by sentiments expressed in the capitals of other nations such as Russia, Mexico, Turkey, and Venezuela.[29]

The kinds of criticisms being made by government officials in these other nations are made increasingly by human rights-based organizations in the United States as well. In 2005 the US Human Rights Network (an association of more than 160 U.S.-based human rights organizations, to be discussed later in this chapter) issued a public memorandum to President George W. Bush.[30] This memorandum was also in response to the State Department's annual *Country Reports on Human Rights Practices.* The network noted the failure of the United States to ratify important international human rights treaties, including those addressing economic human rights. Much like China, besides charging the U.S. government with civil and political human rights violations, the network addressed violations of the right to health, housing, and work providing fair wages and a decent living for workers and their families. The network memorandum concluded that "the human rights situation within the U.S. calls for serious self-assessment and reflection" and noted that the United States "is at grave risk of becoming a place where human dignity and freedom are routinely denied."[31]

The failure of the U.S. government to implement economic human rights standards domestically led the PPEHRC to take the unprecedented step of filing formal complaints about the United States in the international human rights arena.

Petitioning the Inter-American Commission on Human Rights

For several years the PPEHRC and its allies have gathered individual testimonies to document economic human rights violations in the United

States and have sought to bring them to the attention of the United Nations and other international organizations. Its principal legal strategy, however, has focused on petitioning the Inter-American Commission on Human Rights (IACHR), which meets in Washington, D.C. This commission was established under the charter of the Organization of American States (OAS), a regional organization in which the United States holds membership.

The United States is one of thirty-four member-nations of the OAS and ratified its charter in 1968. OAS nations are located in the Western hemisphere and include Canada as well as nations in Central and South America and the Caribbean. The purpose of the IACHR is to promote the observance and protection of international human rights. It advises the OAS, but has no independent enforcement powers. In the past its findings regarding human rights violations have often been disputed or ignored by the United States. For a variety of legal and practical reasons, PPEHRC chose IACHR as the international body before which to make its case.[32]

The PPEHRC filed a petition with the IACHR in 1999 that broadly challenged federal welfare reform legislation for violating, among other things, people's rights to an adequate standard of living, food, housing, and social security.[33] The PPEHRC charged that the United States was not helping people progressively realize their economic human rights consistent with available resources, as was called for under the International Covenant of Economic, Social and Cultural Rights.[34] In asking the IAHRC to find the United States in violation of the principles of international human rights law, the PPEHRC stated that U.S. welfare reform legislation was "a cruel and illegal retrogression in the provision of survival benefits to the poor."[35] As the PPEHRC put it, despite a healthy national economy in the 1990s and federal government surpluses to which this economic health had contributed, "social welfare policies in the United States have led to increasing inequality of income, with the harshest consequences, such as hunger, lack of health care, and homelessness, falling principally on single mothers and their children."[36]

The 1999 petition was later withdrawn for procedural reasons, and its contents were then reworked by some of the legal allies of the PPEHRC. In 2004, the PPEHRC again petitioned the IACHR, reiterating the retrogression in the protection of economic human rights occurring in the United States and charging that the U.S. government's actions "are now being emulated by less economically powerful OAS member states, causing untold damage to the progressive realization of social and economic rights in the Americas."[37] In its 2004 petition, the PPEHRC questioned the United States' failure to protect rights to housing, health care, and social security.

U.S. actions, it stated, were in violation of international and regional human rights treaties, such as the American Declaration of the Rights and Duties of Man—a human rights agreement considered binding on all OAS members, though the United States has chosen not to ratify it and in the past has refused to be bound by its provisions. In its petition, the PPEHRC took specific note of federal welfare reform legislation's abolition of entitlement to cash welfare benefits and the time limits on receipt of benefits it imposed. Such actions were not undertaken, the PPEHRC noted, because of a lack of available resources. They were "policy choices taken which are incompatible with human rights standards."[38]

In early 2005, the PPEHRC followed up its petition by requesting that the IAHRC hold an immediate hearing on violations of the human right to housing and also that later hearings be held on violations of the right to health care and adequate income security. The hearing on housing rights was quickly granted by the IAHRC. At that historic hearing, IAHRC commissioners accepted testimony from organizations concerned with housing rights violations not only in the United States, but also in Canada and Brazil. Those testifying on the United States addressed such topics as the U.S. government's withdrawal of commitment to public housing, forced evictions and the demolition of existing public housing facilities without adequate replacement, the lack of affordable housing for families with low incomes, and the problem of homelessness.[39] The PPEHRC issued a formal invitation to IAHRC commissioners to view some of the public housing conditions in Chicago and Philadelphia and to interact with people suffering housing rights violations.

The PPEHRC, along with KWRU and other allies, has been making important strides in calling international attention to the U.S. government's economic human rights record. In concert with a number of organizations not formally affiliated with it, the PPEHRC has also begun working on the individual state level to pressure state governments to integrate human rights standards into their laws and policies.

Bringing Human Rights Standards to the Individual States

The Pennsylvania Campaign

Economic Human Rights–Pennsylvania (EHR–PA) offers a model for how other economic human rights activists might use legislative tactics to open up public debate and to build awareness regarding the need to apply international human rights standards at the individual state level.[40] EHR–PA is a joint project of PPEHRC, KWRU, and the Pennsylvania Chapter of the National Association of Social Workers. In 2002, EHR–PA enlisted the help of a Democratic state representative, Lawrence Curry, from a district outside of Philadelphia. While Curry's district was over-whelmingly Republican, he had previously demonstrated support of the activities of KWRU and agreed to assist EHR–PA in a new and unusual undertaking.

EHR–PA was not interested in using the legislative process as a possible solution to end poverty, as it believed only a mass movement led by the poor could produce that result. Rather, it wanted to use the legislative pro-cess to educate people about and to organize them around economic human rights issues as a part of building that mass movement. At the urg-ing of EHR–PA, in spring 2002 Curry introduced a resolution into the state's House (HR 473), which called for the establishment of a select com-mittee that would "study and investigate the integration of human rights standards in Pennsylvania laws and policies."[41] This select committee would be empowered to hold public hearings and to receive testimony. Following a major lobbying effort by EHR–PA and its supporters, the reso-lution passed in the Republican-dominated Pennsylvania state legislature. EHR–PA participants then worked with Curry to organize hearings in communities around the state.

Throughout the hearing process, people living in poverty and their allies presented testimonies regarding their experiences with the violation of economic human rights, testimonies prepared under the guidance and with the support of EHR–PA. The community hearings received a good deal of media attention, thus fulfilling the intention of EHR–PA that the legislative process be used as an awareness-building and grassroots orga-nizing tool to help build support for ending economic human rights viola-tions. The EHR–PA campaign brought together groups of people that typically did not unite and work collectively for a common cause, such as social work professionals and the unemployed and impoverished. Cam-paign organizers viewed this unity as important to building a mass move-ment to end poverty.

Some matters arose in the course of testimonies on rights violations to which legislators felt state government could rather easily attend. Encour-aged by that feature of the hearings, in 2003 the legislature unanimously approved a new resolution (HR 144) to continue the study and to allow for more hearings. This resolution opened the way for even more awareness building and organizing by EHR–PA around economic human rights in Pennsylvania, and local economic human rights committees began to form as a consequence of this process of movement building.

In late 2004, the select committee issued a final report in which it made the following statements: "The Committee finds that in development of economic and social policy to address the issues brought forth in these hearings, it is critical to define economic human rights as those basic individual rights to health care, nutrition, housing, quality education, and sustainable employment at a living wage. It is further critical to view poverty as an individual, family, and a community's inability to access even one of these basic rights… [T]he General Assembly should continue to appropriately investigate the systems and barriers that are in place, which inhibit the fulfillment of an individual's economic human rights. This recognition and analysis of how to move forward in an effort to improve these systems will benefit all Pennsylvanians."[42]

Having opened up discussion of the need for Pennsylvania state government to respect economic human rights, it is expected that efforts to keep this discussion going will continue to be used by EHC–PA as a valuable organizing tool. Its successful efforts have already begun serving as a model for action elsewhere at the individual state level.

The Massachusetts Human Rights Bill

The success of the economic human rights efforts of EHC–PA in Pennsylvania helped to spark a movement to pass similar legislation in Massachusetts. This more recent effort came about under the leadership of the Massachusetts Convention on the Elimination of All Forms of Discrimination Against Women (CEDAW) Project, a coalition of organizations and individuals interested in bringing international human rights law to bear on domestic issues, especially discrimination. The convention is an international treaty signed by President Jimmy Carter in 1980 but never ratified by the U.S. Senate. The CEDAW Project's collaborators include Amnesty International USA, the Massachusetts Welfare Rights Union, Survivors, Inc. (also a welfare rights group), and Women's International League for Peace and Freedom.[43] While the CEDAW Project is not affiliated with the PPEHRC, it shares its concern with "bringing human rights home." One of its collaborators, the Massachusetts Welfare Rights Union, is a PPEHRC member.

In 2005 the CEDAW Project and its allies, organizing under the umbrella name The Massachusetts Human Rights for All Initiative, were successful in gaining support for the introduction of the Massachusetts Human Rights Bill.[44] House Bill 706, introduced by Representative Ellen Story of Amherst, Massachusetts, is similar to the two resolutions passed in the Pennsylvania legislature. It calls for the creation of a special commission "to investigate the integration of international human rights standards into Massachusetts state law and policies."[45] However, the Massachusetts bill is unique in that it not only requests a series of hearings in which the public will be able to report on human rights abuses, including violations of their economic human rights; it also requires a technical review of Massachusetts law to be undertaken from a human rights legal perspective.

The CEDAW Project is hopeful that the recommendations of this special commission will ultimately result in legislation bringing international human rights standards to bear throughout the Massachusetts legal code. An open letter issued by the CEDAW Project, calling for organizational endorsements of House Bill 706, put it this way: "Approaching state governance from a human rights perspective will have enormous implications for those populations most vulnerable to human rights abuses: prisoners, immigrants, recipients of state benefits, especially women, children, and the elderly."[46]

The CEDAW Project takes note of the fact that the U.S. government is not a party to important human rights treaties, including the International Covenant on Economic, Social, and Cultural Rights. It points out that these treaties have higher standards of rights protection than does the U.S. Constitution and require that government take proactive steps to prevent human rights violations from occurring. In literature calling for support and endorsements of the Massachusetts Human Rights Bill, the CEDAW Project discusses the significance of undertaking a strategy pressing for the adoption "of human rights standards at the nonfederal level. Local use of treaties is an innovative strategy that enables activists to bypass federal resistance to international human rights standards, and instead focus on putting those standards to work right in our own communities… Local human rights legislation can be a first step towards progressive adoption of international law at the federal level."[47]

In its literature, the CEDAW Project also makes specific reference to human rights deficiencies of the state's TANF policies, administered by the Massachusetts Department of Transitional Assistance. The CEDAW Project cites mandatory work requirements that lead to jobs with poverty-level wages, cash-benefit time limits, the denial of cash assistance to children born to mothers on the welfare rolls, and the lack of supporting social services that would help mothers balance work and family responsibilities. All of these policies are, in its view, contrary to international human rights law and principles. The treatment of lone-mother-headed families in Massachusetts will require significant change if evaluated through a human rights lens.

California's Statewide Economic Human Rights Campaign

Not all economic human rights activities aimed at the individual state level involve strategies whereby human rights activists make use of state legislatures. The California Poor People's Economic Human Rights Campaign is a case in point. The California Campaign is spearheaded by the Women's Economic Agenda Project (WEAP), based in Oakland, and the Community Homeless Alliance Ministry, based in San Jose, a collaboration of which the campaign is an outgrowth.[48] The Women's Economic Agenda Project is a social justice organization in existence since 1982. Both organizations are members of the national PPEHRC. In 1998 WEAP was visited by the director of KWRU, Cheri Honkala, and was invited to join KWRU and other grassroots groups in being a member of what was to become the PPEHRC. In light of subsequent vigorous involvement in economic human rights activities, which have included organizing protest marches, teach-ins, demonstrations, tribunals, and statewide freedom bus tours of California poverty areas, WEAP could easily be characterized as "the KWRU of the West Coast."

Among its numerous other activities, including a major effort to promote health care as a human right in cooperation with labor organizations and other groups, the California Campaign has undertaken the formation of local Poor People's Economic Human Rights Committees throughout the state. The activities of these local committees, of which there are over two dozen, include collecting documentation of economic human rights violations. By 2005, some 2,000 violations had been documented. The California Campaign believes that it is important for such committees to record people's experiences with human rights abuses but that it should be done not just for the sake of evidence gathering. Documentation activities are seen as an important part of the process by which people can be educated about their economic human rights, as set forth in such documents as the Universal Declaration of Human Rights.[49]

The significance the California Campaign (and the PPEHRC in general) attaches to documentation of human rights violations for educational purposes should not be viewed casually. It has been mentioned already here that the United States lacks a "human rights culture" for which government and political elites at all levels bear responsibility. In the United States, human rights discourse is not a normal part of people's lived experience.[50] People in the United States have been left abysmally ignorant about just what their human rights are. Moreover, most do not realize that the U.S. government acknowledged the importance of respecting these rights when it voted for the United Nations to adopt the Universal Declaration of Human Rights in 1948.

In 1997, Human Rights U.S.A. commissioned a national survey in connection with the then-upcoming fiftieth anniversary of the Universal Declaration. The survey included the following question: "As far as you know, is there an official document that sets forth human rights for everyone worldwide? (If so) Can you tell me the name of that document?" Only 8 percent of U.S. adults and 4 percent of U.S. high school juniors and seniors were aware of the Universal Declaration of Human Rights and able to correctly name it.[51] This is the kind of ignorance the California Campaign and many other human rights-based groups are now seeking to overcome.

The California Campaign urges its economic human rights committees to frame local issues in human rights terms and to link these issues to the goals of the PPEHRC: "If you are engaged in local battles over housing, healthcare, a living wage or any other economic human rights issue, link it to the broader movement to end poverty in the U.S. This broader vision keeps us clear on our long-term goals as we engage in our local battles. This way we can articulate what we are for, not only what we are against."[52] The strategy is to encourage people to think about their poverty-related problems in ways that call upon a set of values that are not parochial but that instead speak to universal human needs. These values can be found in human rights discourse.

Linking Local Economic Human Rights Violations to International Law

The Urban Justice Center is a nongovernmental organization founded in New York City in 1984. The center performs outreach work in impoverished communities and advocates for changes in social policy and for legal reforms that will serve the interests of low-income people in the city. For some years now, the center's Human Rights Project has been addressing economic human rights, including rights violated by welfare reform.

In 2000, the Human Rights Project issued a hard-hitting report, *Hunger Is No Accident*, which documented the ways in which both New York and federal welfare reform policies were violating people's human right to food.[53] The project noted that the right to food is guaranteed under international human rights law; it is mentioned in the Universal Declaration as well as in various human rights treaties, but is not recognized by the U.S. government or, apparently, by New York City officials. In the words of *Hunger Is No Accident*, "In New York City, government officials (under welfare reform) routinely deny needy applicants access to welfare and food stamps through the use of diversion, programmatic barriers, discrimination, degradation and arbitrary and inappropriate case closings."[54] One result, according to the report, is that 400,000 residents of New York City live in households suffering from hunger, and demands being placed on emergency food assistance, soup kitchens, and food pantries are outpacing resources. The project recommended to the New York City government that it "acknowledge the obligation to 'respect,' 'protect,' and 'fulfill' the human right to food."[55]

The Human Rights Project also looked into the relationship between skin color and people's treatment under welfare reform, an issue addressed in chapter 4. In a report on this topic, the project noted that the adverse impacts of welfare reform were not equally distributed along racial lines and pointed out that this was frequently hidden by New York City's use of "race-blind" aggregate data to describe the welfare recipient population.[56] The project's survey of 335 people at 35 New York City social service agencies found that people of color frequently experienced discriminatory treatment when they visited welfare offices. Although African Americans and Latino families were more likely than whites to live in severe poverty conditions and to experience food insecurity, they were also more likely than whites to confront unlawful tactics being used to divert applicants from accessing the welfare rolls.

While citing welfare reform in general as a human rights violation, the project drew attention to the fact that racial discrimination in the administration of welfare is also a human rights violation.[57] In New York City, some 80 percent of adult TANF recipients—who for the most part are women—were African-American or Latino in 2000. In 2001 the project sent a report to the United Nations in which it criticized both the U.S. government's and New York City's failure to comply with the economic human rights provisions of the International Convention on the Elimination of Racial Discrimination (ICERD).[58] Access to and the adequacy of public benefits such as welfare and food stamps were singled out as being problematic, especially for impoverished women of color.[59]

In a 2002 report, subtitled *Pushing Recipients Deeper into Poverty*, the Human Rights Project systematically examined the economic human rights violations that were an outcome of welfare reform. In the project's words, "Welfare reform has done little to promote poverty reduction… Instead, it has caused increased deprivation of many fundamental human rights, such as the right to food, health, and housing. These conditions are not luxuries, but rather, basic human rights linked to the right to education, the right to employment, and the right to an adequate standard of living. As a member of the United Nations, the U.S. has an obligation to fulfill these rights, which are outlined in numerous international documents, particularly the Universal Declaration of Human Rights."[60]

In 2004, the Urban Justice Center sent a representative to Geneva, Switzerland, to testify before the sixtieth session of the UN Commission on Human Rights. The United States is one of two nations—the other is Somalia—that has not ratified the Convention on the Rights of the Child.

This international human rights treaty, like a number of others, contains important economic human rights provisions. The center's representative urged the commission to consider child poverty in New York City a human rights violation for which the U.S. government should be held responsible. The representative urged the United States to put children at the center of its concern and to ratify the convention.

The Urban Justice Center's Human Rights Project is one of the coordinators of the New York City Human Rights Initiative (along with Amnesty International USA and several other organizations). The initiative, formed in 2002, is a citywide coalition and has over eighty members.[61] At its urging, in 2004 the New York City Council agreed to consider the adoption of an ordinance that would bring two international human rights treaties, CEDAW and ICERD, to bear on city governance. Hearings on this ordinance to amend the New York City administrative code were held in 2005. With the adoption of this ordinance, New York would be only the second city in the nation to implement CEDAW (the other is San Francisco, discussed following) and the very first city to implement ICERD. The Human Rights Government Operations Audit Law would require that the city's agencies take a variety of steps to proactively root out racial and gender discrimination in resource allocation, service delivery, and employment practices. The most direct beneficiaries of bringing these human rights standards to bear on New York City governance would be women, people of color, and the poverty population.

The Urban Justice Center is only one of a growing number of grassroots groups and established organizations that are framing poverty in economic human rights terms. The next section discusses a new network structure that is knitting these groups and organizations together. This network is striving to address human rights, including economic human rights, and to build a human rights culture within the United States, drawing upon the strength of collective action.

The US Human Rights Network

Genesis of the Network

Since its formation in 1996, the Women's Institute for Leadership Development in Human Rights (WILD) has led a largely grassroots campaign to get the United States to ratify the Convention on the Elimination of All Forms of Discrimination Against Women.[62] Its campaign has included bringing the human rights standards of CEDAW into play in local communities. WILD led the effort that pressured San Francisco in 1998 to become the first city in the nation to adopt an ordinance implementing

CEDAW locally. This ordinance requires that San Francisco apply the human rights principles contained in this international treaty to eliminate gender discrimination in employment, resource allocation, and the delivery of services.[63]

In 1999, WILD held a ground-breaking conference of U.S. human rights activists from across the United States—people framing domestic issues in international human rights terms. The twenty-two attendees were all women, most of whom were human rights attorneys, academics, or leaders of various nongovernmental organizations, but they had interests and experiences in a wide range of different human rights areas besides gender. Cheri Honkala, the director of KWRU, was one of the participants involved in economic human rights issues. At this conference, those present closely examined and assessed the state of human rights work and human rights-based social change strategies within the United States.

WILD subsequently issued a comprehensive report intended to contribute to the development and momentum of the newly emerging interest in addressing human rights within the United States.[64] In it, WILD identified a number of needs to be met, including the "expanded use of information and communications technology for information-sharing, outreach, advocacy, and networking."[65] WILD also saw the need for "the creation of an organizing/networking structure that integrates U.S. human rights work both vertically and horizontally," which it called a "U.S. Human Rights Network."[66] It would not be long before such a network began to be created.

Birth of the Network

In 2002, a large leadership summit of human rights activists took place at the Howard University Law School in Washington, D.C. The summit meeting was titled "Ending Exceptionalism: Strengthening Human Rights in the United States." It brought together greater numbers of people and broadened the diversity of those engaged in the conversation WILD began. The US Human Rights Network was an outcome of this summit meeting. The network's birth was announced on December 10, 2003, a date annually celebrated worldwide as International Human Rights Day. The network's founding members ranged from well-known international human rights watchdog organizations, such as Amnesty International USA and Human Rights Watch, to on-the-ground grassroots groups such as KWRU, WEAP, The Urban Justice Center, and WILD.[67] The presence of such founding organizations as Amnesty and Human Rights Watch in the network is highly significant, as these organizations had traditionally limited their focus to civil and political rights and to violations of these human rights abroad. In recent years these two organizations have shifted their focus to include the United States and have also begun to address economic human rights violations.[68]

At the time the network's creation was announced in late 2003, over fifty organizations had agreed to become members and to join the movement to end human rights violations in the United States. These numerous organizations' interests are reflected in the various caucuses the network has formed, which include an Economic and Social Rights caucus. In 2004, the caucus elected Cheri Honkala from KWRU as its representative in the network and also elected the director of WEAP as an alternate representative. As has been discussed, both of those grassroots organizations have been important participants in the Poor People's Economic Human Rights Campaign.

The US Human Rights Network has a number of core principles to which members must adhere. Among these principles are: (1) human rights are protected by building social movements; and (2) social movement leadership must be by the people most directly affected by human rights violations. The mission statement of the Economic and Social Rights Caucus reflects both these principles and is clearly also consistent with the philosophy and goals of the PPEHRC: "The US Human Rights Network Economic and Social Rights Caucus (ESRC) addresses the full range of economic and social rights within the U.S. context, including health, housing, social security, food, education, and work. The ESRC takes its leadership from poor communities—those most affected by economic and social rights violations. It supports the organized poor and takes the position that nothing short of the elimination of poverty meets universal human rights standards. The current mandate of ESRC is to increase public understanding of poverty as a human rights violation, and to support within a human rights framework the efforts of poor people to claim their human rights."[69]

Helping to Build the U.S. Economic Human Rights Movement

Those wanting to contribute to building the movement for economic human rights in the United States have many resources upon which to draw. The US Human Rights Network provides news and information on human rights education and training opportunities and disseminates a resource guide on human rights in the United States,[70] which contains sections on domestic human right abuses, including poverty. The guide also offers guidance on methods and strategies human rights activists are finding useful in their human rights work and in their efforts to create a human rights culture. These include

1. Educating communities about human rights standards
2. Organizing public protest and response to human rights violations
3. Documenting human rights violations
4. Infusing international human rights standards into the U.S. legal system
5. Assessing and shaping U.S. rights policy in human rights terms
6. Producing scholarship that reflects and supports U.S. human rights work.[71]

Most individuals can readily find a useful role to play when it comes to carrying out one or more of the activities in this list, regardless of their station in life.

People doing human rights work, or who are interested in doing so, do not necessarily have to be part of a group or organization to become a participant in the US Human Rights Network's caucuses, including the Economic and Social Rights Caucus. Individuals can join the network and get involved in the caucuses by going to its website (www.ushrnetwork.org) to register. For people wanting to establish organizational ties, the many human rights-based groups and organizations mentioned in this chapter, including the Poor People's Economic Human Rights Campaign, are eager for additional support. All welcome monetary donations and, particularly in the case of grassroots groups, rely heavily on volunteers, collaborators, and allies.

Persons feeling like they lack knowledge about international human rights should not view this as an obstacle to becoming involved. Learning more about human rights is an easy matter. Human rights education materials—both appropriate for use with adults as well as geared toward children and schools—are readily available on the Internet. Particularly helpful websites include

1. Center for Economic and Social Rights (http://www.cesr.org)
2. National Center for Human Rights Education (http://www.nchre.org)
3. University of Minnesota's Human Rights Resource Center (http://www.hrusa.org)
4. People's Movement for Human Rights Education (http://www.pdhre.org)

The numerous human-rights based organizations mentioned in this chapter all have websites that can be highly informative regarding economic human rights issues. (Refer to the endnotes.) Finally, a great deal can be learned about economic human rights from the PPEHRC's University of the Poor (http://universityofthepoor.org).

The "Second Phase" of the Civil Rights Movement: Economic Human Rights

Before his life was taken from him in 1968, Dr. Martin Luther King, Jr., hoped to create a multiracial social movement that would lead to the eradication of gross economic inequalities and poverty in the United States. King envisioned this as the "second phase" of the civil rights movement, the first having been directed at bringing down the barriers posed by racial segregation. He proclaimed, "I think it is necessary to realize that we have moved from the era of civil rights to the era of human rights."[72]

To honor its lost civil rights leader, shortly after King's death the Southern Christian Leadership Conference went forward with the first phase of the Poor People's Campaign King had been busy organizing.[73] They created Resurrection City, a tent shanty town near the Mall in Washington, D.C., which housed poor people from all across the United States. They and their supporters demonstrated in the streets of the nation's capital for over a month, while lobbying U.S. government officials for an "economic bill of rights." Among protestors' demands were a living-wage job for every employable citizen and an adequate and guaranteed income for those who could not work or who could not find jobs. Unfortunately, without King's leadership and inspiration, the Poor People's Campaign and, more generally, the "second phase" of the civil rights movement, soon lost momentum and halted.

The opportunity to complete the second phase of the civil rights movement is, however, here once again. Committed people, many of whom are already working together across the nation, are building a movement to once and for all establish respect for economic human rights within the United States. Such a movement can only draw inspiration from these words by King: "True compassion is more than flinging a coin to a beggar. It comes to see that an edifice which produces beggars needs restructuring."[74] Not only can King's economic human rights agenda be completed—it must be.

Notes

Preface

1. Sharon Parrott, Edwin Park, and Robert Greenstein, "Assessing the Effects of the Budget Conference Agreement on Low-Income Families and Individuals" (Washington, D.C.: Center on Budget and Policy Priorities, December 20, 2005). Available at http://www.cbpp.org/12-20-05bud.htm.

Chapter 1

1. Connecticut Alliance for Basic Human Needs, *Jobs First! (Families Last?): The Lives of Connecticut Families after Welfare Reform* (Hartford, CT: CABHN, 2002), 7.
2. In this book the term *lone mother* is used rather than the more conventional *single mother*. *Lone mother* is frequently used by European scholars in their discussions of welfare policy and is a term that helps to capture the inability of many never-married and divorced mothers to rely on former male partners, family, or personal social networks to help them adequately meet their children's subsistence needs. Such women are, in effect, "on their own." See Jane Lewis, ed., *Lone Mothers in European Welfare Regimes* (London: Jessica Kingsley Publishers, 1997), 3.
3. Sandi Nelson, "Trends in Parents' Economic Hardship," *Snapshots of America's Families3*, no. 21 (March 2004), 2. Available at http://www.urban.org/UploadedPDF/310970_snapshots3_no21.pdf
4. Annual welfare caseload statistics are available at U.S. Department of Health and Human Services. "ACF News, Statistics," http://www.acf.hhs.gov/news/stats/newstat2.shtml. Last accessed October 21, 2005.
5. U.S. Bureau of the Census, *Poverty in the United States: 2002* (Washington, D.C.: U.S. Government Printing Office, 2003), 4. Annual poverty statistics are available at "U.S. Census Bureau, Poverty," http://www.census.gov/hhes/www/poverty/poverty.html. Last accessed October 21, 2005.
6. Sharon Parrott, "House Budget Reconciliation Bill Includes Highly Flawed TANF Provisions That Have Repeatedly Failed to Garner Support" (Washington, D.C.: Center on Budget and Policy Priorities, November 30, 2005). Available at http://www.cbpp.org/11-29-05tanf.htm.
7. This section draws upon Robert F. Drinan, *The Mobilization of Shame* (New Haven, CT: Yale University Press, 2001), ch. 1; David Forsythe, *Human Rights in International Relations* (New York: Cambridge University Press, 2000), ch. 2; and Paul Gordon Lauren, *The*

Evolution of International Human Rights: Visions Seen (Philadelphia: University of Pennsylvania Press, 1998), chs. 7, 8.

8. Center for the Study of Human Rights, *Twenty-Five Human Rights Documents*, 2d ed. (New York: Columbia University Press, 1994), 6.

9. Ibid., 8.

10. Ibid., 8–9.

11. See Cass R. Sunstein, *The Second Bill of Rights: FDR's Unfinished Revolution and Why We Need It More than Ever* (New York: Basic Books, 2004).

12. Franklin D. Roosevelt, "Four Freedoms Speech," *Congressional Record* 87 (1941), 44–47.

13. The quotes immediately following are from that speech. See Franklin D. Roosevelt, "State of the Union Message," *Congressional Record* 90 (1944), 55–57.

14. Ibid.

15. Center for the Study of Human Rights, *Twenty-Five Human Rights Documents*, 12.

16. Ibid., 10–11.

17. See Mathew C. R. Craven, *The International Covenant on Economic, Social, and Cultural Rights: A Perspective on Its Development* (New York: Oxford University Press, 1995).

18. Joseph Wronka, *Human Rights and Social Policy in the 21st Century*, rev. ed. (Lanham, MD: University Press of America, 1998).

19. See Robert Justin Goldstein, "The United States," in *International Handbook of Human Rights*, ed. Jack Donnelly and Rhoda E. Howard (Westport, CT: Greenwood Press, 1987), 429–456; and Drinan, *Mobilization of Shame*, chs. 8–11.

20. Rhoda E. Howard-Hassmann and Claude E. Welch, "Looking at Ourselves," in *Economic Rights in Canada and the United States*, eds. Rhoda Howard-Hassmann and Claude E. Welch (Philadelphia: University of Pennsylvania Press, forthcoming 2006).

21. See Joseph Wronka, "A Little Humility Please: Human Rights and Social Policy in the United States," *Harvard International Review Annual* 64 (1998), 72–75.

22. See, for example, Samantha Power, *A Problem from Hell: America and the Age of Genocide* (New York: Basic Books, 2002).

23. Natalie Hevener Kaufman, *Human Rights Treaties and the Senate: A History of Opposition* (Chapel Hill, NC: University of North Carolina Press, 1990).

24. See Asbjorn Eide, Catarina Krause, and Allan Rosas, eds., *Economic, Social, and Cultural Rights: A Textbook*, 2nd rev. ed. (The Hague, The Netherlands: Kluwer Law International, 2001); and Paul Hunt, *Reclaiming Social Rights: International and Comparative Perspectives* (Aldershot, UK: Dartmouth Publishing Company, 1996).

25. Rhoda E. Howard, *Human Rights and the Search for Community* (Boulder, CO: Westview Press, 1995), ch. 7.

26. Amartya Sen, *Development as Freedom* (New York: Anchor Books, 2000), 8.

27. A guaranteed income, in the form of a negative income tax, was also proposed by President Richard Nixon (1968–1974) in 1969. Aimed primarily at reducing growing welfare costs rather than reducing poverty, Nixon's program was condemned by welfare rights activists for inadequate benefit levels and was criticized by those in Congress opposed in principle to a guaranteed minimum income. It failed to receive congressional approval.

28. Anuradha Mittal and Peter Rosset, eds., *America Needs Human Rights* (Oakland, CA: Food First Books, 1999).

29. Anuradha Mittal, "The Politics of Hunger," *Earth Island Journal* 12 (Spring 1997). Available at http://www.earthisland.org/eijournal/new_articles.cfm?articleID=304&journalID=50.

30. David Weissbrodt, "International Law of Human Rights: A U.S. Perspective," in Howard-Hassmann and Welch, *Economic Rights in Canada and the United States*.

31. Ibid.

32. Ibid.

33. Jeffrey Reiman, *The Rich Get Richer and the Poor Get Prison: Ideology, Class, and Criminal Justice* (Needham Heights, MA: Pearson Allyn & Bacon, 2004).

34. Gwendolyn Mink, *Welfare's End* (Ithaca, NY: Cornell University Press, 2002).

35. William F. Schultz, *In Our Own Best Interest: How Defending Human Rights Benefits Us All* (Boston: Beacon Press, 2002). Schultz, executive director of Amnesty International USA, focuses primarily upon the benefits to the United States of respecting civil and political rights domestically and abroad.

Chapter 2

1. Kenneth J. Neubeck, "Establishing Respect for Economic Human Rights," in *The Promise of Welfare Reform: Results or Rhetoric?*, eds. Keith Kilty and Elizabeth Segal (Binghamton, NY: Haworth Press, forthcoming 2006).

2. Bruce S. Jansson, *The Reluctant Welfare State: A History of American Social Welfare Policies* (Belmont, CA: Wadsworth, 1988).

3. Mimi Abramovitz, *Regulating the Lives of Women: Social Welfare from Colonial Times to the Present* (Boston: South End Press, 1996), 321.

4. Linda Gordon, *Pitied but Not Entitled: Single Mothers and the History of Welfare, 1890–1935* (New York: Free Press, 1994).

5. James T. Patterson, *America's Struggle against Poverty: 1900–1994* (Cambridge, MA: Harvard University Press, 1994), 13. Such percentages are estimates, since official poverty statistics did not begin to be issued by the federal government until 1959.

6. Theda Skocpol, *Protecting Soldiers and Mothers: The Political Origins of Social Policy in the United States* (Cambridge, MA: Belknap Press of Harvard University Press, 1992).

7. Ibid.

8. Gordon, *Pitied but Not Entitled*.

9. Ibid.

10. Winifred Bell, *Aid to Dependent Children* (New York: Columbia University Press, 1965).

11. Kenneth J Neubeck and Noel A. Cazenave, *Welfare Racism: Playing the Race Card against America's Poor* (New York: Routledge, 2001), 44–45.

12. Bell, *Aid to Dependent Children*, 19.

13. Frances Fox Piven and Richard A. Cloward, *Regulating the Poor: The Functions of Public Welfare*, updated ed. (New York: Vintage Books, 1993), ch. 2.

14. Charles Noble, *Welfare as We Knew It: A Political History of the American Welfare State* (New York: Oxford University Press, 1997), ch. 4.

15. Ibid.

16. Piven and Cloward, *Regulating the Poor*, ch. 3.

17. Neubeck and Cazenave, *Welfare Racism*, 47–48.

18. Bell, *Aid to Dependent Children*, 34.

19. Neubeck and Cazenave, *Welfare Racism*, 51–53.

20. Bell, *Aid to Dependent Children*, 29.

21. Theda Skocpol, *Social Policy in the United States: Future Possibilities in Historical Perspective* (Princeton, NJ: Princeton University Press, 1995), 164.

22. Michael Katz, *The Undeserving Poor: From the War on Poverty to the War on Welfare* (New York: Pantheon Books, 1989).

23. Piven and Cloward, *Regulating the Poor*, part 3.

24. Ibid.

25. Martin Gilens, "How the Poor Became Black," in *Race and the Politics of Welfare Reform*, ed. Sanford F. Schram, Joe Soss, and Richard C. Fording (Ann Arbor: University of Michigan Press, 2003), 105.

26. Abramovitz, *Regulating the Lives of Women*, 321.

27. Katz, *Undeserving Poor*, ch. 2.

28. Ibid.

29. Douglas S. Massey and Nancy A. Denton, *American Apartheid: Segregation and the Making of the Underclass* (Cambridge, MA: Harvard University Press, 1993).

30. Raymond S. Franklin, *Shadows of Race and Class* (Minneapolis: University of Minnesota Press, 1991).

31. Neubeck and Cazenave, *Welfare Racism*, 3–7.

32. Martin Gilens, *Why Americans Hate Welfare: Race, Media, and the Politics of Antipoverty Policy* (Chicago: University of Chicago Press, 1999).

33. Kathryn Edin and Laura Lein, *Making Ends Meet: How Single Mothers Survive Welfare and Low-Wage Work* (New York: Russell Sage Foundation, 1997).

34. Noble, *Welfare As We Knew It*, ch. 6.

35. Ibid.

36. Jill Quadagno, *The Color of Welfare: How Racism Undermined the War on Poverty* (New York: Oxford University Press, 1994), ch. 5.

37. Ellen Reese, *Backlash Against Welfare Mothers: Past and Present* (Berkeley: University of California Press, 2005), 6–12.
38. Ibid., 178.
39. Alan Weil and Kenneth Finegold, eds., *Welfare Reform: The Next Act* (Washington, D.C.: Urban Institute Press, 2002). See also U.S. Department of Health and Human Services, Office of the Assistant Secretary for Planning and Evaluation, "Comparison of Prior Law and the Personal Responsibility and Work Opportunity Reconciliation Act of 1996" (P.L. 104–193), http://aspe.os.dhhs.gov/hsp/isp/reform.htm.
40. Lawrence M. Mead, ed., *The New Paternalism: Supervisory Approaches to Poverty* (Washington, D.C.: Brookings Institution Press, 1997). Mead laid the foundations for the *new paternalism* in Mead, *Beyond Entitlement: The Social Obligations of Citizenship* (New York: Basic Books, 1986).
41. Randy Albelda and Chris Tilly, *Glass Ceilings and Bottomless Pits: Women's Work, Women's Poverty* (Boston: South End Press, 1997), app. B.
42. See 108th Congress, 2003–2004, U.S. House of Representatives, H.R.4, "Personal Responsibility, Work, and Family Promotion Act of 2003," available at THOMAS, "HR 4," http://thomas.loc.gov/cgi-bin/query/D?c108:1:./temp/~c108EmhN0o::.
43. Holly Sklar, Laryssa Mykyta, and Susan Wefald, *Raise the Floor: Wages and Policies that Work for All of Us* (Boston: South End Press, 2001).
44. G. William Domhoff, *Who Rules America?: Power and Politics,* 4th ed. (Boston: McGraw-Hill, 2002).
45. Piven and Cloward, *Regulating the Poor.*
46. Ibid., 3–48.
47. Richard L. Zweigenhaft and G. William Domhoff, *Diversity in the Power Elite: Have Women and Minorities Reached the Top?* (New Haven: Yale University Press, 1999).
48. Linda Gordon, ed., *Women, Welfare, and the State* (Madison: University of Wisconsin Press, 1990); and Mimi Abramovitz, *Under Attack, Fighting Back: Women and Welfare in the United States* (New York: Monthly Review Press, 1996).
49. Abramovitz, *Under Attack, Fighting Back,* 102–108.
50. See Albelda and Tilly, *Glass Ceilings and Bottomless Pits,* 65–77.
51. Abramovitz, *Regulating the Lives of Women.*
52. Ibid., 36–40.
53. Mink, *Welfare's End,* 7.
54. Eduardo Bonilla-Silva, *White Supremacy and Racism in the Post-Civil Rights Era* (Boulder, CO: Lynne Rienner, 2001).
55. Stephen Jay Gould, *The Mismeasure of Man,* rev. ed. (New York: W. W. Norton, 1996).
56. Audrey Smedley, *Race in America: Origins and Evolution of a Worldview,* 2nd ed. (Boulder, CO: Westview Press, 1999).
57. Eduardo Bonilla-Silva, *Racism without Racists: Color-Blind Racism and the Persistence of Racial In-equality in the United States* (Lanham, MD: Rowman & Littlefield, 2003).
58. Amy Elizabeth Ansell, *New Right, New Racism: Race and Reaction in the United States and Britain* (New York: New York University Press, 1997).
59. Joe R. Feagin, *Racist America: Roots, Current Realities, and Future Reparations* (New York: Routledge, 2001).
60. This phrase was popularized by the title of William J. Wilson's *The Declining Significance of Race: Blacks and Changing American Institutions* (Chicago: University of Chicago Press, 1978).
61. Bonilla-Silva, *Racism without Racists.*
62. Neubeck and Cazenave, *Welfare Racism.* See also Kenneth J. Neubeck and Noel A. Cazenave, "Welfare Racism and Its Consequences: The Demise of AFDC and the Return of the States' Rights Era," in *Work, Welfare and Politics: Confronting Poverty in the Wake of Welfare Reform,* ed. Frances Fox Piven, Joan Acker, Margaret Hallock, and Sandra Morgen (Eugene: University of Oregon Press, 2002), 35–53.
63. Neubeck and Cazenave, *Welfare Racism,* 36.
64. Ibid., 143–144.
65. Dorothy Roberts, *Killing the Black Body: Race, Reproduction, and the Meaning of Liberty* (New York: Vintage Books, 1997).

66. Neubeck and Cazenave, *Welfare Racism*, 69–114.

67. Ibid., 117–144.

68. Ibid., 213–214.

69. Benjamin Bowser and Raymond G. Hunt, eds. *Impacts of Racism on White Americans* (Thousand Oaks, CA: Sage Publications, 1996).

70. Kenneth J. Neubeck, "Welfare Racism and Human Rights," in Howard-Hassmann and Welch, *Economic Rights in Canada and the United States*.; Kenneth J. Neubeck, "Attacking Welfare Racism/Honoring Poor People's Human Rights," in *Lost Ground: Welfare Reform, Poverty, and Beyond*, eds. Randy Albelda and Ann Withorn (Boston: South End Press, 2002); and Linda Burnham, "Welfare Policy: A Human Rights Issue," Working Paper No. 2 (Oakland, CA: Women of Color Resource Center, 2002), available at http://coloredgirls.org/content.cfm?cat=publication&file=addition.

71. See Patricia Hill Collins, *Black Feminist Thought: Knowledge, Consciousness, and the Politics of Empowerment*, 2nd ed. (New York: Routledge, 2000).

72. Margaret L. Andersen and Patricia Hill Collins, eds., *Race, Class, and Gender,* 5th ed. (Belmont, CA: Wadsworth, 2004).

73. See Reese, *Backlash against Welfare Mothers.*

Chapter 3

1. Institute for Women's Policy Research, "Women's Earnings Fall; U.S. Census Bureau Finds Rising Gender Wage Gap," press release (Washington, D.C.: IWPR, August 27, 2004).

2. "Welfare Receipt (AFDC/TANF)," *Child Trends DataBank*, 2003, available at http://childtrendsdatabank.org/indicators/50AFDCTANF.cfm.

3. Reese, *Backlash Against Welfare Mothers*, 3–19.

4. Federal statistics on recipients of Aid to Families with Dependent Children (AFDC) and Temporary Assistance for Needy Families (TANF) are available at "ACF News, Statistics," http://www.acf.hhs.gov/news/stats/newstat2.shtml. Last accessed October 21. 2005.

5. U.S. Department of Health and Human Services, "HHS Releases Data Showing Continuing Decline in Number of People Receiving Temporary Assistance," news release, September 3, 2003.

6. Edin and Lein, *Making Ends Meet.*

7. Arloc Sherman, Shawn Fremstad, and Sharon Parrott, "Employment Rates for Single Mothers Fell Substantially during Recent Period of Labor Market Weakness" (Washington, D.C.: Center on Budget and Policy Priorities, June 22, 2004), 10, note 19.

8. Sklar, Mykyta, and Wefald, *Raise the Floor*, 118. On the approximately eighteen state-level EITCs, see State EITC Online Resource Center, "State Materials," http://www.stateeitc.org/materials/fact_shts.asp. Last accessed on October 25, 2005.

9. See, for example, Rebecca M. Blank, "Evaluating Welfare Reform in the United States," *Journal of Economic Literature* 40, no. 4 (2002), 1105–1166.

10. Douglas J. Besharov, ed., *Family and Child Well-Being after Welfare Reform* (Somerset, NJ: Transaction Publishers, 2004).

11. U.S. Census Bureau, *Income, Poverty, and Health Insurance Coverage in the United States: 2003* (Washington, D.C.: U.S. Government Printing Office, August 2004), 40.

12. Robert Pear, "Despite the Sluggish Economy, Welfare Rolls Actually Shrank," *New York Times* (March 22, 2004), A21.

13. National Campaign for Jobs and Income Support, "Kicked Off, Kept Off: How TANF Keeps Low-Income People Poor" (Washington, D.C.: NCJIS, February 2002).

14. Michael L. Brown, "Ghettos, Fiscal Federalism, and Welfare Reform," in Schram, Soss, and Fording, eds., *Race and the Politics of Welfare Reform*, 63–68.

15. National Campaign for Jobs and Income Support, "Kicked Off, Kept Off."

16. Sheila R. Zedlewski, Linda Giannarelli, Joyce Morton, and Laura Wheaton, "Extreme Poverty Rising, Existing Government Programs Could Do More," New Federalism Series B, No. B-45 (Washington, D.C.: Urban Institute, April 2002).

17. Gregory Acs, Katherin Ross Phillips, and Sandi Nelson, "The Road Not Taken? Changes in Welfare Entry during the 1990s" (Washington, D.C.: The Urban Institute, December 2003).

18. Fremstad, "Falling TANF Caseloads Amidst Rising Poverty Should Be a Cause of Concern," (Washington, D.C.: Center on Budget and Policy Priorities, September 5, 2003).

19. Center on Budget and Policy Priorities, "Poverty Increases and Median Income Declines for Second Consecutive Year," press release (Washington, D.C.: CBPP, September 26, 2003).

20. Shawn Fremstad, "Falling TANF Caseloads Amidst Rising Poverty Should Be a Cause of Concern."

21. Center on Budget and Policy Priorities, "Poverty Increases and Median Income Declines for Second Consecutive Year."

22. Shawn Fremstad, "Recent Welfare Reform Research Findings: Implications for TANF Reauthorization and State TANF Policies," press release (Washington, D.C.: Center on Budget and Policy Priorities, January 30, 2004).

23. "Children in Working Poor Families," *Child Trends DataBank*, 2003, available at http://childtrendsdatabank.org/indicators/74WorkingPoor.cfm.

24. Pamela Loprest, "Fewer Welfare Leavers Employed in Weak Economy," *Snapshots3*, no. 5 (Washington, D.C.: Urban Institute, August 2003), 1. Available at http://www.urban.org/UploadedPDF/310837_snapshots3_no5.pdf.

25. Ibid.

26. Jeff Chapman and Jared Bernstein, "Falling Through the Safety Net: Low Income Mothers in the Jobless Recovery," *EPI [Economic Policy Institute] Brief* #191 (April 11, 2003), 1.

27. Loprest, "Fewer Welfare Leavers Employed."

28. Ibid.

29. Beth Barrett, "75 Percent of Los Angeles County Welfare Recipients in Poverty," *Los Angeles Daily News* (July 23, 2003), N1.

30. Demetra Smith Nightingale, "Work Opportunities for People Leaving Welfare," in Weil and Finegold, *Welfare Reform,* 104.

31. Heidi Goldberg, "Improving TANF Program Outcomes for Families with Barriers to Employment" (Washington, D.C.: Center on Budget and Policy Priorities, January 22, 2002).

32. See Katherine S. Newman, *No Shame in My Game: The Working Poor in the Inner City* (New York: Vintage Books, 2000).

33. Goldberg, "Improving TANF Program Outcomes for Families with Barriers to Employment," 5.

34. Karen C. Tumlin and Wendy Zimmermann, "Immigrants and TANF: A Look at Welfare Recipients in Three Cities" (Washington, D.C.: Urban Institute, October 2003), 12.

35. Sheila R. Zedlewski and Jennifer Holland, "How Much Do Welfare Recipients Know about Time Limits?" (Washington, D.C.: Urban Institute, December 18, 2003).

36. Pamela Loprest, "Disconnected Welfare Leavers Face Serious Risks," *Snapshots3*, no. 7 (Washington, D.C.: Urban Institute, August 2003), 1.

37. Ibid., 2.

38. Heather Boushey, "Former Welfare Families Need More Help: Hardships Await Those Making Transition to Workforce," *Economic Policy Institute Briefing Paper* (April 1, 2002), 1.

39. Sherman, Fremstad, and Parrott, "Employment Rates for Single Mothers Fell," 3.

40. Heather Boushey and David Rosnick, "For Welfare Reform to Work, Jobs Must Be Available" (Washington, D.C.: Center for Economic and Policy Research, April 2004).

41. Mark Nord, Margaret Andrews, and Steven Carlson, "Household Food Security in the United States, 2002," Food Assistance and Nutrition Research Report No. 35 (Washington, D.C.: U.S. Department of Agriculture, October 2003).

42. Ibid., 9 and 16.

43. Ibid., 14.

44. Food Research and Action Center, "Hunger in the U.S.," 2004, available at http://www.frac.org/html/hunger_in_the_us/hunger_index.html.

45. "Food Stamp Receipt," *Child Trends DataBank*, 2003, available at http://.childtrendsdatabank.org/56FoodStampReceipt.cfm.

46. "Welfare Receipt (AFDC/TANF)."

47. "Food Stamp Receipt."

48. Sheila Zedlewski, "Are Shrinking Caseloads Always a Good Thing?," *Short Takes on Welfare Policy* No. 6 (Washington, D.C.: Urban Institute, June 2002).

49. Sheila Zedlewski, "Recent Trends in Food Stamp Participation: Have New Policies Made a Difference?" (Washington, D.C.: Urban Institute, May 19, 2004), 1.

50. United States Conference of Mayors, "Hunger and Homelessness Survey, 2003" (Washington, D.C.: U.S. Conference of Mayors/Sodexho, December 2003).
51. Centers for Disease Control and Prevention, "Summary Health Statistics for U.S. Adults: National Health Interview Survey, 1997," *Vital and Health Statistics* 10, no. 205 (May 2002), 53.
52. National Center for Health Statistics, *Health, U.S.A.: 2001* (Washington, D.C.: NCHS, 2001).
53. U.S. Census Bureau, *Income, Poverty, and Health Insurance Coverage in the United States 2003*.
54. Kaiser Commission on Medicaid and the Uninsured, *Women Who Left Welfare: Health Care Coverage, Access, and Use of Health Services* (Washington, D.C.: Henry J. Kaiser Family Foundation, June 2002), 1.
55. Ibid., 5, 7.
56. National Low Income Housing Coalition, *Out of Reach 2003: America's Housing Wage Climbs* (Washington, D.C.: NLIHC, September 2003), available at http://www.nlihc.org/oor2003/.
57. Ibid., 6.
58. Sandi Nelson, "Trends in Parents' Economic Hardship," *Snapshots3*, no. 21 (Washington, D.C.: Urban Institute, March 2004), 2.
59. Boushey, "Former Welfare Families Need More Help," 5.
60. Fremstad, "Recent Welfare Reform Research Findings," 17.
61. Ibid.
62. Neubeck and Cazenave, *Welfare Racism*, 147–176.
63. Reese, *Backlash Against Welfare Mothers*, 3–19.
64. Rebecca Cook, "Group Decries Tactics to Reduce Welfare Cases," *Seattle Post-Intelligencer* (August 24, 2004). Available at http://seattlepi.nwsource.com/local/187614_welfare24.html.
65. Ibid.
66. See National Women's Law Center, "NWLC Analysis of New Census Data Finds Poverty of Women and Children Increases for Third Straight Year," press release, August 26, 2004, available at http://www.nwlc.org/details.cfm?id=1986&section=newsroom; Center on Budget and Policy Priorities, "Census Data Show Poverty Increased, Income Stagnated, and the Number of Uninsured Rose to a Record Level in 2003," press release, August 27, 2004, available at http://www.cbpp.org/8-26-04pov.htm.
67. See also Greg J. Duncan and Lindsay Chase-Lansdale, eds., *For Better and for Worse: Welfare Reform and the Well-Being of Children and Families* (New York: Russell Sage, 2002).
68. Boushey, "Former Welfare Families Need More Help," 6.
69. Center for the Study of Human Rights, *Twenty-Five Human Rights Documents*, 10–13.
70. Sunstein, *The Second Bill of Rights*. (See note 11, chapter 1.)

Chapter 4

1. The term *welfare mother* makes receipt of welfare the defining criterion of whom and what a mother is. Given that the term *welfare* itself carries negative connotations for so many people, *welfare mother* can only be considered a derogatory term. It ignores the many other (and often more positive) foundations on which mothers on the welfare rolls base their social identity.
2. Jennifer Friedlin, "Welfare Series: Services for Abused Women Scarce," *Women's eNews* (August 27, 2004), 1, available at http://womensenews.org/article/cfm/dyn/aid/1964.
3. NOW Legal Defense and Education Fund, *Surviving Violence and Poverty: A Focus on the Link between Domestic and Sexual Violence, Women's Poverty and Welfare* (Washington, D.C.: NOWLDEF, September 18, 2002), 1, available at http://www.legalmomentum.org/issues/wel/Surviving.pdf.
4. See National Domestic Violence Hotline, "Abuse in America," http://www.ndvh.org/educate/abuse_in_america.html. Last accessed October 25, 2005.
5. Richard M. Tolman and Jody Raphael, "A Review of Research on Welfare and Domestic Violence," *Journal of Social Issues* 56 (Winter 2000): 655–682.
6. NOW Legal Defense Fund, *Surviving Violence and Poverty*, 1.
7. Ibid., 2–5.
8. Ibid., 2.

9. Michelle Ganow, "Strategies for TANF Agencies to Identify and Address Domestic Violence," *WIN (Welfare Information Network) Issue Notes* (December 2001), available at www.financeprojectinfo.org.

10. Ibid., 1, 2.

11. Friedlin, "Welfare Series."

12. Dorian Solot and Marshall Miller, "Let Them Eat Wedding Rings: The Role of Marriage Promotion in Welfare Reform" (Boston: Alternatives to Marriage Project, 2002), available at http://www.unmarried.org/rings.php.

13. "Domestic Violence: The Hidden Peril of Marriage Promotion" (New York: NOW Legal Defense and Education Fund, May 6, 2003). Available at http://www.legalmomentum.org/issues/wel/hiddenperil.pdf.

14. Urvashi Vaid, "Pro-Marriage and Anti-Gay: Closer Look at Implications of Welfare Reform," *The Advocate* (April 16, 2002), 72.

15. Joseph DeFilippis, "City View: Poor Understanding," *City Limits Monthly* (February 2001), 1. Available at http://citylimits.org/content/articles/articleView.cfm?articlenumber=184.

16. Vaid, "Pro-Marriage and Anti-Gay."

17. Sean Cahill and Kenneth T. Jones, *Leaving Our Children Behind: Welfare Reform and the Gay, Lesbian, Bisexual, and Transgender Community* (Washington, D.C.: National Gay and Lesbian Task Force, December 2001), available at http://www.thetaskforce.org/downloads/WelfRef.pdf.

18. DeFilippis, "City View: Poor Understanding."

19. Cahill and Jones, *Leaving Our Children Behind*, 2.

20. See Kavan Peterson, "Same-Sex Unions—A Constitutional Race," September 8, 2005, http://www.stateline.org/live/ViewPage.action?siteNodeId=136&languageId=1&contentId=20695.

21. From statements by mothers collected by Maine Equal Justice Partners, quoted in National Council on Disability, *TANF and Disability: Importance of Supports for Families With Disabilities in Welfare Reform* (Washington, D.C.: NCD, 2003), 4.

22. David Wittenburg, "A Health-Conscious Safety Net?: Health Problems and Program Use among Low-Income Adults with Disabilities" (Washington, D.C.: Urban Institute, September 2004), 2.

23. U.S. Centers for Disease Control and Prevention, "Summary Health Statistics for U.S. Adults: National Health Interview Survey, 1997," *Vital and Health Statistics* 10, no. 205 (May 2002), 53.

24. Ibid.

25. Sunhwa Lee, Melissa Sills, and Gi-Taik Oh, "Disabilities among Children and Mothers in Low-Income Families" (Washington, D.C.: Institute for Women's Policy Research, June 2002), 1.

26. U.S. Government Accounting Office, *Welfare Reform: Former TANF Recipients with Impairments Less Likely to Be Employed and More Likely to Receive Federal Supports* (Washington, D.C.: GAO, December 2002), 8.

27. Ibid.

28. Ibid.

29. Ibid., 3.

30. Lee, Sills, and Oh, "Disabilities among Children and Mothers."

31. Joseph Shapiro, *No Pity: People with Disabilities Forging a New Civil Rights Movement* (New York: Times Books/Random House, 1993).

32. Mary Jo Deegan and Nancy A. Brooks, eds., *Women and Disability: The Double Handicap* (New Brunswick, NJ: Transaction Books, 1988); Michelle Fine and Adrienne Asch, eds., *Women with Disabilities* (Philadelphia: Temple University Press, 1988).

33. Mitchell LaPlante, Jae Kennedy, H. Stephen Kaye, and Barbara L. Wenger, "Disability and Employment," *Disability Statistics Abstracts*, no. 11 (January 1996), available at http://www.oregon.gov/ODC/tadoc/stat11.pdf.

34. Eileen Sweeney, "Recent Studies Indicate that Many Parents Who Are Current or Former Welfare Recipients Have Disabilities or Other Medical Conditions" (Washington, D.C.: Center on Budget and Policy Priorities, February 2000).

35. National Council on Disability, *TANF and Disability*, 7–8.

36. Friedlin, "Welfare Series," 1, 6.

37. Bruce Weber, Greg Duncan, and Leslie Whitener, "Rural Dimensions of Welfare Reform," *Poverty Research News* 4, no. 5 (September–October 2000), 1, available at http://www.jcpr.org/newsletters/vol4_no5/index.html.

38. Bruce Weber, Greg Duncan, and Leslie Whitener, eds., *Rural Dimensions of Welfare Reform* (Kalamazoo, MI: W. E. Upjohn Institute, 2002).

39. U.S. Census Bureau, *Income, Poverty, and Health Insurance Coverage in the United States: 2003*, 11, 13.

40. Kathleen K. Miller and Bruce Weber, "How Do Persistent Poverty Dynamics and Demographics Vary Across the Rural-Urban Continuum?" *Measuring Rural Diversity*, 1, no. 1 (November 2003). See also Monica G. Fisher and Bruce Weber, "The Importance of Place in Welfare Reform: Common Challenges for Central Cities and Remote-Rural Areas," Center on Urban and Metropolitan Policy Research Brief (Washington, D.C.: The Brookings Institution, June 2002).

41. U.S. Census Bureau, *Income, Poverty, and Health Insurance Coverage: 2003*, 10.

42. Leslie Whitener, Bruce Weber, and Greg Duncan, "Reforming Welfare: Implications for Rural America," *Rural America* 16, no. 3 (Fall 2001), 1–2.

43. U.S. Government Accounting Office, *Welfare Reform: Rural TANF Programs Have Developed Many Strategies to Address Rural Challenges* (Washington, D.C.: GAO, September 2004), 1.

44. Ibid., 6.

45. Weber, Duncan, and Whitener, *Rural Dimensions of Welfare Reform*, 1.

46. U.S. Government Accounting Office, *Welfare Reform*, 14.

47. Weber, Duncan, and Whitener, *Rural Dimensions of Welfare Reform*, 11.

48. Ibid., 10.

49. U.S. Government Accounting Office, *Welfare Reform*, 13–18. See also Jill Findeis et al., *Welfare Reform in Rural America: A Review of Current Research* (Columbia, MO: Rural Policy Research Institute, University of Missouri, February 2001).

50. George Rucker, "Status Report on Public Transportation in Rural America" (Washington, D.C.: U.S. Department of Transportation, 1994).

51. Weber, Duncan, and Whitener, *Rural Dimensions of Welfare Reform*, 12–14.

52. Betty Reid Mandell, "Welfare Reform: The War against the Poor," *New Politics* 8 (Winter 2001), 10.

53. National Coalition for the Homeless, "People Need Livable Incomes" (Washington, D.C.: NCH, 2003), 2, available at http://www.nationalhomeless.org/facts/income.html.

54. National Low Income Housing Coalition, *America's Neighbors: The Affordable Housing Crisis and the People It Affects* (Washington, D.C.: NLIHC, February 2004).

55. National Coalition for the Homeless, "People Need Livable Incomes," 1.

56. Ibid.

57. U.S. Department of Housing and Urban Development, *Trends in Worst Case Needs for Housing* (Washington, D.C.: HUD, December 2003).

58. National Coalition for the Homeless, "How Many People Experience Homelessness?," NCH Fact Sheet #2 (Washington, D.C.: NCH, 2002), 2, available at www.nationalhomeless.org.

59. National Law Center on Homelessness and Poverty, "Key Data Concerning Homeless Persons in America" (Washington, D.C.: NLCHP, July 2004), available at http://www.nlchp.org/FA_HAPIA/HomelessPersonsinAmerica.pdf.

60. Ralph da Costa Nunez and Laura M. Caruso, "Are Shelters the Answer to Family Homelessness?" *USA Today (Society for the Advancement of Education)*, January 2003. Available at http://www.looksmarthighschool.com/p/articles/mi_m1272/is_2692_131/ai_96268300.

61. See U.S. Conference of Mayors and Sodexho USA, "Hunger and Homelessness Survey," (Washington, D.C.: U.S. Conference of Mayors, 2005), available at http://www.usmayors.org/uscm/hungersurvey/2004/onlinereport/HungerAndHomelessnessReport2004.pdf.

62. National Coalition for the Homeless, "Why Are People Homeless?," NCH Fact Sheet #1 (Washington, D.C.: NCH, 2002), 3, available at http://www.nationalhomeless.org.

63. Ibid., 4.

64. Ibid., 3.

65. National Alliance to End Homelessness, "Research on Homelessness and TANF" (Washington, D.C.: NAEH, 2002), available at http://www.endhomelessness.org/pol/papers/tanf-leavers.pdf.

66. Institute for Children and Poverty/Homes for the Homeless, "Deja Vu: Family Homelessness in New York City" (New York: ICP, April 2001), 1. Available at http://www.homesforthehomeless.com/PDF/reports/NYC.pdf?Submit1=Free+Download.

67. Ibid.
68. Fernanda Santos and Robert Ingrassia, "Family Surge at Shelters," *New York Daily News* (April 18, 2002). Available at http://www.nydailynews.com/front/story/12076p-11345c.html.
69. National Coalition for the Homeless, "People Need Livable Incomes," 2.
70. See Kirsten Cowal et al., "Mother–Child Separations among Homeless and Housed Families Receiving Public Assistance in New York City," *American Journal of Community Psychology* 30 (October 2002): 711–731.
71. National Coalition for the Homeless, "Homeless Families with Children," NCH Fact Sheet #12 (Washington, D.C.: NCH, June 2005), available at http://www.nationalhomeless.org/facts/families.pdf. See also National Law Center on Homelessness and Poverty, "Key Data Concerning Homeless Persons in America," 1.
72. Sheila Rafferty Zedlewski, "The Importance of Housing Benefits to Welfare Success" (Washington, D.C.: Brookings Institution and Urban Institute, April 2002).
73. Nina Bernstein, "Side Effect of Welfare Law: The No-Parent Family," *New York Times* (July 29, 2002), A1.
74. U.S. Department of Health and Human Services, *Indicators of Welfare Dependence: Annual Report to Congress, 2004* (Washington, D.C.: DHHS, 2004), app. A, table 7.
75. Nina Bernstein, "Child Only Cases Grow in Welfare," *New York Times* (August 14, 2002), A1.
76. Mathematica Policy Research, Inc., "The Status of Child-Only TANF Families: Evidence from New Jersey," Issue Brief Number 3 (June 2002), available at http://mathematica-mpr.com/publications/PDFs/wfnjchildbrief.pdf.
77. Ibid., 2–3.
78. Center for Law & Social Policy, "TANF and Kinship Care" (Washington, D.C.: CLASP, October 2002), 1, available at http://www.clasp.org/publications/doc_TANF_and_kinship_care.pdf.
79. Nina Bernstein, "Child Only Cases Grow in Welfare," A1.
80. Center for Law & Social Policy, "TANF and Kinship Care,"1.
81. Nina Bernstein, "Child Only Cases Grow in Welfare," A1.
82. Jason DeParle, "As Welfare Rolls Shrink, Burden on Relatives Grows," *New York Times* (February 21, 1999), 1.
83. Cynthia Andrews Scarcella, Jennifer Ehrle, and Rob Geen, "Identifying and Addressing the Needs of Children in Grandparent Care" (Washington, D.C.: Urban Institute, August 2003), 2–3.
84. Holly S. Kleiner, Jodie Hertzog, and Dena Targ, "Grandparents Acting as Parents: Background Information for Educators," in *Grandparents Raising Grandchildren: A Resource Guide for Professionals,* ed. Parentlink (Raleigh: North Carolina State University, Cooperative Extension Service, January 1998), app. C, 1–2, available at http://www.ces.ncsu.edu/depts/fcs/nnfr/grandman/appendices.shtml.
85. Scarcella, Ehrle, and Geen, "Identifying and Addressing the Needs of Children," 3–4.
86. Ibid., 2–3.
87. Generations United, "Kinship Care–Public Benefits" (Washington, D.C.: GU, June 2004), 1, available at http://www.gu.org/projg&opubbene.htm.
88. Scarcella, Ehrle, and Geen, "Identifying and Addressing the Needs of Children," 4.
89. Faith Mullen and Monique Einhorn, "The Effect of State TANF Choices on Grandparent-Headed Households" (Washington, D.C.: AARP, November 2000), available at http://www.aarp.org/research/assistance/lowincome/aresearch-import-548-2000-18.html.
90. Center for Law and Social Policy and Community Legal Services, Inc., *Every Door Closed: Barriers Facing Parents with Criminal Records* (Washington, D.C.: CLASP and CLS, 2002), 30.
91. Jon Morgenstern et al., "Barriers to Employability among Substance Dependent and Non-substance-Affected Women on Federal Welfare: Implications for Program Design," *Journal of Studies on Alcohol* 64 (March 2003), 239–247.
92. Andrea Wilkins, "Substance Abuse and TANF" (Denver, CO: National Conference of State Legislatures, April 2003), 1, available at http://ncsl.org/statefed/welfare/substance.pdf.
93. Ibid., 2.
94. Edin and Lein, *Making Ends Meet,* 176–178.
95. Center for Law and Social Policy, *Every Door Closed,* ch. 2.

96. Human Rights Watch, *No Second Chance: People with Criminal Records Denied Access to Public Housing* (New York: HRW, 2004), available at http://www.hrw.org/reports/2004/usa1104.

97. Center for Law and Social Policy, *Every Door Closed*, 28.

98. Dorothy Roberts, *Shattered Bonds: The Color of Child Welfare* (New York: Basic Books, 2002).

99. Rebecca Gordon, *Cruel and Usual: How Welfare Reform Punishes Poor People* (Oakland, CA: Applied Research Center, 2001).

100. Neubeck and Cazenave, *Welfare Racism;* and Reese, *Backlash against Welfare Mothers.*

101. Ibid.; see also Schram, Soss, and Fording, *Race and the Politics of Welfare Reform.* (See chapter 2, note 25.)

102. Neubeck and Cazenave, *Welfare Racism*, ch. 7; Linda Burnham, "Welfare Reform, Family Hardship, and Women of Color," in Albelda and Withorn, *Lost Ground*, 43–56.

103. Joe Soss et al., "Setting the Terms of Relief: Explaining State Policy Choices in the Devolution Revolution," *American Journal of Political Science* 45 (2001), 378–403. On the harmful effects of family caps in general, see Jodie Levin-Epstein, "Lifting the Lid Off the Family Cap: States Revisit Problematic Policy for Welfare Mothers," *CLASP [Center for Law and Social Policy] Policy Brief* (December 2003), available at http://www.clasp.org/publications/family_cap_brf.pdf.

104. U.S. Commission on Civil Rights, "A New Paradigm for Welfare Reform: The Need for Civil Rights Enforcement" (Washington, D.C.: U.S. Commission on Civil Rights, August 2002). Available at http://www.usccr.gov/pubs/prwora/welfare.htm.

105. Ibid., 1.

106. See, for example, U.S. Senate Bill S770, titled "Fair Treatment and Due Process Protection Act of 2003," introduced into the 108th Congress by Senators Russell Feinberg, Edward Kennedy, and Mary Landrieu on April 2, 2003, available at "S770," http://thomas.loc.gov/home/c108query.html. This bill had the backing of some forty national civil rights, labor, legal assistance, faith-based, women's, and antipoverty organizations.

107. U.S. Commission on Civil Rights, "A New Paradigm for Welfare Reform."

108. Ibid., 1.

109. Ibid., 4.

110. Ibid., 3 and 4.

111. Ibid., 4.

112. Ibid., 3.

113. Ibid.

114. Ibid, 4.

115. Ibid.

116. Ibid., 5.

117. Ibid.

118. Neubeck and Cazenave, *Welfare Racism*, 35–36.

119. Scott Martelle and Mai Tran, "More Vietnamese Immigrants Reaching End of Welfare Benefits," *Los Angeles Times* (November 1, 2003), B1.

120. U.S. Census Bureau, *Statistical Abstract of the United States, 2004–2005* (Washington, D.C.: U.S. Government Printing Office, 2004), 8.

121. Ibid., 9.

122. Ibid., 10.

123. Tumlin and Zimmerman, *Immigrants and TANF.* See also Shawn Fremstad, "Immigrants and Welfare Reauthorization" (Washington, D.C.: Center on Budget and Policy Priorities, February 2002). Available at http://www.cbpp.org/1-22-02tanf4.pdf.

124. Michael Fix and Jeffrey S. Passel, "Assessing Welfare Reform's Immigrant Provisions," in Weil and Finegold, *Welfare Reform*, 179–202.

125. Audrey Singer, "Welfare Reform and Immigrants: A Policy Review," in *Immigrants, Welfare Reform, and the Poverty of Policy*, ed. Philip Kretsedemas and Ana Aparicio (New York: Praeger Publishers, 2004), 26–27.

126. Ibid.

127. Kretsedemas and Aparacio, *Immigrants, Welfare Reform, and the Poverty of Policy.*

128. Fix and Passel, "Assessing Welfare Reform's Immigrant Provisions," 179.

129. Audrey Singer, "Welfare Reform and Immigrants," 25–26.

130. Shawn Fremstad, "Immigrants, Persons with Limited Proficiency in English, and the TANF Program: What Do We Know?" (Washington, D.C.: Center on Budge and Policy Priorities, March 2003). Available at http://www.cbpp.org/1-22-02tanf4.pdf.

131. Leighton Ku, Shawn Fremstad, and Matthew Broaddus, "Noncitizens' Use of Public Benefits Has Declined since 1996" (Washington, D.C.: Center on Budget and Policy Priorities, April 2003), 1.

132. Ibid., 4.

133. Fix and Passel, "Assessing Welfare Reform's Immigrant Provisions," 184–185.

134. Jane Reardon-Anderson, Randy Capps, and Michael Fix, "The Health and Well-Being of Children in Immigrant Families" (Washington, D.C.: The Urban Institute, November 2002), 1–2.

135. Ibid., 3–6.

136. Ibid.

137. Fix and Passel, "Assessing Welfare Reform's Immigrant Provisions," 187–189.

138. Ronnie Lupe, "Chairman's Corner: If the Welfare Reform Act Remains as It Is, Human Misery Is Certain to Follow," *Fort Apache Scout*, 34, 1996), 2. Cited in Layne K. Stromwell et al., "The Implications of 'Welfare Reform' for American Indian Families and Communities," *Journal of Poverty*, 2 (1998), 7.

139. U.S. Census Bureau, *Income, Poverty, and Health Insurance Coverage: 2003*, 12.

140. Ward Churchill, *A Little Matter of Genocide: Holocaust and Denial in the Americas, 1492 to the Present* (New York: City Lights Books, 1998).

141. Wakina Scott, "Welfare Reform and American Indians: Critical Issues for Reauthorization," National Health Policy Forum Issue Brief, no. 778 (June 17, 2002), 2–3, available at http://nhpf.org/pdfs_ib/IB778%5FWelfare%26AmerIndians%5F6%2D19%2D02%2Epdf.

142. "American Indian Families and Tribes: Key Issues in Welfare Reform Reauthorization" (Menlo Park, CA: Kaiser Family Foundation, April 2002), 1–2. Available at http://www.kff.org/minorityhealth/loader.cfm?url=/commonspot/security/getfile.cfm&PageID=14161.

143. Patricia L. Kirk, "Running Out of Time: Congress Considers TANF Reauthorization as Some Native Recipients Face the End of Benefits," *American Indian Report*, 20 (June 2004), 12–17.

144. Scott, "Welfare Reform and American Indians," 3.

145. Shanta Pandey, Min Zhan, and Shannon Collier-Tenison, "Families' Experience with Welfare Reform on Reservations in Arizona," *Social Work Research* 28 (June 2004), 93–104.

146. Eddie F. Brown and Stephen Cornell, *Welfare, Work, and American Indians: The Impact of Welfare Reform* (Washington, D.C.: National Congress of American Indians, November 2001), available at http://udallcenter.arizona.edu/nativenations/pubs/welfare_reform.pdf.

147. U.S. General Accounting Office, *Welfare Reform: Tribal TANF Allows Flexibility to Tailor Programs, but Conditions on Reservations Make It Difficult to Move Recipients into Jobs* (Washington, D.C.: GAO, July 2002). Available at http://www.gao.gov/new.items/d02768.pdf.

148. Ibid., 20.

149. Brown and Cornell, *Welfare, Work, and American Indians*, i.

150. Ibid., 42.

151. Albelda and Withorn, *Lost Ground*; Louis Kushnick and James Jennings, eds., *A New Introduction to Poverty: The Role of Race, Power, and Politics* (New York: New York University Press, 1999); Applied Research Center, *From Poverty to Punishment: How Welfare Reform Punishes the Poor* (Oakland, CA: ARC), 20.

152. Ange-Marie Hancock, *The Politics of Disgust: The Public Identity of the Welfare Queen* (New York: New York University Press, 2004), ch. 4.

Chapter 5

1. Center for the Study of Human Rights, *Twenty-Five Human Rights Documents*, 12.

2. See Daniel H. Weinberg, "Measuring Poverty: Issues and Approaches," Poverty Measurement Working Papers (Washington, D.C.: U.S. Bureau of the Census, December 14, 1995), available at http://www.census.gov/hhes/poverty/povmeas/papers/yaled95.html.

3. Azza Salama Layton, *International Politics and Civil Rights Policies in the United States, 1941–1960* (New York: Cambridge University Press, 2000).

4. Michael Harrington, *The Other America: Poverty in the United States* (New York: Scribner, 1997).
5. Mollie Orshansky, "Counting the Poor: Another Look at the Poverty Profile," *Social Security Bulletin*, 28 (January 1965), 3–29.
6. Poverty thresholds are determined annually by the U.S. Bureau of the Census. Thresholds for 2004 and earlier years are available at U.S. Census Bureau, "Poverty Thresholds," http://www.census.gov/hhes/www/poverty/threshld.html. Last accessed on October 26, 2005.
7. See Food Marketing Institute, "Food Prices," http://www.fmi.org/facts_figs/foodprices.pdf. Last accessed October 24, 2005.
8. See Barbara Ehrenreich, *Nickeled and Dimed: On (Not) Getting By in America* (New York: Owl Books, 2002).
9. This has been empirically well established by the University of Michigan's Panel Study of Income Dynamics. Established to assess the impact of the federal War on Poverty, it has followed the economic fortunes of nearly 8,000 families since 1968. See Panel Study of Income Dynamics, "An Overview of the Panel Study on Income Dynamics," http://psidonline.isr.umich.edu/Guide/Overview.html. Last accessed on October 24, 2005.
10. Information on the Self-Sufficiency Standard is available at Wider Opportunities for Women, "Six Strategies for Family Economic Self-Sufficiency," http://www.sixstrategies.org. Last accessed on October 24, 2005. The standard has been calculated for over thirty states, plus New York City and Washington, D.C.
11. Diana Pearce, *The Self-Sufficiency Standard for Pennsylvania* (June 2004), available at Wider Opportunities for Women, "The Self-Sufficiency Standard for Pennsylvania," http://www.sixstrategies.org/states/stateproject.cfm?strStateProject=PA.
12. National Research Council, *Measuring Poverty: A New Approach* (Washington, D.C.: National Academy Press, 1996). See http://www.census.gov/hhes/poverty/povmeas/toc.html.
13. Bradley R. Schiller, *The Economics of Poverty and Discrimination*, 9th ed. (Upper Saddle River, NJ: Pearson Prentice Hall, 2004), 37–40.
14. See Luxembourg Income Study, "Introduction," at http://www.lisproject.org/introduction/history.htm. Last accessed on October 24, 2005.
15. Timothy M. Smeeding, Lee Rainwater, and Gary Burtless, "U.S. Poverty in a Cross-National Context," in *Understanding Poverty*, ed. Sheldon H. Danziger and Robert H. Haveman (Cambridge, MA: Harvard University Press, and New York: Russell Sage Foundation, 2002), 162.
16. Ibid., 162–163.
17. See Alice O'Connor, *Poverty Knowledge: Social Science, Social Policy, and the Poor in Twentieth-Century U.S. History* (Princeton, NJ: Princeton University Press, 2001), 3.
18. Smeeding, Rainwater, and Burtless, "U.S. Poverty in a Cross-National Context," 170–171.
19. Ibid., 171.
20. Ibid.
21. Gary Martin and Vladimir Kats, "Families and Work in Transition in 12 Countries, 1980–2001," *Monthly Labor Review* 126 (September 2003), 3–31. On European Union nations, see also Petra Lehmann and Christine Wirtz, "Household Formation in the EU—Lone Parents," *Statistics in Focus* (May 2004), 1–7.
22. Martin and Kats, "Families and Work in Transition," 13.
23. Janet C. Gornick and Marcia K. Meyers, *Families that Work: Policies for Reconciling Parenthood and Employment* (New York: Russell Sage Foundation, 2003).
24. On the varied rates of employment of lone mothers in fifteen European Union nations, see Lehmann and Wirtz, "Household Formation in the EU—Lone Parents."
25. Martin and Kats, "Families and Work in Transition."
26. Mary Daly and Katherine Rake, *Gender and the Welfare State: Care, Work and Welfare in Europe and the United States* (Cambridge, UK: Policy Press, 2003). On ways in which many European nations' policies address the balance between work and family life, see Organization for Economic Cooperation and Development, *Employment Outlook 2001* (Paris: OECD, June 2001), ch. 4. Available at OECD, "Balancing Work and Family Life," http://www.oecd.org/dataoecd/11/12/2079435.pdf. On how this balance is treated in the United States, see Gornick and Meyers, *Families that Work*.
27. Karen Christopher, "Family-Friendly Europe," *American Prospect* 13 (April 8, 2002), 59.
28. Lee Rainwater and Timothy M. Smeeding, *Poor Kids in a Rich Country: America's Children in Comparative Perspective* (New York: Russell Sage Foundation, 2003), 110–112.

29. Sen, *Development as Freedom*, 89.
30. Rainwater and Smeeding, *Poor Kids in a Rich Country*, 147.
31. David R. Francis, "It's Better to Be Poor in Norway than in the U.S.," *Christian Science Monitor* (April 14, 2005), 17. Available at http://www.csmonitor.com/2005/0414/p17s02-cogn.html.
32. Ibid. See also The Century Foundation, *The New American Economy: A Rising Tide that Lifts Only Yachts* (New York: The Century Foundation, 2004), available at http://www.tcf.org/Publications/EconomicsInequality/wasow_yachtrc.pdf.
33. Rainwater and Smeeding, *Poor Kids in a Rich Country*, ch. 7.
34. See the European Social Charter website at Council of Europe, "Human Rights: European Social Charter," http://www.coe.int/T/E/Human_Rights/Esc/. Last accessed on October 24, 2005.
35. Cass Sunstein, *The Second Bill of Rights*, 102. (See chapter 1, note 11.)
36. Rainwater and Smeeding, *Poor Kids in a Rich Country*, ch. 8. See also Sheila B. Kamerman et al., "Social Policies, Family Types, and Child Outcomes in Selected OECD Countries," OECD Social, Employment, and Migration Working Papers no. 6 (Paris: Organization for Economic Co-operation and Development, May 20, 2003), available at http://www.childpolicyintl.org/publications/SOCIAL%20POLICIES,%20FAMILY%20TYPES,%20AND%20CHILD%20OUTCOMES%20IN%20SELECTED%20OECD%20COUNTRIES.pdf.
37. See, for example, Jane Lewis, ed., *Lone Mothers in European Welfare Regimes: Shifting Policy Logics* (Bristol, PA: Jessica Kingsley Publishers, 1997); and Majella Kilkey, *Lone Mothers between Paid Work and Care: The Policy Regime in Twenty Countries* (Burlington, VT: Ashgate Publishing Company, 2000).
38. Christopher, "Family-Friendly Europe," 59–60.
39. See, for example, Gornick and Meyers, *Families that Work*, chs. 4–7; and U.S. Social Security Administration, *Social Security Programs throughout the World: Europe, 2004* (Washington, D.C.: SSA, September 2004), available at http://www.ssa.gov/policy/docs/progdesc/ssptw/2004–2005/europe/ssptw04euro.pdf. On policies specifically benefiting children, see Jonathan Bradshaw and Naomi Finch, "A Comparison of Child Benefit Packages in 22 Countries," Department for Work and Pensions Research Report no. 174 (York, UK: University of York, 2002), available at http://www.dwp.gov.uk/asd/asd5/rrep174.as.
40. Michael B. Katz, *The Price of Citizenship: Redefining the American Welfare State* (New York: Metropolitan Books, 2001).
41. Rainwater and Smeeding, *Poor Kids in a Rich Country*, 117, 119.
42. Ibid., 117–118. See also Sheila Kamerman et al., "Social Policies, Family Types, and Child Outcomes"; and Gornick and Meyers, *Families that Work*.
43. Rainwater and Smeeding, *Poor Kids in a Rich Country*, 134.
44. Ibid., 123–131.
45. Vicki Turetsky, "The Child Support Program: An Investment that Works" (Washington, D.C.: Center for Law and Social Policy, July 2005), 1, available at http://clasp.org/publications/cs_funding_072605.pdf.
46. Ibid., 2.
47. Cynthia Miller et al., *The Interaction of Child Support and TANF: Evidence from Samples of Current and Former Welfare Recipients* (New York: MDRC, January 2005), available at http://www.mdrc.org/publications/397/full.pdf.
48. Edin and Lein, *Making Ends Meet*, 218–219.
49. Elaine Sorensen, "Child Support Gains Some Ground," *Snapshots3*, no.11 (Washington, D.C.: Urban Institute, October 2003), 1, available at http://www.urban.org/UploadedPDF/310860_snapshots3_no11.pdf.
50. Rainwater and Smeeding, *Poor Kids in a Rich Country*, 125–126.
51. Joel F. Handler, *Social Citizenship and Workfare in the United States and Western Europe: The Paradox of Inclusion* (Cambridge, UK: Cambridge University Press, 2004).
52. Christopher, "Family-Friendly Europe," 60.
53. Abby J. Cohen, "A Brief History of Federal Financing for Child Care in the United States," *Financing Child Care*, 6 (Summer/Fall 1996), 32.
54. See Child Care Bureau, "Child Care Development Fund," http://www.acf.hhs.gov/programs/ccb/geninfo/development.htm. Last accessed on October 24, 2005.

55. See Sen, *Development as Freedom*.

56. On this issue, see Physicians for a National Health Program, "International Health Systems," http://www.pnhp.org/facts/international_health_systems.php. Last accessed on October 24, 2005.

57. Gornick and Meyers, *Families that Work*, 117–121.

58. Ibid., 118.

59. Jane Waldfogel, "International Policies toward Parental Leave and Child Care," *Caring for Infants and Toddlers* 11 (Spring/Summer 2001), 99–111. See also Jody Heymann et al., *The Work, Family, and Equity Index: Where Does the United States Stand Globally?* (Cambridge, MA: The Project on Global Working Families, Harvard School of Public Health, 2004).

60. Sheila B. Kamerman and Shirley Gatenio, "Mother's Day: More Than Candy and Flowers, Working Parents Need Paid Time-Off," Issue Brief (New York: Clearinghouse on International Developments in Child, Youth and Family Policies, Columbia University, Spring 2002).

61. Ibid., 4.

62. Gornick and Meyers, *Families that Work*, 129.

63. In 2005, the French government adopted measures to relax the thirty-five-hour work week requirement and to allow private employers more flexibility in assigning overtime. But the thirty-five hours remains a requirement in the public sector and the standard work week for the private sector.

64. Gornick and Meyers, *Families that Work*, 153–154.

65. Ibid., 163–172.

66. Ibid., 179–181.

67. Handler, *Social Citizenship and Workfare*, ch. 5.

68. Matt Barnes et al., eds., *Poverty and Social Exclusion in Europe* (Northampton, MA: Edward Elgar, 2002).

69. Gerry Rodgers, Charles Gore, and Jose B. Figueiredo, eds., *Social Exclusion: Rhetoric, Reality, Responses* (Geneva, Switzerland: International Labour Organization, 1995).

70. Matt Barnes, "Social Exclusion and the Life Course," in Barnes et al., *Poverty and Social Exclusion in Europe*, 1–23.

71. Hilary Silver and S. M. Miller, "Social Exclusion: The European Approach to Social Disadvantage," *Poverty & Race*, 11 (September–October 2003), 1–2, 11–14.

72. See the paper by Philippe Van Parijs, "Basic Income: A Simple and Powerful Idea for the 21st Century," available at http://www.etes.ucl.ac.be/BIEN/Files/Papers/2000VanParijs.pdf.

73. Basic Income European Network's mission statement can be found at Basic Eureopean Network, "BIEN Mission Statement," www.etes.ucl.ac.be/BIEN/BIEN/MissionStatement.htm. Last accessed on October 24, 2005.

74. Phillippe Van Parijs, *What's Wrong with a Free Lunch?* Joshua Cohen and Joel Rogers, eds. (Boston: Beacon Press, 2001).

75. Phillippe Van Parijs, "A Basic Income for All," in Ibid., 14.

76. Ibid., 19–20.

77. Ironically, the federal EITC was introduced in 1975 by members of Congress opposed to negative income tax proposals, fearing that they would go to many families lacking working heads and would undermine their incentives to work.

78. Arloc Sherman, "Social Security Lifts 1 Million Children above the Poverty Line" (Washington, D.C.: Center on Budget and Policy Priorities, May 2005), 1.

79. U.S. Census Bureau, *Poverty in the United States, 2002*, 7.

80. Sheldon Danziger, "After Welfare Reform and an Economic Boom: Why is Child Poverty Still So Much Higher in the U.S. than in Europe?" Paper presented at the 8th International Research Seminar on Social Security, Sigtuna, Sweden, June 16–19 2001, available at http://www.fordschool.umich.edu/research/poverty/pdf/sigtuna.pdf.

81. Ibid., 2.

82. Ibid., 5.

83. Ibid., 6.

84. Everett Carll Ladd and Karlyn H. Bowman, *Attitudes toward Economic Inequality* (Washington, D.C.: AEI Press, 1998), 118.

85. Ibid., 120.

86. Neubeck and Cazenave, *Welfare Racism*. (See chapter 2, note 11.)

87. Herbert Gans, *The War against the Poor: The Underclass and Antipoverty Policy* (New York: Basic Books, 1996).

88. Sanford F. Schram, *Welfare Discipline: Discourse, Governance, and Globalization* (Philadelphia: Temple University Press, forthcoming 2006).

89. Handler, *Social Citizenship and Workfare*. See also Jamie Peck, *Workfare States* (New York: Guilord Press, 2001).

Chapter 6

1. See Office of Management and Budget, "Department of Homeland Security," http://www.whitehouse.gov/omb/budget/fy2005/homeland.html. Last accessed October 24, 2005.

2. Dana Milbank and Spencer S. Hsu, "Cheney: Kerry Victory Risky," *Washington Post* (September 8, 2004), A1.

3. David Cay Johnston, "Richest Are Leaving Even the Rich Far Behind," *New York Times* (June 5, 2005), 1.

4. Schram, *Welfare Discipline,* ch.1 (See chapter 5, note 88.)

5. On federal deficit spending and the national debt, see Ed Hall, "U.S. National Debt Clock," http://www.brillig.com/debt_clock/. Last accessed on October 24, 2005.

6. For 2006 federal budget figures, see Office of Management and Budget, "Budget of the United States Government, Fiscal Year 2006," http://www.whitehouse.gov/omb/budget/fy2006/. Last accessed on October 24, 2005.

7. NETWORK, "The President's FY 06 Budget Proposal–Is It a Just Budget?" (Washington, D.C.: NETWORK, February 2005), available at http://www.networklobby.org/issues/budget.html.

8. Frances Fox Piven, *The War at Home: The Domestic Costs of Bush's Militarism* (New York: New Press, 2004).

9. Roosevelt is quoted in Sunstein, *The Second Bill of Rights,* 11. (See chapter 1, note 11.)

10. Ibid., 13.

11. Ibid., 72.

12. Ibid.

13. Ibid., 77.

14. See Kensington Welfare Rights Union, "About the Kensington Welfare Rights Union," http://kwru.org/kwru/abtkwru.html. Last accessed on October 24, 2005.

15. Kensington Welfare Rights Union, *Poor People's Human Rights Report on the United States,* 1st ed. (Philadelphia: KWRU, 1999).

16. For discussion of the role of KWRU in the PPEHRC, see Ford Foundation, *Close to Home: Case Studies of Human Rights Work in the United States* (New York: Ford Foundation, 2004), chs. 2, 6.

17. See Poor People's Economic Human Rights Campaign, "Mission," http://economichuman-rights.org/about/mission.html. Last accessed on October 25, 2005.

18. See University of the Poor, "About," http://www.universityofthepoor.org/about.html. Last accessed October 25, 2005.

19. A summary of "The Declaration of the Poor People's Economic Human Rights Campaign on the Full Realization of Human Rights in the United States" is available at Center for Economic and Social Rights, "Summary," http://cesr.org/node/view/83. Last accessed on October 25, 2005.

20. Poor People's Economic Human Rights Campaign, "The Declaration of the Poor People's Economic Human Rights Campaign on the Full Realization of Human Rights in the United States" (2003), 1, para 4. Available at http://globalization.icaap.org/content/v3.1/10_declaration.html.

21. Ibid., 2.

22. Ibid., 3.

23. Ibid., 6.

24. Sunstein, *The Second Bill of Rights* (See chapter 1, note 11.); and Wronka, *Human Rights and Social Policy.* (See chapter 1, note 18.)

25. Wronka, "A Little Humility, Please." (See chapter 1, note 21.)

26. See U.S. Department of State, *Country Reports and Practices,* 2004 (Washington, D.C.: U.S. Department of State, 2005). Available at http://www.state.gov/g/drl/rls/hrrpt/2004/index.htm.

27. See, for example, People's Republic of China State Council, *The Human Rights Record of the United States in 2004* (Beijing, China: State Council, March 3, 2005). Available at People's

Daily Online, "Full Text of the Human Rights Record of the U.S. in 2004," http://english.people.com.cn/200503/03/eng20050303_175406.html. Last accessed on October 25, 2005.

28. Ibid., 13.

29. Edward Cody, "China, Others Criticize U.S. Report on Rights," *Washington Post* (March 4, 2005), A14.

30. US Human Rights Network, "A Memorandum to President Bush in Response to the U.S. State Department's Country Reports on Human Rights Practices" (Atlanta, GA: USHRN, February 2005). Available at http://www.ushrnetwork.org/pubs/humanrightsmemorandumFINAL-edited%20pdf.pdf.

31. Ibid., 9.

32. Ford Foundation, *Close to Home*, 30.

33. "Poor People's Economic Human Rights Campaign [et al.] vs . The United States of America," Petition to the Inter-American Commission on Human Rights, October 1, 1999. Available at http://www.university of the poor.org/library/IACpetition.pdf.

34. See Center for Economic and Social Rights, *Economic, Social and Cultural Rights: A Guide to the Legal Framework* (New York: CESR, January 2000).

35. Poor People's Economics Human Rights Campaign [et al.] *vs* The United States of America, Petition to the Inter-American Commission, 2.

36. Ibid.

37. Letter addressed to the Executive Secretary, Inter-American Commission on Human Rights, from the Poor People's Economic Human Rights Campaign et al., August 26, 2004, available at http://www.kwru.org/LEGAL/Challengingunjustlaws.htm#petition.

38. Ibid., 2.

39. See Poor People's Economic Human Rights Campaign, "PPEHRC Travels to Washington D.C. for Hearing," http://www.economichumanrights.org/updates/oashearing.htm. Last accessed on October 25, 2005.

40. This discussion is largely drawn from Mary Bricker-Jenkins, "Legislative Tactics in a Movement Strategy: The Economic Human Rights-Pennsylvania Campaign," unpublished manuscript (September 3, 2003); "Social Worker Honored for Efforts to End Poverty," *Temple Times Online Edition* 34 (October 16, 2003), available at http://www.temple.edu/temple_times/10-16-03/socialwork.html; and the Pennsylvania Chapter of the National Association of Social Workers, "Economic Human Rights-PA Campaign," http://www.nasw-pa.org/displaycommon.cfm?an=1&subarticlenbr=60. Last accessed on October 25, 2005.

41. Pennsylvania House Resolution no. 473, introduced on March 25, 2002, available at http://www2.legis.state.pa.us/WU01/LI/BI/BT/2001/0/HR0473P3466.pdf.

42. "Findings," *Report of the Select Committee on House Resolution 144 Investigation of Integration of Human Rights Standards in Pennsylvania Laws and Policies*, November 30, 2004, available at http://www.nasw-pa.org/displaycommon.cfm?an=1&subarticlenbr=60.

43. Information about the Massachusetts CEDAW Project can be found at Suffolk University, "The Massachusetts CEDAW Project," http://www.suffolk.edu/cwhhr/Mass_CEDAW.html. Last accessed on October 25, 2005.

44. The Massachusetts Human Rights Bill, along with discussion of the reasoning behind it, is available at Suffolk University, "Human Rights for All," www.suffolk.edu/cwhhr/endorsement.pdf. Last accessed on October 25, 2005.

45. Ibid.

46. See "Human Rights for All," open letter dated April 2005, issued by representatives of Massachusetts CEDAW Project, at Suffolk University, "Human Rights for All," http://www.suffolk.edu/cwhhr/Mass_CEDAW.html.

47. Leaflet on The Massachusetts Human Rights for All Initiative, n.d., available at Suffolk University, "The Massachusetts Human Rights for All Initiative," http://www.suffolk.edu/cwhhr/endorsement.pdf. Last accessed on October 25, 2005.

48. Women's Economic Agenda Project, "The California Statewide Poor People's Economic Human Rights Campaign," http://www.weap.org/ppehr/ppehr.html#what. Last accessed on October 5, 2005.

49. Ibid. ·

50. On the idea of human rights culture and human rights as a lived experience, see Joseph Wronka, "Toward the Creation of a Human Rights Culture," http://www.humanrightsculture.org. Last accessed on October 25, 2005.

51. For results of the adult survey, see University of Minnesota Human Rights Library, "Final Adult Survey Data," http://www1.umn.edu/humanrts/edumat/adultsur.htm. Last accessed on October 25, 2005. The survey was conducted by Peter D. Hart Research Associates on November 3–4 and 7–8, 1997.
52. See Women's Economic Agenda Project, "The California Statewide Poor People's Economic Human Rights Campaign" 3, para 4.
53. Urban Justice Center, "Hunger Is No Accident: New York and Federal Welfare Policies Violate the Human Right to Food" (New York: Urban Justice Center, Human Rights Project, July 2000), available at http://urbanjustice.org/publications/index.html.
54. Ibid., 1.
55. Ibid., 5.
56. Urban Justice Center, "Key Survey Findings: Assessing the Intersection of Race and Welfare Reform for New York City Households," Brief no. 1 (New York: Urban Justice Center, Human Rights Project, April 2001), available at http://urbanjustice.org/publications/index.html.
57. Ibid., 2–4.
58. The ICERD is one of the few international human rights treaties the U.S. Senate has ratified, albeit only after adding significant reservations that serious limit the obligation of the United States to be held accountable for abiding by its provisions.
59. Urban Justice Center, *Compliance with Article 5: Economic, Social, and Cultural Rights Under the International Convention on the Elimination of Racial Discrimination* (New York: Urban Justice Center, Human Rights Project, August 3, 2001), available at http://urbanjustice.org/publications/index.html.
60. Urban Justice Center, *Human Rights Violations in Welfare Legislation: Pushing Recipients Deeper Into Poverty* (New York: Urban Justice Center, Human Rights Project, April 2002), available at http://urbanjustice.org/publications/index.html.
61. See New York City Human Rights Initiative, "About the New York City Human Rights Initiative," http://www.nychri.org. Last accessed on October 25, 2005.
62. See Women's Institute for Leadership Development for Human Rights, "Purpose and History," http://www.wildforhumanrights.org/about/index.html. Last accessed on October 5, 2005. See also Ford Foundation, *Close to Home*, ch. 9.
63. See San Francisco Commission on the Status of Women, "CEDAW," http://www.sfgov.org/site/cosw_index.asp?id=10848. Last accessed on October 25, 2005.
64. WILD for Human Rights, *Making the Connections: Human Rights in the United States* (San Francisco: WILD, 2000), available at http://www.wildforhumanrights.org/pdfs/makingthe-connections.pdf.
65. Ibid., 32.
66. Ibid.
67. See US Human Rights Network, "Why a U.S Human Rights Network?," http://www.ushr-network.org/home.cfm . Last accessed on October 25, 2005.
68. See Amnesty International USA, "USA, Human Rights Concerns," http://www.amnesty-usa.org/countries/usa/index.do. Last accessed October 25, 2005. See also Human Rights Watch, "United States," http://hrw.org/doc/?t=usa. Last accessed October 25, 2005.
69. See US Human Rights Network, "Economic and Social Rights Caucus," http://www.ushr-network.org/page159.cfm. Last accessed on October 25, 2005.
70. US Human Rights Network, *Something Inside So Strong: A Resource Guide on Human Rights in the United States* (Atlanta, GA: USHRN, 2003), available at http://www.ushrnetwork.org/page2.cfm.
71. Ibid., 40.
72. Quoted in Ford Foundation, *Close to Home*, 3.
73. See Robert T. Chase, "Class Resurrection: The Poor People's Campaign of 1968 and Resurrection City," *Essays in History*, 40 (1998), Department of History, University of Virginia, available at http://etext.lib.virginia.edu/journals/EH/EH40/chase40.html.
74. Martin Luther King, Jr., "Beyond Vietnam—A Time to Break Silence," April 4, 1967, available at American Rhetoric, "Martin Luther King: Beyond Vietnam," http://www.ameri-canrhetoric.com/speeches/mlkatimetobreaksilence.htm. A speech given at a meeting of Clergy and Laity Concerned at Riverside Church, New York City. Last accessed on October 25, 2005.

Index